D1124070

Rafael Alberti's

Poetry of the Thirties

Judith Nantell

Rafael Alberti's

Poetry of the Thirties

The Poet's Public Voice

The University of Georgia Press

Athens and London

© 1986 by the University of Georgia Press
Athens, Georgia 30602

Designed by Kathi L. Dailey
Set in 10 on 12 Linotron 202 Times Roman
with Antique Olive display

The paper in this book meets the guidelines for
permanence and durability of the Committee on
Production Guidelines for Book Longevity of the
Council on Library Resources.

Printed in the United States of America

90 89 88 87 86   5 4 3 2 1

Library of Congress Cataloging in Publication Data

Nantell, Judith.
Rafael Alberti's poetry of the thirties.

(South Atlantic Modern Language Association award study)
English and Spanish.
Bibliography: p.
Includes index.
1. Alberti, Rafael, 1902–   —Criticism and interpretation. 2. Alberti,
Rafael, 1902–   —Political and social views. I. Title. II. Series.
PQ6601.L2Z79   1985   861'.62   84-28029
ISBN 0-8203-0777-7 (alk. paper)

The frontispiece is the Guernica Study and Postscript of *Horse's Head*
by Pablo Picasso. Courtesy of VAGA and Museo del Prado, Madrid.
© SPADEM, Paris/VAGA, New York, 1985.

South Atlantic
Modern Language Association
Award Study

For Chris, with love

Es memorable y desgarrador para el poeta haber encarnado para muchos hombres, durante un minuto, la esperanza.

Pablo Neruda, *Confieso que he vivido*

Contents

Acknowledgments

Since my interest in investigating the poetic production of Rafael Alberti spans nearly a decade, any enumeration of the people who encouraged me along the way and assisted me in bringing this research to fruition would be lengthy indeed. Still, I would like to express my sincere gratitude to at least some of those who were especially helpful.

Several people deserve special thanks because without their cooperation my book never could have been published. Above all, my most grateful acknowledgment is to be given to Rafael Alberti for graciously granting me permission to draw on his poetry, *La arboleda perdida,* and *El poeta en la calle: Obra civil.* In addition, my gratitude goes to the Carmen Balcells Literary Agency representing Rafael Alberti. I would like to express my heartfelt thanks to Rafael Gómez Sánchez Iglesias, Director, Biblioteca-Museo José María de Cossío, Tudanca, Spain, for his warm hospitality, admission to the library, and permission to cite Alberti's correspondence with Cossío. I would also like to thank Josefina Manresa Marhuenda for granting me permission to quote from the poetry of her late husband, Miguel Hernández. My thanks go to María-Rosario Prados not only for allowing me to quote from Emilio Prados's poetry but also for her interest in my study. The Carmen Balcells Literary Agency, representing Pablo Neruda, is also to be thanked for its authorization to quote from his poetry. My gratitude also goes to the Hogar Clínica San Juan de Dios, Lima, Peru, and its Director, Hermano Lázaro Simón Canovas, for permission to cite César Vallejo's poetry. I wish to thank Maxwell Adereth for kindly allowing me to draw on his study. I would also like to express my thanks to E. J. Brill, Leiden, the Netherlands, for allowing me to quote from Johan Lechner's work. For permission to reproduce the studies and "postscripts" to Pablo Picasso's *Guernica* I am grateful to S.P.A.D.E.M., Paris, France/V.A.G.A., New York, New York. I would also like to express my gratitude to the Prado Museum, Madrid, Spain, for providing the necessary photographs for reproduction. Lastly, I wish to offer special thanks to Pamela Lewis and Todd McDaniel of the Museum of Modern Art, New York, for their assistance.

I would like to acknowledge my former professors. Luis Beltrán, under whose guidance I began my investigation into Alberti's poetry, has been an inspiration. Olga Impey, Miguel Enguídanos, and Anita Rozlapa have nurtured my understanding of Hispanic poetry.

To a number of my Hispanist colleagues I would like to express my thanks for helping this book to be. Andrew Debicki, C. Brian Morris, and Antonio Sánchez Barbudo carefully read portions of the present study, shared their wisdom, and offered helpful suggestions. Juan Cano-Ballesta also read a portion of the study and assisted me in locating the first editions of many of Alberti's poems of the early thirties. Juan Loveluck's thoughtful reading of the entire manuscript offered both insightful observations and genuine encouragement. Ignacio Aguilera y Santiago, José Luis Cano, and Alonso Zamora Vicente aided me in my search for the rare editions of Alberti's poetry of the early thirties that I eventually found in private libraries in Spain. William Risley, early in my career, took an interest in my research on Alberti's poetry and urged me to publish the results. My colleague David Darst advised me regarding a portion of the manuscript and accommodated me with a teaching schedule conducive to my research. To these and other Hispanist colleagues I am most grateful.

I would like to thank Robert Johnson, Dean of Graduate Studies and Research, Florida State University, for financial assistance in preparing the manuscript. My thanks are also extended to the Graduate School of the University of Wisconsin–Madison, especially in the person of Peter Smith, for a faculty research grant in the summer of 1979 that enabled me to acquire useful material in Spain.

Especial gratitude goes to the 1984 South Atlantic Modern Language Association (SAMLA) Studies Award Committee for the careful and expert attention given to my manuscript. In particular, I would like to thank Alistair Duckworth, Chairperson, for guiding my manuscript through the various stages of the Book Award Competition. I would also like to take this opportunity to thank Malcolm Call, Director and Editor, the University of Georgia Press, and the members of his editorial staff for seeing the manuscript through to book form. My special thanks go to Ellen Harris, Managing Editor, for her patience and advice, to Joanne Ainsworth, copyeditor, for her close reading of the text and her many helpful suggestions, to Sandy Hudson for helping with the illustrations, and to Kathi Dailey for designing the book.

I applaud both Janet Horton, for her attentive, efficient preparation of the manuscript, and Cathy Butler, for helping me with the necessary correspondence.

I would like to thank a few very special friends who have helped me in important ways. I cherish my parents, Jack and Ruth Nantell, and I appreciate greatly their endless encouragement and limitless love. My sisters, Mary Nantell Pearce and Sharon Nantell, always have been wonderfully supportive, even in the teeth of horrendous long-distance telephone charges. I would like to thank my friend and fellow Hispanist, Margo Persin, for her encouragement. My English colleague and frequent running companion, Bonnie Braendlin, I wish to thank for her concern and, most of all, her friendship. I am forever grateful to Chris Maloney, my husband, who listened to many of my ideas in rehearsal, shared many of his own insights and ideas with me, and nourished me continually with his firm commitment both to our marriage and his own career as a philosopher. Without him many of my own efforts might not have been realized. Finally, I wish to thank Tagmeme and Watson, my ever-present, although not everlasting, muses.

Abbreviations

AP	Rafael Alberti, *La arboleda perdida: Libro I y II de memorias* (Barcelona: Seix Barral, 1976)
C	Rafael Alberti, *Consignas* (Madrid: "Octubre," 1933)
CPE	Johan Lechner, *El compromiso en la poesía española del siglo XX,* vol. 1 (Leiden: Universitaire Pers, 1968)
CV	Pablo Neruda, *Confieso que he vivido: Memorias* (Buenos Aires: Losada, 1974)
CMFL	Maxwell Adereth, *Commitment in Modern French Literature: Politics and Society in Peguy, Aragon, and Sartre* (London: Gollancz, 1967)
FF	Sergei Eisenstein, *Film Form: Essays in Film Theory,* ed. and trans. Jay Leyda (Cleveland: World, 1967)
FS	Sergei Eisenstein, *The Film Sense,* ed. and trans. Jay Leyda (Cleveland: World, 1967)
HE	*Hora de España*
MA	*El Mono Azul*
MP	Louis MacNeice, *Modern Poetry: A Personal Essay* (New York: Oxford University Press, 1968; originally published 1938)
O	*Octubre: Escritores y artistas revolucionarios*
OC	Federico García Lorca, *Obras completas,* 16th ed. (Madrid: Aguilar, 1971)
OPC	*Miguel Hernández: Obra poética completa,* 3d ed., introduction and notes by Leopoldo de Luis and Jorge Urrutia (Bilbao: Edita Zero, 1976)
P	Sergei Eisenstein, "Introduction, *The Battleship Potemkin,*" in *Potemkin: A Film by Sergei Eisenstein,* trans. Gillon R. Aitken (New York: Simon and Schuster, 1968)
PC	Rafael Alberti, *Poesías completas* (Buenos Aires: Losada, 1961)
PEPR	Juan Cano-Ballesta, *La poesía española entre pureza y revolución (1930–1936)* (Madrid: Gredos, 1972)

PEC   Rafael Alberti, *El poeta en la calle: Obra civil (Madrid: Aguilar, 1978).*

PP   Cecil Maurice Bowra, *Poetry and Politics, 1900–1960* (Cambridge: Cambridge University Press, 1966)

PPC   Emilio Prados, *Poesías completas,* edited by Carlos Aguinaga and Antonio Carreira (Mexico City: Aguilar, 1975)

SS   C. B. Morris, *Surrealism and Spain, 1920–1936* (Cambridge: Cambridge University Press, 1972)

TA   Stephen Spender, *The Thirties and After: Poetry, Politics and People (1933–1975)* (London: Macmillan, 1978)

TLD   C. B. Morris, *This Loving Darkness: The Cinema and the Spanish Writers, 1920–1936* (New York: Oxford University Press, 1980)

UFRE   Rafael Alberti, *Un fantasma recorre Europa* (Madrid: Tentativa Poètica, 1933)

Rafael Alberti's

Poetry of the Thirties

Chapter 1

Introduction

R afael Alberti is undeniably one of the most well known, original, and revolutionary poets of twentieth-century Spanish literature. His poetry, written during the past six decades, is a compendium of the most significant artistic and literary tendencies of the modern era and has been the object of much critical attention and praise. As a member of the Generation of 1927, Alberti will always be associated with such renowned poets as Vicente Aleixandre, Luis Cernuda, Federico García Lorca, Jorge Guillén, and Pedro Salinas. The achievements and innovations made by these poets during the twenties in Spain not only were and continue to be recognized by readers and literary artists in other countries but also have had a lasting and important effect on the generations of Spanish poets that were to follow. Alberti's poetry published between 1925 and 1929 is, as Solita Salinas de Marichal affirms, "un fiel espejo de su generación poética" and thus represents the accomplishments attained by these unique and imaginative poets.[1]

Alberti's fame, however, does not rest solely on the poetry he wrote in the mid- and late twenties, most notably *Marinero en tierra, La amante, El alba del alhelí, Cal y canto, Sobre los ángeles, Sermones y moradas,* and the series of poems entitled *Yo era un tonto y lo que he visto me ha hecho dos tontos.*[2] During the thirties Rafael Alberti was one of the first to advocate "la utilidad pública de la poesía," thereby distinguishing himself as one of Spain's most militant political poets. Recalling Alberti's poetry of the thirties, Pablo Neruda writes in his memoirs: "Este poeta de purísima estirpe enseñó la utilidad pública de la poesía en un momento crítico del mundo. En eso se parece a Mayakovski. Esta utilidad pública de la poesía se basa en la fuerza, en la ternura, en la alegría y en la esencia verdadera. Sin esta calidad la poesía suena pero no canta. Alberti siempre canta" (*CV,* 188). Alberti is a revolutionary poet not only because works such as *Cal y canto* and *Sobre los ángeles* marked radical stylistic change in the course of modern Spanish poetry but also because in the thirties, especially, his poetry urged fundamental change in society.

The Poet and His Era

The reorientation from a poet studying and writing about the personal world *within* to a poet examining the public world *without* is the subject of this book. My investigation of public themes and voices in Alberti's poetry of the thirties explores what constitutes the world without, the social domain, and how poetry itself can be either a useful and practical instrument or a more reflective and meditative method for analyzing and attempting to comprehend the world.

Throughout both his lifetime and poetic production Rafael Alberti has remained ever attentive to what the poet himself describes as "el compás del pulso de mi época."[3] This book concerns a particular era in Alberti's life and work and the poetry that echoes that era. The thirties in Europe, as well as in other parts of the world, were years of feverish social turmoil. Rafael Alberti's poetry from the first day of January 1930 through the closing months of 1939 transcribes and evaluates the volatile tempo of that decade.

Poetry and politics; the word and the deed. These constituted Rafael Alberti's life in the thirties. That decade found Alberti and other Western poets intensely involved in critical public events and crucial social issues. Stephen Spender recalls:

> The thirties was the decade in which young writers became involved in politics. The politics of this generation were most exclusively those of the left. They were mainly so for two reasons: first, on account of the events of the time . . . secondly, because even during the twenties when most of the well-known writers dissociated themselves from politics in their literary work, there was nevertheless an underlying leftwing orthodoxy among writers which went back to the end of the First World War. . . .
>
> Politics, when it overtook our generation, meant for us the partial abrogation of a passive, receptive, analytical poetry . . . in favour of a poetry of will and the directed analytic intellect. (*TA,* 13, 17)

Alberti himself was dedicated to the revolution, and his "poetry of will" represents and advocates social change and the construction of the "nueva era del mundo" (*PC,* 375). This self-proclaimed "poeta en la calle" explains: "Since 1931 my life and work have been placed at the service of the Spanish revolution and the international proletariat." This statement and its expressed attitude of commitment is seminal to the poetry that Alberti would write not only during the thirties but also for the next fifty years.[4]

Alberti's first political poem, "Con los zapatos puestos tengo que morir (Elegía cívica) (1° de enero de 1930)," (1930), and *Consignas* (1933), *Un fantasma recorre Europa* (1933), *El burro explosivo, Nuestra diaria palabra* (1936), *De un momento a otro (poesía e historia) (1932–1937)* (1937), and *El poeta en la calle (1931–1936)* (1938) have a dual focus: politics and man as a "political animal."[5] The subject matter of this poetry is the art of government and the affairs of state. Concerned with public events, Alberti's political poetry of the thirties extends beyond the private inner world of the poet and often responds to sociopolitical circumstances, frequently incorporating them as themes. At times, this poetry discloses an underlying ideological and normative thesis that is often polemical and even perhaps presented in a highly didactic, doctrinaire manner. Alberti's poetry of the thirties is also concerned with man, "Functioning Man," to borrow Louis MacNeice's phrase, a vital and active participant in the community (*MP,* 29).

The poet and the role the poet ought to assume as a "man among men," as a committed, politically sensitive, and politically active poet of the *pueblo,* the common people, are other concerns of Alberti's poetry of the thirties.[6] For Alberti, the poet not only represents but also is the spokesperson for and the persuasive and vocal guide of the people. The public themes of his poetry are often presented by various public voices who transcribe and, occasionally, criticize the sociopolitical reality of the common man.

Throughout the era under consideration, Rafael Alberti both presents man's reality as it is and envisions how it should be. Whether recording the effects of a dictatorship ("Elegía cívica"), the course and the impact of the Marxist-socialist revolution (*Un fantasma recorre Europa*), or the "catastrophe" and the "glory" of the Spanish Civil War (*Capital de la gloria*), Alberti writes about man, the problems facing man, and the course of action that must be taken in order for man to change his present circumstance and create and construct the Just Society of his future.

In his poetry of the thirties, Rafael Alberti assumes the public voice of the spokesperson for the pueblo of whom he sings. Louis MacNeice observed in 1938 that "the poet is primarily a spokesman, making statements or incantations on behalf of himself or others—usually for both, for it is difficult to speak for oneself without speaking for others or to speak for others without speaking for oneself" (*MP,* 1). Aware of his role as the poet of the people and forever speaking on behalf of the collectivity to whom his life and work are actively committed, Alberti provides a self-portrait of the public spokesperson of his poetry:

> Yo soy Rafael Alberti . . . el que vuelve a su patria como poeta en la calle, a nivelar su voz con la del pueblo, a ser suyo en la lucha, a cantarlo, ayudarlo, sostenerlo. . . .
>
> Creo que soy un hombre comprometido con el hombre, y mi literatura es una literatura de servicio, de virtud. . . . Estoy comprometido porque he sido un hombre libre, y el hombre libre elige. Y elegí el amor y el dolor del hombre de España, del mundo. . . . yo soy un poeta de la vida. El compromiso mío no es

cantar, sino cantarles a ellos, y ésta es la diferencia de gargantas. . . . He exaltado en mi verso la liberación de los hombres y el amor y la fraternidad y la paz. Creo que mi mano puede estrechar la de todos los hombres.[12] (*PEC*, 616, 617, 618)

The Poet and the Pueblo

I shall develop three significant elements of Alberti's poetry of the thirties. The first is Alberti's identification with the people. For the poet, the common man constitutes the essence of not only the Spanish nation but also the universal and ideologically unified nation of the world. Poetry of the people is, as Alberti writes in one of his poems on the Spanish Civil War, a public poetry where the poet's public voice is the "pulmón de todo un pueblo" (*PC*, 416).[7] In this poetry reverberates the singular voice of the poet, essentially the "eco de un canto collectivo." Jaime Concha's observation regarding Pablo Neruda's revolutionary poetry also applies to Rafael Alberti's poetry of the thirties: "Poesía y revolución aquí se hermanan: la voz individual de nuestro máximo poeta no es sino el eco de un canto colectivo, el rumor inconmovible de una sociedad que labra en la práctica, y paso a paso, su destino soberano."[8]

The second element recurrent in Alberti's poetry of this period is a Marxist view of political events and issues, a Marxist vision of the present and future eras. In referring to the political poets of his own generation in Great Britain in the thirties, Louis MacNeice observes that many of his contemporaries converted to Marxism because it offered a "creed" to the artist who "must move in a concrete world" (*MP*, 25).[9] Stephen Spender offers another reason why Marxism appealed to so many writers in the thirties. Spender writes: "Perhaps one reason for the attraction to communism was that the communists also had their vision of final crisis, though they regarded it as one involving the destruction of capitalism rather than of civilization" (*TA*, 24). Rafael Alberti, a man among men in the concrete world he daily surveyed as a poet of politics, adopted in 1931 the creed of Marxism and throughout the remainder of his political poetic production advocated the destruction of the old political order and the construction of the Marxist-socialist new era.

Pablo Neruda, César Vallejo, Louis Aragon, W. H. Auden, Stephen Spender, and many other poets of the thirties underwent a political conversion similar to that of Alberti and each also held and expressed similar Marxist views in many of his works. Alberti's poetic trajectory closely parallels that of other poets of this same era. The best analysis, however, of Alberti's own conversion to Marxism and the subsequent change in the subject matter of his poetry lies in his poetry itself. In chapters 3 and 4, I discuss the poet's affirmation of the "other world" (*PC*, 350) he embraced and the social circumstances that engendered his commitment to the people's future.

The third important element of Alberti's poetry of the period under consideration is his optimistic vision of the people's nascent era. Like other committed poets of the thirties, Alberti is ever-hopeful and never loses sight of the emergent "dawn" of the people's era, a prevalent and symbolic motif in his and others' poetry of the period. Even in the midst of the Spanish Civil War and the destruction of his dream of the Just Society, Alberti optimistically sings of the "new child of victory" who will triumphantly usher in the people's era of "glory" (*PC*, 402).

Poetry, Politics, and Prophesy

In *La arboleda perdida*, Alberti remembers the years 1928–29 and himself as a non-"political animal": "Poco o nada sabía yo de política, entregado a mis versos solamente en aquella España hasta entonces de apariencia tranquila. Mas de repente mis oídos se abrieron a palabras que antes no había escuchado o nada me dijeran: como república, fascismo, libertad" (*AP*, 276). However, with the continuing and ever-increasing threat to freedom posed by the dictatorship of Miguel Primo de Rivera, Alberti came to see, as his memoirs and first political poem "Con los zapatos puestos tengo que morir (Elegía cívica) (1° de enero de 1930)" reveal, that he could no longer remain apolitical but would have to speak on behalf of the Spanish people:

> El grito y la protesta que de manera oscura me mordían rebotando en mis propias paredes, encontraban por fin una puerta de escape, precipitándose, encendidos, en las calles enfebrecidas de estudiantes, en las barricadas de los paseos, frente a los caballos de la guardia civil y los disparos de sus máusers. Nadie me había llamado. Mi ciego impulso me guiaba. La mayor parte de aquellos muchachos poco sabía de mí, pero ya todos eran mis amigos. ¿Qué hacer? ¿Cómo darles ayuda para no parecer únicamente un instigador, uno de esos 'elementos extraños' a los que la prensa se atribuía siempre cualquier suceso contra el régimen? Ni los poemas de *Sermones y morades,* aún más desesperados y duros que los de *Sobre los ángeles*, podían servirles. A nadie, por otra parte, se le ocurría entonces pensar que la poesía sirviese para algo más que el goce íntimo de ella. A nadie se le ocurría. Pero los vientos que soplaban ya iban henchidos de presagios. (*AP*, 277)

During the thirties and in the decades that followed, Rafael Alberti would urge "la utilidad pública de la poesía," appreciating the value of a poetry that promised more than "el goce íntimo de ella."

Alberti's poetry is allied with that of many committed British poets of the same period. In *The Thirties and After: Poetry, Politics and People*, Stephen Spender, assessing the works of his contemporaries, recalls: "One had the sense of belonging to a small group who could see terrible things which no one else saw" (*TA*, 23). Pablo Neruda remarks in his memoirs that Rafael Alberti had this prophetic vision: "Yo conocí a Rafael Alberti en las calles de Madrid con camisa azul y corbata colorada. Lo conocí militante del pueblo cuando no había muchos poetas que ejercieran ese difícil destino. Aún no habían sonado las campanas para España, pero ya él sabía lo que podía venir" (*CV*, 188).

This clairvoyant, prophetic, public voice of the thirties in Spain anticipates the emergence of the common people as the vital force capable of securing the social revolution and the Just Society. In 1930, however, when Alberti wrote his first political poem, the "Elegía cívica," his hopes for the Just Society were menaced by an ominous political regime. This apocalyptic poem, which I examine in chapter 2, depicts in gruesome detail the nightmare of living in a stifling ambience of death and social disorder. Alberti predicts the *pueblo*'s doom if the people do not act collectively in order to bring about change in the existing social system. Seeing "the terrible things that no one else saw," this "poeta en la calle" of 1 January 1930, grounded in his contemporary reality and intent on recording and changing this reality, undertakes a threefold mission he will pursue throughout his poetry of the thirties. This mission entails disclosing his vision of the present social circumstance of the people, predicting what must be done in order to effect the people's new era, and advocating "la utilidad pública de la poesía."

In chapter 3, I examine the years 1931–35 in Alberti's poetic production and his conception of the people's contribution to "a new human history."[10] During these years Alberti, as a novice to political poetry, experiments with revolutionary modes of political writing. He discovers not only the instrumental value of poetry but also the meditative and reflective potential of poetry concerned with public rather than private matters. I focus on specific poems in the collections *Consignas* and *Un fantasma recorre Europa* as examples of either utilitarian political poetry or reflective political poetry. In addition, I examine the prevalent public themes and voices that first emerge in these works in relation to their subsequent development in other poems of the same era and Alberti's collections of political poetry written during and after the Spanish Civil War.

The fratricidal conflict that took place in Spain between 1936 and 1939 was both a prominent and poignant example to the world of the people's desire to change the existing social order and to create the new society of the future. The theme of the people's role in erecting the Just Society culminates in

Capital de la gloria, Alberti's intimate poetic diary of the people's struggle. This war poetry, in which Alberti's public voice both proudly celebrates the heroic deeds of the common man in the war and pensively attempts to comprehend the significance and the purpose of the conflict, is the subject of chapter 4. The poems of *Capital de la gloria* probe the meaning of the Spanish Civil War, a public event that shaped and determined the destiny of the Spanish people and also had grave repercussions throughout the free world.

"Putting the Subject Back into Poetry"

Stephen Spender, in his evaluation of the thirties, observed: "This was one of those intervals of history in which events make the individual feel that he counts. His actions or his failure to act could lead to the winning or the losing of the Spanish Civil War, could even decide whether or not the Second World War was going to take place" (*TA*, 25). Rafael Alberti, in speaking on behalf of other individuals in his public poetry of that decade, knew that direct action was needed if the freedom of the people was to be secured. He believed this so firmly and so deeply that he dedicated his life and work to poetry and to politics, to the word and to the deed. His poetry of the thirties reveals a keen awareness of both the power and the necessity of discourse used to realize social action and change. Spender's observations regarding British political poets of the thirties sheds further light on many of Alberti's political poems written during that same era: "In writing about politics, we were using the instrument of language provided for us by our predecessors to express what they lacked in their work, an overt subject matter. We were putting the subject back into poetry. We were taking the medium of poetry which to them was an end in itself and using it as an instrument for realizing our felt ideas about the time in which we were living" (*TA*, 26).

In his political poetry Alberti communicates his observations, concerns, and aspirations either in an aggressive, agitative, and highly doctrinaire manner or in a more subdued, reflective, and meditative manner. In the latter type of poetry, figurative language rather than political rhetoric is used. This social poetry transcends the realm of public politics, conveying the reader to the poet's personal political conclusions. Much of this reflective poetry, especially in the case of Alberti's poems of the Spanish Civil War, is a unique synthesis of politics and poetics, a poetry in which the poet approaches his external subject by drawing from his own personal involvement in and reactions to pressing public events.[11]

The Present Study

Throughout Alberti's political poetry of the thirties he delineates features of the *pueblo*-protagonist while explaining the role of this symbolic collective engaged in political activity. In this study I trace both the evolution of this protagonist in Alberti's poetry and also examine how the poet expresses, explains, and evaluates the role of this collective force within society. Because Alberti's poetry of this period is concerned with Spain, Europe, the USSR, North and South America, or wherever his travels and his survey of public issues would take him, my study also considers the poet's political and historical milieu. It is thus, in part, an "extrinsic" study in that it is an attempt to interpret Alberti's poetry of the period "in light of its social context."[12] This poetry is not divorced from its social setting; rather, it is a poetry where the setting itself figures prominently, be it the regime of Primo de Rivera, peasant unrest in the early thirties in Spain, the embracing of Marxism by the European common man, or the battlefields of the Spanish Civil War.

In addition to considering the concrete world that is the subject matter of this poetry, I also closely examine the poem itself, offering detailed analyses of many of the most representative poems of this period in Alberti's poetic production. Style, structure, diction, tone, rhythm, and metaphoric language and tensions are among the many aspects of the work that I investigate in my attempt to determine what and how this poetry communicates.

I have selected and adjusted my approach to Alberti's poetry according to the specific text under consideration.[13] Alberti's earliest political poem, the "Elegía cívica," is a cryptic and disquieting examination of the social climate of Spain in the late twenties. In chapter 2, I show that the poet's hermetically surrealist vision of the relation of the populace to the social order makes sense only if the reader identifies the specific thematic and structural formulas that both create and order the chaos that seems to be the poem itself. The poet's difficult surrealist style, however, aids rather than hinders his horrifying descriptions of the social reality transcribed in the "Elegía cívica." Alberti's political allegory not only presents the reader with the poet's own personal vision of the social disorder experienced by the citizens of Spain on 1 January 1930, but also effectively uses a montage of complex and colliding images, often reminiscent, as I demonstrate, of early surrealist films. In addition, numerous surrealist motifs, metaphoric inversions, and varied anaphoric and rhythmical patterns aid the poet in embodying linguistically his personal vision of the social chaos prompting his "Elegía cívica." I also study Alberti's verbal montage of confusing, clashing images in relation to the cinematic "intellectual montage" method developed by Sergei Eisenstein.[14] A filmic interpretive strategy thus aids in my ordering the chaos of Alberti's "Elegía cívica."

In 1933, with the publication of *Consignas* and *Un fantasma recorre Europa*, Alberti abandons the enigmatic and oneiric images of the "Elegía cívica" and adopts instead a new image that both verbally incarnates and succinctly expresses the social message underlying this poetry. This image does not record the fantasies of the mind or the afflictions of the poet's own self, but rather it is conceived as a social message chronicling the actions and aspirations of the common people. The public speakers of Alberti's poetry of the early thirties, as discussed in chapter 3, focus on special sociopolitical circumstances experienced by the *pueblo* as it attempts to create its own destiny. The poet, inspired by Marxist ideology and the people of whom and for whom he now writes, uses the discourse of the poem both to transcribe the collectivity's social reality as it is and also to envision how it could be.

Much of *Consignas* and *Un fantasma recorre Europa* is poetry of direct language and statement, political discourse and rhetoric, calls to action, and mandates to participate in the social revolution. The speakers of these poems, the party's spokesperson, the "we" of the people, and the narrator representing the common man, are public voices didactically proclaiming the poem's fundamental social command. I show that in the poetry of 1933–34, especially, Alberti adopts a clear, simple, and direct style that could be apprehended immediately by the people to whom his assumed public voices speak. "Poetic diction" has been replaced by "political diction" as the poet, immersed in the people's social reality and intent on carrying out his newfound role as the agitator of the masses, attempts to persuade and educate his audience regarding the goals of the revolution. Marxian dictums, obvious political clichés, didactic statements, and often-belligerent mandates to act abound in Alberti's political verse of the early thirties. The poet thus engages in what I call an agitative mode of political writing. Here, the declaration and acceptance of the poem's social message take precedence over a more refined and reflective interpretation of public issues. Alberti's agitative works of the early thirties, as I demonstrate in chapter 3, place Spanish political poetry at the fore of revolutionary verse not only in Spain but also in other European countries.

Close examination of the overtly stated social theses, commonplace political diction, prosaic rhyming and rhythmical patterns, aggressive tone, and the abundance of popular verse forms in this poetry illuminates the new role the political poem was to have for Alberti in the early thirties. Conceived and used as a weapon in the social struggle, the poem must be appraised in terms of its instrumental rather than aesthetic value. The reader, therefore, must learn to approach the poem in a new way, namely as a verbal means to obtain a specific political end. In chapter 3, I address the issues raised by poetry written for the sake of politics and discuss the problems often associated with such verse.

The advent of the Spanish Civil War in 1936 and the grave and sobering experience of this conflict bring Alberti to a new understanding of the role of language within the realm of political events. For the poet of *Capital de la gloria,* as I show in chapter 4, the paradox of the struggle is to be resolved on both an ideological and a metaphoric level. Marxism provides Alberti with a unity of vision and the underlying meaning of the role of the common man in the war. Metaphoric language, however, is the means by which the poet is able to penetrate conceptually and emotionally the death/life dialectic manifested in war and also to imagine and sketch in verse the war's synthetic result—the new destiny of the people in the new era.

In my study of representative poems of *Capital de la gloria,* I attempt to clarify how poetic discourse helps to formulate the enigma that is war. Calls to action, political rhetoric, and agitative tones do not serve the poet who wishes to reflect upon and give voice to his more personal response to the public event that is both a "catástrofe" and a "gloria," a "vida muerta y nueva vida" (*PC,* 402, 417).[15] My examination of various poems of the period reveals that the poet uses language in a creative manner as he investigates the cause and consequence of the Spanish Civil War. Campestral imagery of germination and growth, the symbolic motifs of spring and autumn, personification, paradox, and apostrophe are among the many stylistic devices that Alberti uses to mold linguistically his thoughts on the nature of war and the role of the people in the conflict.

Throughout *Capital de la gloria* Alberti's rigorous search for "la palabra precisa . . . el verbo exacto . . . el justo adjetivo" (*PC,* 445), which will, he hopes, impose order on the "desorden impuesto"[16] of the conflict, is intensified by the use of alexandrine quartets, hendecasyllabic tercets, *silvas,* and ballads that further help both to make precise and to give form to the amorphous enigma of war. When Alberti is able to harness his impulse to preach and propagandize, abandon his public role as the agitator of the masses, and use the poem's discourse as a means to discover and communicate the paradoxical nature of the political event, as he does in *Capital de la gloria,* then the poet offers his personal insight into the collectivity's efforts to create a new future.

Only a few critics have analyzed, interpreted, or evaluated poems of Alberti's political poetic production.[17] Often, studies of his poetic trajectory ignore his political poetry or dismiss it altogether, stressing Alberti's earlier, more lyrical stage, where he is concerned with the troubled states of his own soul.

These studies often disregard or dispense with his more politically tendentious stage and his concerns with public events.[18] Although some critics have examined Alberti's political poetry in more general studies of either Spanish commitment poetry of the twentieth century (Lechner) or the evolutionary pattern of Spanish poetry of the thirties "entre pureza y revolución" (Cano-Ballesta), no single work focuses on Alberti alone as the most significant revolutionary poet of politics that Spain produced in the thirties. Alberti's evolution as a poet is similar to that of other important political poets of his lifetime, most notably Vladimir Mayakovsky, Louis Aragon, W. H. Auden, Pablo Neruda, César Vallejo, Luis Cernuda, Emilio Prados, and Miguel Hernández, to name but a few, and these similarities need to be established and explored. The public themes and voices of Alberti's poetry of the thirties are constant in the remainder of his political poetic production. There exist, then, thematic and stylistic elements binding Alberti's political poetry into an organic whole, and these should be investigated if his political poetry is to be appreciated as an integral part of his life and his work. In this book I try to remedy the deficiencies in the existing bibliography of Rafael Alberti while exploring the nature and the value of political poetry as a genre.

Throughout my investigation of Rafael Alberti's political poetry I attempt to interpret the poem itself, survey the concrete world of the era it records, and highlight the problems raised by this type of poetry. I also heed and recommend the advice of C. M. Bowra: "No problem in poetry can ever have a final solution, and the problems raised by political poetry are no exceptions to this rule. We must take it as we find it and ask what poets have tried to do and how far they have succeeded in doing it" (*PP*, 33).

Chapter 2

The Poet, Society, and the Image of Disorder

Será en ese momento cuando los caballos sin ojos
se desgarren las tibias contra los hierros en punta
de una valla de sillas indignadas junto a los
adoquines de cualquier calle recién absorta en la
locura. . . .

Rafael Alberti, "Elegía cívica"

You cannot say, or guess, for you know only
A heap of broken images. . . .

T. S. Eliot, *The Waste Land*

C on los zapatos puestos tengo que morir (Elegía cívica) (1° de enero de
1930)" is Rafael Alberti's obscure and disquieting examination and critique of the social climate of the twenties in Spain. This extensive narrative
poem is a complex political allegory where, with surrealist discourse and what
André Breton had called the "verbo profético,"[1] Alberti explains, reflects,
and attempts to order the chaos pervading the ambience in which his narrator
roams. On this first day of January 1930, the date accompanying the poem's
title, nothing makes sense, the paradoxical and the inexplicable happen, and
everyday existence is transformed into an unreality that soon becomes the
norm. Here, figurative forces embodying death clash with and seem to be
victorious over those embodying life as an ominous "alba de las náuseas"
looms (l. 29).

The events, episodes, and characters presented and described in Alberti's
fiction refer to circumstances and personages of Spain's sociopolitical order in

a particular moment in history. Specifically, the poet focuses on the art of government and the affairs of state of King Alfonso XIII and the dictatorship of General Miguel Primo de Rivera.[2] This poem, however, is not merely the story of Spanish politics as told by the poet's assumed narrative voice. The "Elegía cívica" is, above all, a subjective, probing and, at times, strident critique of the sociopolitical order and, particularly, of the relation of the monarchy and the dictatorship to the Spanish people.

Ordering the Chaos

The plot of the "Elegía cívica" is quite simple. A first-person narrator witnesses, records, and responds to the cause of death, destruction, repression, social unrest, political disorder, and street demonstrations taking place in the Spain he observes.[3] The resulting ruin, chaos, frenzy, and "madness" (l. 1) are linked to the poem's antagonists, "vosotros" (l. 2) and "tú" (l. 5). In the course of the narrative, the collective, as a cohesive, life-filled force, openly confronts the "tú" and eventually destroys this figure (ll. 43–60). Throughout the "Elegía cívica," the poem's narrator repeatedly declares the role that he plays in the events recreated in the poem.

It is the telling of the "Elegía cívica" that is complicated, confusing, and often enigmatic. A series of bizarre, obscure, disjunctive, unsettling, and perplexing word-images must be made sense of, interrelated, ordered, and finally united before the semantic message of the poem can be reconstructed and ultimately understood. The poem's inherent ambiguities and cryptic allusions make sense only if the reader relates them to something outside of the poem itself, namely the sociopolitical circumstances of a specific moment in Spanish history. Making sense of the word-images, discerning the identity of the mysterious antagonist, and ordering the chaos that seems to be the poem itself are the most difficult tasks facing the reader upon beginning the poem. There are, however, specific and interrelated structural, stylistic, and thematic formulas that, when deciphered, will render the poem meaningful:

Será en ese momento cuando los caballos sin ojos se desgarren las tibias   1
    contra los hierros en punta de una valla de sillas indignadas junto a los
    adoquines de cualquier calle recién absorta en la locura.
Vuelvo a cagarme por última vez en todos vuestros muertos   2
en este mismo instante en que las armaduras se desploman en la casa del rey,   3
en que los hombres más ilustres se miran a las ingles sin encontrar en ellas   4
    la solución a las desesperadas órdenes de la sangre.
Antonio se rebela contra la agonía de su padrastro moribundo.   5
Tú eres el responsable de que el yodo haga llegar al cielo el grito de las   6
    bocas sin dientes,

de las bocas abiertas por el odio instantáneo de un revólver o un sable.   7

Yo sólo contaba con dos encías para bendecirte,   8

pero ahora en mi cuerpo han estallado 27 para vomitar en tu garganta y   9
hacerte más difíciles los estertores.

¿No hay quien se atreva a arrancarme de un manotazo las vendas de estas   10
heridas y a saltarme los ojos con los dedos?

Nadie sería tan buen amigo mío,   11

nadie sabría que así se escupe a Dios en las nubes   12

ni que mujeres recién paridas claman en su favor sobre el vaho   13
descompuesto de las aguas

mientras que alguien disfrazado de luz rocia de dinamita las mieses y los   14
rebaños.

En ti reconocemos a Arturo.   15

Ira desde la aguja de los pararrayos hasta las uñas más rencorosas de las   16
patas traseras de cualquier piojo agonizante entre las púas de un peine
hallado al atardecer en un basurero.

Ira secreta en el pico del grajo que desentierra las pupilas sin mundo de los   17
cadáveres.

Aquella mano se rebela contra la frente tiernísima de la que le hizo   18
comprender el agrado que siente un niño al ser circuncidado por su
cocinera con un vidrio roto.

Acércate y sabrás la alegría recóndita que siente el palo que se parte contra   19
el hueso que sirve de tapa a tus ideas difuntas.

Ira hasta en los hilos más miserables de un pañuelo descuartizado por las   20
ratas.

Hoy sí que nos importa saber a cuántos estamos hoy.   21

Creemos que te llamas Aurelio y que tus ojos de asco los hemos visto   22
derramarse sobre una muchedumbre de ranas en cualquier plaza pública.

¿No eres tú acaso ése que esperan las ciudades empapeladas de saliva y de   23
odio?

Cien mil balcones candentes se arrojan de improviso sobre los pueblos   24
desordenados.

Ayer no se sabía aún el rencor que las tejas y las cornisas guardan hacia las   25
flores,

hacia las cabezas peladas de los curas sifilíticos,   26

hacia los obreros que desconocen ese lugar donde las pistolas se hastían   27
aguardando la presión repentina de unos dedos.

Oíd el alba de las manos arriba,   28

el alba de las náuseas y los lechos desbaratados,   29

de la consunción de la parálisis progresiva del mundo y la arterioesclerosis   30
del cielo.

No creáis que el cólera morbo,   31

la viruela negra,   32

el vómito amarillo,   33

la blenorragia,   34

las hemorroides,   35

los orzuelos y la gota serena me preocupan en este amanecer del sol como   36
un inmenso testículo de sangre.

En mí reconoceréis tranquilamente a ese hombre que dispara sin importarle   37
la postura que su adversario herido escoge para la muerte.

Unos cuerpos se derrumban hacia la derecha y otros hacia la izquierda,   38

pero el mío sabe que el centro es el punto que marca la mitad de la luz y la   39
sombra.

Veré agujerearse mi chaqueta con alegría.   40

¿Soy yo ese mismo que hace unos momentos se cagaba en la madre del que   41
parió las tinieblas?

Nadie quiere enterrar a este arcángel sin patria.   42

Nosotros lloramos en ti esa estrella que a las dos en punto de la tarde tiene   43
que desprenderse sin un grito para que una muchedumbre de tacones haga
brotar su sangre en las alamedas futuras.

Hay muertos conocidos que se orinan en los muertos desconocidos,   44

almas desconocidas que violan a las almas conocidas.   45

A aquel le entreabren los ojos a la fuerza para que el ácido úrico le queme   46
las pupilas y vea levantarse su pasado como una tromba extática de
moscas palúdicas.

Y a todo esto el día se ha parado insensiblemente.   47

Y la ola primera pasa el espíritu del que me traicionó valiéndose de una gota 48
de lacre

y la ola segunda pasa la mano del que me asesinó poniendo como disculpa   49
la cuerda de una guitarra

y la ola tercera pasa los dientes del que me llamó hijo de zorra para que al   50
volver la cabeza una bala perdida le permitiera al aire entrar y salir por
mis oídos

y la ola cuarta pasa los muslos que me oprimieron en el instante de los   51
chancros y las orquitis

y la ola quinta pasa las callosidades más enconadas de los pies que me   52
pisotearon con el único fin de que mi lengua perforara hasta las raíces de
esas plantas que se originan en el hígado descompuesto de un caballo a
medio enterrar

y la ola sexta pasa el cuero cabelludo de aquel que me hizo vomitar el alma   53
por las axilas

y la ola séptima no pasa nada   54

y la ola octava no pasa nada   55

y la ola novena no pasa nada   56

ni la décima   57

ni la undécima   58

ni la duodécima . . .   59

Pero estos zapatos abandonados en el frío de las charcas son el signo   60
    evidente de que el aire aún recibe el cuerpo de los hombres que de pie y
    sin aviso se doblaron del lado de la muerte.

The reader must identify and isolate the biographical, social, political, historical, and artistic factors that will aid in determining and recreating the composite portraits of each of the three central figures in the allegory: the first-person narrator, the "tú" addressed, and the collective victim of the actions of the "tú." Relationships between the characters in the poem and pertinent extrinsic contexts must be established; these relationships, in turn, will help to explain why the figures are portrayed as they are and behave as they do in the "Elegía cívica." In this way, the poem and its characters not only are linked to particular periods in the poet's life, the history of art and ideas, and the sociopolitical climate but also are more meaningful and more fully developed if interpreted in light of such contexts.[4]

Antithetical dualities or elements in opposition are essential components of the narrator's description of the ambience. Throughout the poem, Alberti juxtaposes elements in conflict in order, on one level, to represent the tensions existing in the social climate and, on another level, to vivify, sustain, and portray realistically the essential thematic tensions of the poem: death/life, evil/good, frenzy/equilibrium, destruction/construction, disease/health, present/future, ending/beginning. The development of these contrapuntal thematic pairs both structures the poem and conveys its fundamental theme.

Inversion of these antithetical dualities is another formula of the "Elegía cívica." As the narrative develops, all opposites are momentarily fused and then rapidly inverted as the poet portrays a surging force of life, metaphorically embodied in the gigantic, dynamic "wave." Adversary becomes victim as the life-force overwhelms death itself and ushers in a new era in the poem's prophetic closing moments (ll. 43–60). Within this schema of reversal, a significant set of negative, metaphoric symbols are inverted as life supplants death, good triumphs over evil, and the beginning of a new epoch signals the end of an old political system.

Another formula used by the poet, intimately related to the formulas of conflict and inversion, is that of the method of "montage." Sergei Eisenstein defines "intellectual montage" in the following passage: "By what, then, is montage characterized and, consequently, its cell—the shot? By collision. By the conflict of two pieces in opposition to each other. By conflict. By collision. . . . From the collision of two given factors arises a concept. . . . Montage is conflict."[5] Applying Eisenstein's concept of filmic montage to the "Elegía cívica," from the collision of word images, scenes, episodes, characters, emotions, tones, temporal periods, and methaphoric symbols a synthesis is ultimately reached, "the thematic matter," as Eisenstein calls it, "the image of the theme itself." This "thematic matter" is the political allegory of the poem.[6]

Identifying and deciphering a significant set of common surrealist motifs also form a part of the method of writing and producing the meaning of the "Elegía cívica."[7] The motifs graphically depict the setting, emotional climate, protagonist, and antagonist of the narrative. In addition, unusual and shocking verbal associations, multiple word images rapidly shifting in content and perspective, and the conflict and inversion of incongruent realities all reflect the poet's adaptation of both cinematic and vanguardist techniques to the poem. These techniques enable the poet to present dramatically his own version of the encroachment of the nightmare on reality, of the horror imagined or the horror experienced.

The poem can be divided into two general moments where the first (ll. 1–47) is, in content, in direct opposition to the second (ll. 48–60). Part 1 describes a tumultuous ambience where the "órdenes de sangre" (l. 4) issued by the poem's central antagonist, "tú eres responsable" (l. 5), attempt to destroy the poem's protagonist, the collective victim of such "orders." In part 2 the roles of persecutor and victim are dramatically inverted as the collectivity rises in order to assault its adversary. The principle of inversion functions, thus, both as a structural and a thematic component of the poem.

The two overall moments of the "Elegía cívica" can be further divided into six sections, four in the first and two in the second. In each, and in the poem conceived as an organic whole, the progressive struggle between forces of death and destruction and a single force of life is graphically and vividly described. Section 1 (ll. 1–15, "Será en ese momento . . .") establishes the setting of the poem, a turbulent cityscape where multiple elements are simultaneously viewed in the process of being destroyed. The opening line establishes the poem's prophetic tone and the fusion of present and future temporal planes. During this day of reckoning the citizenry and the narrator respond to both the political affairs of state and the enigmatic figure held responsible for these affairs. Section 2 (ll. 16–21, "Ira desde la aguja . . .") intensifies the feverish emotional climate where rage and anger permeate every element engaged in the death/life conflict and where barbaric and inhumane acts of violence are an everyday occurrence. In section 3 (ll. 22–27, "Creemos que te llamas Aurelio . . .") further dimensions are added to the setting, the principal antagonist, and the collective protagonist of the political allegory. Section 4 (ll. 28–47, "Oíd el alba de las manos arriba . . .") establishes the poet's complex symbol of the dawn together with the inversion of the opposed dualities developed in the three previous sections. Section 5 (ll. 48–59, "Y la ola primera pasa . . .") marks the narrative's climax. An all-powerful, vital force subverts the personified regime of death. Section 6 (1. 60, "Pero estos zapatos . . .") is the poem's denouement. This prophetic epilogue, together with the poem's title "Con los zapatos puestos tengo que morir," interrelates the envisioned and figurative burial of the cause of death with the narrator's own response and stance.

"Aquellas horas españolas"

In *La arboleda perdida* Alberti summarizes not only the political events of the period under consideration but also his personal response to them. They are, as he reveals, the underpinnings of the "Elegía cívica":

> Me sentí entonces un poeta en la calle, un poeta 'del alba de las manos arriba,' como escribí en ese momento. Intenté componer versos de trescientas o cuatrocientas sílabas para pegarlos por los muros, adquiriendo conciencia de lo grande y hermoso de caer entre las piedras levantadas, con los zapatos puestos, como desea el héroe de la copla andaluza:
>
>> Con los zapatos puestos
>> tengo que morir,
>> que, si muriera como los valientes,
>> hablarían de mí.
>
> 'Con los zapatos puestos tengo que morir' se tituló el primer poema que me saltó al papel, hecho ya con la ira y el hervor de aquellas horas españolas. Desproporcionado, oscuro, adivinando más que sabiendo lo que deseaba, con dolor de hígado y rechinar de dientes, con una desesperación borrosa que me llevaba hasta morder el suelo, este poema, que subtitulé 'Elegía cívica,' señala mi incorporación a un universo nuevo, por el que entraba a tientas, sin preocuparme siquiera adónde me conducía. . . . Poesía subversiva, de conmoción individual, pero que ya anunciaba turbiamente mi futuro camino. (*AP,* 290–91)

Paraphrasing the poem's opening line, Alberti also sketches a self-portrait of the young Rafael of this period in his introduction to the 1966 edition of a collection of many of his political poems: "Yo soy Rafael Alberti . . . el que aún tuvo fuerzas para lanzarse, flamígero de súbito, precipitándose en las calles enfebrecidas de estudiantes, en las barricadas de los paseos, frente a los caballos de la guardia civil y los disparos de sus fusiles."[8]

The "Elegía cívica" is written in free verse where each line corresponds to the impetus of the poet's mental and intuitive processes and the dynamism inherent in the scenes and episodes of violence and destruction that he sets out to record. A lengthy versicle of more than sixty syllables initiates the poem and establishes its accelerated rhythm.[9] The reader is rapidly thrust into a turbulent atmosphere where death collides with life, and madness is the synthetic result in the particularized locale of "cualquier calle recién absorta en la locura" (l. 1). The movement of the symbolic, speeding horses of blind justice and death, headed in space and time toward the stationary "vallas de sillas indignadas" (l. 1), the figurative embodiment of will, and the response of the people, further underscores the dramatic dialectical process of both the poem and the politics of the era. Readers believe that they are about to witness a lament describing and envisioning the imminent death of the Spanish citizenry.

Indignation, however, provokes the citizens to act (l. 1) and thus, momentarily, the process and progress of destruction is impeded. The entire poem will take place in this suspended moment when the citizenry hovers between death and life and the narrator both foretells and awaits the inversion of this dualism. Indignation also prompts the poem's first-person speaker to action as he openly insults and harshly, and rather crudely, criticizes and denounces the cause of such destruction: "Voy a cagarme por última vez en todos vuestros muertos" (l. 2). This attitude, action, and reaction are echoed later in the poem when the speaker declares: "¿Soy yo ese mismo que hace unos momentos se cagaba en la madre del que parió las tinieblas?" (l. 40). These shocking insults and vulgarities are reminiscent of the acts of denunciation of many surrealists and dadaists.[10] Such extreme, personal reactions were often triggered by an extreme sociopolitical reality over which the poet, writer, painter, filmmaker had no control. The narrator's disgusting and appalling actions in the "Elegía cívica" are no exception. They too have their origins in the discontent, frustration, general feeling of helplessness, and widespread disillusionment experienced by modern man as he attempts to comprehend the stark facts of the social disorder and the senseless violence and death engendered by a political system.

The indignation (l. 1), the ire (ll. 16–20), and the wrath (l. 25) experienced by the collective underlie the individual narrator's own emphatic condemnation heard at the outset of the poem. This single insult is taken one step further when the belligerent first-person speaker declares his disgust for the person held responsible for the state of affairs: "Yo solo contaba con dos encías para bendecirte, / pero ahora en mi cuerpo han estallado 27 para vomitar en tu garganta y hacerte más difíciles los estertores" (ll. 8–9). At twenty-seven years of age, the poet, through his highly personalized assumed narrative voice, affirms his disdain for the harbinger of death and actively participates in the demise of this political figure. The narrator, on the one hand, thus foreshadows the role and attitudes of "the poets of today" that Alberti would advocate in 1931: "The poets of today" should be "cruel, violent, demoniac, frightening."[11] On the other hand, this voice of protest echoes that which had already been witnessed and silently heard on the screen in Luis Buñuel and Salvador Dalí's *Un Chien Andalou*. Such a "violenta protesta" is, as *La arboleda perdida* recalls, the "imagen de una juventud confusamente convulsionada." Alberti goes on to say: "Fue significativa la revelación de esta película en la coincidencia con Madrid ya enfebrecido, no lejos de las vísperas de grandes acontecimientos políticos" (*AP, 278*).

The first showing of the 1928 surrealist film in Spain took place on 8 December 1929, in Madrid's *Cineclub* (*AP, 277–78*). That Alberti saw this film that night and some twenty-three days later composed the "Elegía cívica" must be considered when analyzing this "poesía subversiva" (*AP, 291*). A product of feverish political times and a feverish and violent way to interpret those times, the "Elegía cívica" is, in many ways, a verbal extension of Buñuel and Dali's vision of the same period. This same vision would leave its imprint on Federico García Lorca and an entire generation of Spanish poets.[12]

The "Elegía cívica" is an outcry, a gut reaction, a very real response to what the poet thought to be a life-threatening and life-limiting political situation. The abrasive, aggressive insults hurled at the regime, although perhaps lacking in aesthetic value, are the first indications in Alberti's poetry that the poem could serve something other than itself. In recalling this period Alberti observes: "El grito y la protesta que de manera oscura me mordían rebotando en mis propias paredes, encontraban por fin una puerta de escape, precipitándose, encendidos, en las calles enfebrecidas de estudiantes, en las barricadas de los paseos, frente a los caballos de la guardia civil y los disparos de sus máusers. Nadie me había llamado. Mi ciego impulso me guiaba. . . . A nadie, por otra parte, se le ocurría entonces pensar que la poesía sirviese para algo más que el goce íntimo de ella. A nadie se le ocurría. Pero los vientos que soplaban ya iban henchidos de presagios" (*AP, 277*). The "Elegía cívica" is one such "omen." After 1930, in much of Alberti's political poetic production, as will be demonstrated in chapter 3, the poem will serve as a political weapon. It will become an instrument used to expose, analyze, and criticize social matters, and at the same time it will be used to educate and call to action the masses. The instrumental value of the political poem, in embryo in the "Elegía cívica," is especially evident in the more militant poems of *Consignas, Un fantasma recorre Europa,* those published in *Octubre* and *El Mono Azul, El burro explosivo,* and *Coplas de Juan Panadero.*[13]

The first-person narrative voice of the "Elegía cívica" is the antithesis of the childlike, innocent voices heard in *Marinero en tierra* (1925). It is also different from the confused, tormented, personalized angelic voices expressing and explaining the multiple aspects of a complex, existential crisis in *Sobre los ángeles* (1928). The speakers heard in *Yo era un tonto y lo que he visto me ha hecho dos tontos* (1929), the solitary, bewildered, tragicomic characters of the silent cinema, molded to reflect the poet's own mood, are also distinct from the narrator of the "Elegía cívica." This latter voice, as the poet's assumed persona, no longer probes the enigma of existence in relation to his own troubled self. Rather, his concerns lie with the collective and with the relationship of the collective to the political order. The sociopolitical ambience that is, in many ways, the hidden backdrop for Alberti's poems written between 1927 and 1929 has fully surfaced and come to the foreground as the first day of January 1930 and a new era in Alberti's poetic production begin.[14]

"En ti reconocemos"

The most enigmatic of the characters in the "Elegía cívica" is "tú eres el responsable" (l. 6). At the outset of the poem, the narrator's cameralike eyes move from a panorama of "cualquier calle recién absorta en la locura" (l. 1) to the Royal Palace in ruins (l. 3) and finally to a close-up of the central antagonist (ll. 5–7).

At the close of section 1 (l. 15) and again at the beginning of section 3 (l. 22), the narrator provides two additional, enigmatic close-ups of this figure. In identifying and associating the chief figure issuing and responsible for the "órdenes de sangre" (l. 4) with the three proper names of "Antonio," "Arturo," and "Aurelio," Alberti forces the reader to focus on this cluster, the possible significance of each name, and the extrinsic associations that could be made with each. The common denominator of these names, aside from their initial letter, is the possible allusion to past rulers and statesmen of history or legend. Such references characterize and develop, without directly identifying, the underlying presence of the real "tú" of the "Elegía cívica": King Alfonso XIII.

The first reference, to Antonio, can be associated with Mark Antony, who, obeying "las desesperadas órdenes de la sangre" (l. 4), avenged the death of his patron, his "padrastro moribundo" (l. 5), Caesar. The poet establishes a direct syntactic parallel between the subjects of lines 4 and 5 and thus links both figures to the bloodshed and confrontation of death/life forces described at the outset of the poem. It is perhaps the years of anarchy and the reign of terror experienced by the Roman citizenry during the Second Triumvirate that Alberti finds repeated, centuries later, in the sociopolitical ambience described in the poem. A further parallel might be drawn between the political figure of the past and the "tú." Under Caesar there was increased centralization of executive authority in the hands of the *princeps*. The members of the Second Triumvirate followed this precedent and overruled the Roman Senate, convened and dissolved the Assembly at will, controlled elections, and subordinated the constitution to the paramount authority of the rulers. Throughout his reign, King Alfonso XIII repeatedly sought to concentrate all executive authority in his own hands. The king might also bear resemblance to the Roman statesman if it is recalled that Mark Antony often tried to thwart efforts of the opponents of Caesar to establish a new republic. During the later twenties, both King Alfonso and Primo de Rivera aborted various plots that had as their aim the creation of the Spanish Republic. They also refused to hold general elections that might have indicated, as they did in 1931, that the vast majority of the Spanish people desired a new form of government.[15]

What in the life of the legendary figure of romance might the "we" of the poem "recognize" (l. 15) in the "tú"? In comparing the chief personage of Alberti's poem with the fairy king, King Arthur, the first apparent similarity might be that both became monarchs at a very early age and, as youths, both received extensive military training. The Spanish monarch, however, did not actually lead army excursions, as did the mythic Arthur. The former's role in the international politics of Morocco, however, and in the direction of military operations over the head of his minister of war, could be what the poet wishes to underscore in his association of the soldierly undertakings of the legendary Arthur with the military activities of King Alfonso, although the failure of the Spanish army in Morocco is the antithesis of King Arthur's more successful, legendary military campaigns.[16] There are no mythical elements associated with the "tú" of the poem. Rather, this figure is portrayed as "alguien disfrazado de luz" (l. 14). The legendary Arthur slew monsters and giants, while the demythified figure of Alberti's poem "rocía de dinamita las mieses y los rebaños" (l. 14). Just as the splendor of Arthur's court and the Round Table came to an end, the poem's speaker envisions the moment "en que las armaduras se desploman en la casa del rey" (l. 3).

The last reference to a proper name, Aurelio (l. 22), brings to mind the emperor Marcus Aurelius. History reveals that this Roman leader exerted his absolute power for the benefit of the people. Under the guidance of the virtues and wisdom of the Stoic philosopher, the people were the sole object of government. The Aurelio of the "Elegía cívica," however, is the inverse of the beneficent Marcus Aurelius. The Aurelio portrayed in the poem's third section looks with disdain upon the dehumanized people who gather to hear his words. Metaphorically reduced to a reptilean collective, the people's presence before this elevated figure is insignificant. Human indignation found in "cualquier calle" (l. 1) of the poem's initial section is absent in "cualquier plaza pública" (l. 22) as the dehumanized people face the political figure who, although he is called Aurelio, does not possess the admirable qualities of the emperor whose name he has assumed. It is perhaps King Alfonso's attitude of superiority directed toward the common man that Alberti wishes to capture in his close-up of Aurelio.[17]

Alfonso's name need not actually appear in the poem since the narrator suggests his presence from the outset when the Civil Guards, obeying the king's orders, confront the Spanish citizenry (l. 1). It is also indirectly implied in the vision of the demise of the royal palace (l. 3). As the "Elegía cívica" progresses, the king's presence in the civil affairs of Spain is underscored with allusions to past political figures who have also governed nations and who, in many ways, can be compared with or contrasted to the "tú" of the political allegory. The letter *A*, common to all three proper names, brings to mind the emblem of the "Royal A," picturing a crown superimposed on the apex of this letter. The alphabetical ordering of the cluster of names, in addition, recalls the ancient, although Anglo-Saxon, custom of having the names of the heirs to the throne correspond to a specific alliterative pattern. This pattern might then further suggest the presence of King Alfonso.

These early close-ups of the "tú responsable" force the reader first to associate this figure with a particular time period and social climate of Spain. This familiar figure is, however, made unfamiliar as the poet creates a complex composite portrait with historical, political, and mythical dimensions. This initial sketch culminates in a series of close-ups in sections 5 and 6. The unified portrait presented earlier is rapidly and viciously undermined as the narrator presents, in shocking and gory detail, the mutilated and disembodied features of the "tú." The poet, thus, further jolts the reader and disconnects him or her from what had previously been established as the norm. The unified political-historical portrait is shattered, and a maimed, dismembered figure of useless and mangled parts, a victim of a force more powerful than he, is all that remains. What Alberti wants his readers both to see in a new way and to comprehend more fully, in this final hyberbolic sketch, is that no political figure who is the adversary of the people can escape from a unified life-force once the latter have decided to act and change the existing social order.

"El alba de las náuseas"

The "tú" of Alberti's fiction is both enigmatically portrayed as a political figure and also metaphorically described as a character fostering and embodying death (ll. 2, 6–7, 9). The single agent of death of section 1 is, in section 4, transformed into a personified spatial and temporal moment in which figurative destructive forces are so omnipresent and so omnipotent that the beginning of a new day, a new calendar year, and a new decade is abruptly halted when "el alba de las náuseas" (l. 28) overwhelms all aspects of life itself (ll. 28–36). In this cosmic moment of infectious diseases, even the sun has lost its vitality and ability to engender life. A ruler of death, a sickly leader, oversees the nightmarishly grotesque world imagined by the narrator. In the horrific locale, the "órdenes de sangre" (l. 4) decreed by the "tú" are now figuratively concentrated in the crude and shocking image of the "amancer del sol como un testículo de sangre" (l. 36), as the violence and bloodshed fostered by the political system engulf the entire ambience and have cosmic repercussions. The sun, often associated with the king symbolism of "man transposed to the solar plane,"[18] has become a monstrous, maimed, and morbid force. The governing principle, life itself and the powers of regeneration, is thus dramatically and radically undermined and transformed into its opposite during this hideous dawn. All forms of life and especially daybreak as a symbol of a vital beginning suddenly and paradoxically reach immediate extinction in the mordantly sterile ambience from which not even the laws of nature can escape.

The accelerated tempo maintained by the long versicles of sections 1–3 has been momentarily stopped as the poem's speaker enumerates the figurative ailments inherent in the dawn of doom (ll. 31–35). In these short lines of five to nine syllables, the narrator at once underscores the decaying condition of the personified regime while at the same time graphically and metaphorically stressing the symbolic significance of the "sick king" who projects onto nature his own declining, infected spiritual state.[19]

The "alba de las náuseas . . . de la consunción de la parálisis progresiva del mundo" (ll. 29–30) of the "Elegía cívica" recalls the symbolic "aurora" described by Federico García Lorca in "La aurora" in *Poeta en Nueva York:* "La aurora llega y nadie la recibe en su boca/porque allí no hay mañana ni esperanza posible" (ll. 9–10).[20] There is no dawn of new life in García Lorca's horrifying description of the sociopolitical reality of this metropolis in 1929–30. Rather, "la oscuridad inextinguible" pervades "un mundo de la muerte."[21] All life-forces—animal and human alike—are paralyzed and suffering in the repressive, threatening environment of this "poeta en Nueva York." Both Alberti's long poem and García Lorca's collection share an apocalyptic vision; tones of indignation and denunciation; the underlying themes of the conflicts of death/life, oppressor/oppressed; and two distinct yet similar cityscapes of frenzy and chaos. Both works are intensely personal responses to elements in society that wantonly destroy man's freedom and life.[22]

In the "Elegía cívica," the actions and reactions of the poem's speaker and the collective protagonist, the Spanish people, are often parallel in the course of the narrative. This is particularly evident when their emotional responses are charted and analyzed. At first, unrestrained indignation characterizes the temperament of both the citizenry and the narrator as each witnesses and participates in the death/life struggle depicted in the opening section of the poem. Indignation, on the part of the speaker, is transformed into hatred and open denunciation (ll. 2, 4), emotions that are later manifested by the collective in the closing section. The emotions of the "vallas de sillas" (l. 1) are therefore revolutionized into overpowering hatred as the collective "ola" of the "muchedumbre de tacones" (l. 43) destroys the cause of death (ll. 48–59).

The poem's narrative voice, at first, expresses a desire to be blinded (ll. 10–11) so that his eyes can no longer witness death and destruction. This poet-seer has seen all and wants to see nothing more of the collision of death and life where death is the unwanted victor. The narrator, however, finds no one who will "saltarme los ojos con los dedos" (l. 10). With his eyes wide open he thus becomes the clairvoyant critic of the affairs of state (ll. 22–43), eventually foreseeing the demise of the regime and the emergence of the triumphant people (ll. 48–59).

At first, the narrator of the "Elegía cívica" does not fully comprehend his role in the symbolic death/life struggle. It is only after envisioning the possible advent of a new day, "el alba de las manos arriba" (l. 28), which will eclipse the "alba de las náuseas" (l. 29), that the narrator comprehends and explains his newfound role:

> En mí reconoceréis tranquilamente a ese hombre que dispara
>   sin importarle la postura que su adversario herido
>   escoge para la muerte.
> Unos cuerpos se derrumban hacia la derecha y otros
>   hacia la izquierda,
> pero el mío sabe que el centro es el punto que marca
>   la mitad de la luz y la sombra.
>
> (Ll. 37–39)

Earlier he was an isolated witness to the destruction and disorder, a lone voice denouncing "vuestros muertos" (l. 2). His analysis of the people as victims of destructive political forces together with his identification and denunciation of the political source of such disorder have led him to a clear understanding of his own position as a member of the collectivity and as a declared enemy of all that the regime represents. He is, on the first of January 1930, "este arcángel sin patria" (l. 42) because he awaits a new social system. The poem itself has ordered the disorder; it has shaped the poet's own view of the role of the poet and the people in analyzing, criticizing, and changing the affairs of state.

"A Heap of Broken Images"

Rage in the "Elegía cívica," unlike that molded into angelic form and stemming from an emotional crisis in *Sobre los ángeles,* is politically motivated. This emotion is not peculiar to a particular man and a specifically personal experience. Rather, it belongs to and originates in all men and in the collective experience of the "órdenes de sangre" (l. 4). With horrifying detail and techniques and motifs adapted from surrealist literature and film Alberti, particularly in section 2 of the poem (ll. 16–21), creates a montage of word images graphically describing the multiple facets of this complex emotional state. As the narrator surveys the vast, enraged wasteland, he reveals, in an accumulation and collision of images of disorder, the general cause of the emotion (destruction) and its general effect (death). A series of close-ups of the relentless conflict of elements in opposition and the ultimate triumph of death over life further reveals and sustains his vision of this choleric locale: parrararrayos"/"piojo," "peine"/"basurero," "pupilas-cadáveres"/"grajo," "niño"/"cocinera," "pañuelo"/"ratas." In Alberti's new ordering of reality, familiar elements have been placed into an unreal and gruesome world where death, not new life, and violence, not peace, reign as an ominous new year begins. Additional accumulations of prepositions of location ("desde, hasta, entre, en") and specific verbs of action ("desentierra, se rebela, al ser circunciado, se parte") intensify the correspondences between concrete objects representing disintegrating and victimized matter and the general moribund and incensed state of all of civilization. Essentially pictorial, and it is to be recalled that Alberti is both a poet and an artist, this section is a visual representation of the death/life dialectic pervading the "Elegía cívica."[23]

The use of synecdoche gives the second section of the poem metaphoric unity of expression. Remnants of civilization ("peine, pupilas, niño, pañuelo") have been substituted for mankind and represent the general human situation. Kenneth Burke points out that synecdoche has philosophical implications " 'where the individual entity is seen as recapitulating the nature and structure of the universe.' "[24] Applying this observation to the second section of the "Elegía cívica," each synecdochic entity is a microcosm of the disintegration of life and the omnipresence of death originating in and caused by "tus ideas difuntas" (l. 19)—the sociopolitical order scrutinized and evaluated by the narrator.

In this grisly world, inhumane creatures are sustained by the injury and the death they inflict on others. Human emotion has been reduced to the single, ubiquitous, overpowering ire penetrating all aspects and all elements of this now uncivilized world. Even the ritual of circumcision performed on a small child[25] and the allusion to the feast of the circumcision of the child Jesus on January first are brutally undermined as the narrator hyperbolically portrays the barbarism experienced by the unsuspecting and the innocent.

Many prevalent surrealist motifs, such as violent acts done to children, savage assaults on victims, mutilation, creatures flourishing on carrion, and litanies of rotting civilization,[26] serve to depict in great detail the poet's nightmarish vision of the relation of the populace to the political order. Such horrifying visions juxtaposing the bizarre with the commonplace, the shocking with the norm, follow one another rapidly on the printed page throughout the "Elegía cívica" in long versicles endlessly and realistically describing the irrational and the hideous circumstance enveloping all aspects of society as 1930 begins. This is the last time such excursions into the subconscious, the nightmare, and the underside of man will be undertaken in Alberti's poetry. For the time being, however, as especially sections 2 and 5 indicate, surrealist discourse serves to express and even unite the experience of the political event with the violent emotions used to interpret this event.

C. Brian Morris has observed that "in Spain as elsewhere in the 1920's and 1930's, surrealism's extreme attitudes and actions stimulated extreme responses."[27] Alberti's "Elegía cívica" is one such "extreme response." Grounded in avant-garde experiments, techniques, motifs, collages and montages, the poem describes the "locura-órdenes de sangre-ira-alba de las naúseas-ola" stemming from and engendered by the sociopolitical circumstances underlying the poem. Disillusioned, disenchanted, skeptical, horrified and incensed by World War I, the surrealists and dadaists often sought to reflect in their works the death of a civilization and the tragic anguish of the absurdity of man's fate. Alberti, motivated by different political events, reveals a kindred vision, extended in time, space, and focus, in the "Elegía cívica." In modern Spanish poetry, García Lorca's *Poeta en Nueva York* and Luis Cernuda's *Los placeres prohibidos,* of this same era, manifest a similar tragic vision of and "extreme response" to the social order.

The poem's entire progression of word images and contradictory elements is fused into the single image of the giant "wave" of section 5 (ll. 48–59).[28] The object of destruction, however, has been dramatically reversed as the former victim eventually succeeds in crushing the one held responsible for the atrocities witnessed and described throughout the poem. The people, who earlier had been portrayed as passively dehumanized "frogs" listening to the words of a man called Aurelio (l. 22), have now become active participants in his demise. The "muchedumbre de tacones" (l. 43), who initiated the assault, has itself been transformed into an amorphous, all-powerful life-force that will fulfill the narrator's prophecy of the reversal of roles that will take place when the victimized become the adversary. The horrifyingly realistic descriptions of violent death, hysterical anarchy, and brutal acts found throughout the first four sections of the poem culminate in this final sequence of appalling mutilation, radical and outrageous emotional responses, and the ultimate inversion of the forces of death/life.

"The surrealists' conviction that they had the power to see things invisible to other men" and that the "poet-seer," thus, "was gifted to witness and recreate in words . . . a new arrangement of reality" is noted by Morris.[29] These observations can be applied to the litany of violence in the fifth section of Alberti's political allegory. What is "seen" is that the symbolic dawn of paralysis and death, which formerly "y a todo esto el día se ha parado insensiblemente" (l. 47), has now been transformed into a prolonged interval where a surging, vital force triumphs over death.

The narrative voice creates a new picture of upheaval, a "new arrangement of reality," now emphasizing lifeless, disembodied aspects of the personified regime. The poet links these body features of the victim to the more abstract ruinous force by means of the anaphoric repetition of the phrases "del que" and "y la ola . . . pasa." With cinematographic speed, an accelerated succession of word images depicting barbaric acts accumulates before the reader's eyes and in the reader's imagination until, finally, the victim has been overpowered and nothing is left but three typographical suspension points and white space on the printed page. Free verse, enjambment, anaphora, and extensive poetic lines stylistically capture and mirror the impetus of the raging life-force and the unbridled imaginings of the poet's mind. Unpunctuated versicles allow the succession of word images to flow uninterruptedly into one another as the violent visions recorded in each poetic line are ultimately fused into an apocalyptic vision versicle.

The narrator's central focus, however, is momentarily altered when new thematic matter is introduced in this section of the political allegory. A series of imagined atrocities committed against the *yo* narrator (ll. 47–52) emphasize his personal, violent response to the violence witnessed and experienced. Such visions, however, seem to be more of a catalog of the grotesque than an authentic response to the destructive political order. The vulgar insults heard earlier in the poem have become vindictive visions and shocking, verbalized fantasies as the poet's own hatred and personal inner turbulence are transferred to the political regime. Momentarily losing sight of the collective as victim, something he did not do earlier in the poem, Alberti forgoes investigating the causes of the social disorder in favor of listing, with surrealist rhetoric and hermetically private images, aspects of his own malaise. Such a harangue is out of place not because it is unmotivated; certainly line 2, in particular, and sections 1–4, in general, indicate its motivation. It is out of place in the "Elegía cívica" because it destroys the focus of the poem: the citizenry of Spain and its collective response to the affairs of state. Throughout Alberti's political poetic production, whenever the collective's destiny is eclipsed by the poetic voice's own barbed, scathing, personal attacks on political figures, then the poem itself seems to be nothing more than an ineffective instrument of derision rather than a work that could mold into poetic form the politics of the public event.

Poetry and Prophecy

In the "Elegía cívica" the reader has traveled along the streets "absorbed in madness" (l. 1), through the "plaza pública" of "los pueblos desordenados" (ll. 22, 24). The reader has followed the narrator's own physical and psychological excursions into the irrational and violent ambience of "aquellas horas españolas" (*AP,* 290). On this first day of January 1930, judgment is passed on the negative and ruinous elements of society that limit and destroy human freedom and life. Alberti's first political poem is, in itself, a doomsday prediction affirming the demise of those who have brought about death: "Pero estos zapatos abandonados en el frío de las charcas son el signo evidente de que el aire aún recibe el cuerpo de los hombres que de pie y sin aviso se doblaron del lado de la muerte" (l. 60). All that remains of the personified destructive force, as the epilogue reveals, is "estos zapatos abandonados." The cluttered urban setting of horses, chairs, debris, corpses, and diseases culminates in a simple locale where "air" (l. 60), symbolic of "space as a medium for movement and for the emergence of the life-processes,"[30] absorbs death and prepares for the beginning of the new era foretold earlier in the poem (l. 43). The ending of one epoch signals, in itself, the beginning of another, on this symbolic first day of January 1930, as the new decade, calendar year, month, and day bring with them the poet's hope for the vision of a new future. In such an era, the "alba de las naúseas" (l. 29) will be transformed into that symbolic moment when, "a las dos en punto de la tarde" (l. 43), the metaphoric dualities developed throughout the poem will be inverted and life will be victorious over death.[31]

Constructed on the collision of elements in opposition and the thematic principles of contrast and inversion, the "Elegía cívica" can ultimately be reduced to the underlying, pervasive, antithetical duality of death/life. This, as has been shown, can be further broken down into the following major thematic juxtapositions: destruction/construction, stasis/action, emotional fervor/emotional equilibrium, madness/stability, "alba de la naúseas"/"alba de las manos arriba," dawn/two in the afternoon, disease-decay/poplar groves, present/future, past/future, "órdenes de sangre"/"una muchedumbre de tacones haga brotar su sangre en las alamedas futuras," "tú"/"muchedumbre-ola," ending/beginning, and finally, "zapatos abandonados"/"zapatos puestos." Such opposing pairs are the essential features of Alberti's conceptual montage. Having worked out their interrelations, the reader, thus, provides an inner framework for both the structure and meaning of the "Elegía cívica." The adhesive agents in this process are the subtext of Alberti's political allegory and the reader's own role in deciphering this subtext. Once the poem is understood as a critique of the affairs of state of Spain in the twenties, then each contraposed element takes on political significance. Each antithetical, thematic pair, thus, can be fused into a single conceptual unit revealing the dialectic inherent in both the poem itself and in the sociopolitical climate it reflects and records.

At the close of section 2 of the poem, the narrator affirms: "Hoy sí que nos importa saber a cuántos estamos hoy" (l. 21). The insistent and emphatic repetition of the word "hoy" together with the temporal indicators of "en este mismo instante" (l. 3), "alba" (l. 29), "tarde" (l. 43) and "día" (l. 47) and the predominance of present tense verbs in the poem call attention to the date parenthetically accompanying the poem's title: "1° de enero de 1930" and its significance. The Roman deity Janus, alluded to in the nominalization "enero," is itself identified with the principle of inversion. Janus, as Cirlot points out, represented with two faces looking in opposite directions, is a "symbol of wholeness. . . . Because of its duality, it may be taken to signify all pairs of opposites" and, ultimately, their fusion and inversion. Cirlot further notes that "the Romans associated Janus essentially with destiny, time and war. . . . His faces were turned towards the past and the future, denoting both awareness of history and foreknowledge. . . . Janus also symbolizes the union of the powers of priest and monarch."[32]

The significance of Janus and the symbolic inversion of past/future and present/future is evident especially at the close of section 4. The "tú-estrella"/"muchedumbre de tacones" (1.43) reversal is immediately followed by a brief moment where the elegy's antagonist is assaulted and forced to open his eyes and acknowledge the malaise of the past social order (ll. 44–46). Both the "tú" and the "yo" of Alberti's political allegory have assumed Janus's awareness of history and foreknowledge of the future. Only the first-person narrator, however, clearly comprehends the significance of looking in opposite temporal directions and "seeing" the symbolic apocalypse that is, in fact, a genesis.

"Con los zapatos puestos tengo que morir (Elegía cívica)" is both a critique of the political system and a prophetic affirmation and proclamation of what could be done in order to change this system. At times, the poem suffers from boisterous exaggerations, unevenness in tone and point of view, vulgarisms, and oneiric fantasies. Still, to the reader willing to decipher and reconstruct its hidden and often confusing message, the poem does offer an original, striking, penetrating, and complex exploration and assessment of the political experience here rendered meaningful by the discourse of poetry. It also demonstrates that poetry, as Alberti was soon to realize, could be used to appraise and change the social structure rather than serve solely as a medium for self-analysis.

The "Elegía cívica" signals Alberti's "incorporación a un universo nuevo"

(*AP*, 290) or, to use Aragon's phrase, the "return to reality."[33] This "new universe" has three major components, both in this poem and in those that Alberti would write subsequently. Politics is the subject matter of this poetry; the common man has an instrumental role in determining the course of political actions and events; and the poet's assumed poetic voices are both aligned to and the spokespersons for the aims, aspirations, and undertakings of the common man. This is Alberti's first attempt to write outwardly political poetry and his last undertaking with cryptic imagery portraying the human existential condition. After 1930, Alberti will seek new forms to express the new subject matter of his poetry. Like Aragon, Alberti will eventually find the "new image" that will reflect and envision the new sociopolitical order. In this way, Lucille Becker's observation regarding Aragon's poetry is also applicable to Alberti's poetry written after 1930: "This new image was to bring forth a different message, fraternity instead of individualism, optimistic affirmation of a new world instead of pessimistic despair. . . . Aragon would put language at the service of his party and use words for the creation of a new society."[34] At this point in time, however, as Alberti's "Elegía cívica" demonstrates, the problems inherent in the social order are resolved by means of recording bizarre imaginings and nightmarish experiences in the enigmatic word images in which a political allegory is embedded. Hereafter, for the poet, these problems will be resolved by means of the Marxist ideology and, after 1936, a personalized and authentic response to the Spanish Civil War.

It is unfortunate that such an important poem as the "Elegía cívica" has not received the critical attention it deserves.[35] Any study of Alberti's poetic production must include the "Elegía cívica" because the central conceptual dialectic of this poem is seminal to the political poems which are to follow. The struggle between the figurative death/life forces evaluated in this poem will be transferred to and evaluated in terms of the class struggle in collections such as *Consignas, Un fantasma recorre Europa, De un momento a otro, (poesía e historia),* and *El poeta en la calle,* and the Civil War, in *Capital de la gloria* and much of Alberti's poetry written in exile. The emergence of the common man as the origin of new life and as the vital source instrumental in ushering in a new political order is the fundamental theme of Alberti's entire political poetic production for the next fifty years. This unifying theme is first introduced in the "Elegía cívica."

In Alberti's poetic production, the "Elegía cívica" definitively signals a change in focus and is thus a significant work.[36] Less concerned with his own "alma en pena"[37] and more concerned with the sociopolitical problems of the collective, Alberti, with the writing of this poem, embarks on his journey as a self-proclaimed "poeta en la calle." "Con los zapatos puestos tengo que morir (Elegía cívica)" reveals in embryo the committed attitude Alberti would later adopt and explain in much of his poetry written after 1930. This poetry, ever aware of, never deaf to, and always recording "el compás del pulso de mi época" (*PC*, 790), both demonstrates and parallels the evolutionary pattern characterizing the works of García Lorca, Cernuda, Neruda, Aragon, and Mayakovsky and other poets, writers, artists, and filmmakers of the early decades of the twentieth century.

Chapter 3

The Poet, the People, and a New Human History

Of all living beings on earth we alone are privileged to experience and relive, one after another, the moments of substantiation of the most important achievements in social development. More. We have the privilege of participating collectively in making a new human history.

Sergei Eisenstein, Introduction to *The Battleship Potemkin*

*I*n 1968, Rafael Alberti recalled the final days of his stay in Germany and his first trip to the USSR during the closing months of 1932:

A fines del año 1932, me encontraba en Berlín, con María Teresa, pensionado por la Junta de Ampliación de Estudios para estudiar los movimientos teatrales europeos. En Alemania ya no se podía vivir. Un clima de violencia la sacudía en todas direcciones. El hambre y la desocupación andaban por las calles, cruzadas de las escuadras nazis, que pateaban las aceras, salpicando de agua de los charcos a los aterrados transeúntes. Hitler se disponía, como en gran guiñol, a instalar sus absurdos bigotes y brazos gesticulantes tras el humo y las llamas del incendio del Reichstag. En ese momento viajé por primera vez a la Unión Soviética, que fue para mi entonces como un viaje del fondo de la noche al centro de la luz. (*PEC*, 453)

These words reveal Alberti's acute sensitivity to social injustice, a sensitivity evident in embryo in the thematic content of the "Elegía cívica" written two years earlier. The metaphoric "noche" of gloom and death witnessed by the poet in the Germany of 1932 is merely an extension in time and space of the horrifying "alba de las náuseas" examined in Alberti's first political poem. The metaphoric "luz" that would engender the envisioned "alba de las manos arriba," the object of the narrator's quest in the "Elegía cívica," the poet would ultimately encounter in the USSR in 1932. Alberti's first trip to the Soviet Union, like that of Louis Aragon two years earlier, was to have a dramatic and lasting effect on his life and his work.[1] This illuminating and revealing journey of discovery signaled the beginning not only of revolutionary thematic matter in Alberti's poetry but also of a new mode of writing, a political mode of writing, which would have, in the course of the next fifty years, various manifestations in his poetic production.

The symbolic "light" that would inspire Alberti's earliest political poems of 1931–33, especially, originates in his experiences in the Soviet Union as a young man of thirty, his first impressions of the Five-Year Plan, his friendships with the members of the *Unión Internacional de Escritores Revolucionarios (MORP),* the influence these writers would have on both himself and his work, his conversion to Marxism, and, above all, the poet's sincere commitment to his fellowmen.[2] Alberti's political poetry written in the initial years of the thirties and later published in *Consignas* and *Un fantasma recorre Europa* is also grounded in the social reality of the First Spanish Republic and the poet's own reactions to the general climate of unrest transcribed in his political poetry of that era.[3] Despite its idealistic aims, commitment to liberty, and attempts at social reform, the Republic could not contain the social conflicts present in the Spain of the early thirties. This frenzied and uncertain climate not only would help to precipitate the Spanish Civil War but also would leave its imprint on Alberti and other artists of his generation, thereby shaping their attitudes toward politics and their approaches to art.[4]

"Al volver y empezar"

Thematically, *Consignas* and *Un fantasma recorre Europa* explore many of the same social problems and political solutions considered in the "Elegía cívica." In the collections of 1933, however, the poet's assumed personae have emerged from the fateful, surreal "alba de las naúseas." The speakers heard in these collections walk among their fellowmen and amid the concrete reality of the here and now. The speakers are public voices concerned with public issues: agrarian problems, peasant revolts, the struggle for the land, hunger, poverty, unemployment, economic depression, rural and industrial strikes, the promulgation of Marxism, the promotion of the classless society, and the construction of the new social order. These concerns are rooted in the poet's external circumstance, and ultimately, in *Consignas* and *Un fantasma recorre Europa,* they are transformed into the themes and normative theses of the poems whose overt subject is this circumstance. Throughout Alberti's collections of 1933, public voices not only investigate these concerns of the poet but also encourage their audience to scrutinize, participate in, and in most cases, change the social reality described in the poems.

The chaotic and frightening world described in Alberti's political allegory of 1 January 1930 reflected, in part, the social turmoil of Spain in the late twenties. This world, however, also reflected the poet's own personal and often exaggerated vision of that social situation. The reality described in *Consignas* and *Un fantasma recorre Europa*, however, is based on aspects of the real situation of the people in 1931–33, a situation that the poet and his audience share, a situation that the poet neither personalizes nor distorts in subjectively cryptic, oneiric descriptions. In these two collections of 1933, Alberti seeks to disclose clearly specific aspects of the "living process of reality," to use Adereth's observation (*CMFL,* 175), that have both stimulated his social conscience and awakened in him certain responses that are not peculiarly his own but rather collectively shared.

In *Commitment in Modern French Literature,* Adereth explains: "What committed writers like to stress is that images, no matter how fanciful, have their basis in reality and derive their force from the concentrated view of reality which they give us. . . . Images are not divorced from reality, but rise above it. They make us visualize what our senses alone cannot grasp, and they appeal to our imagination" (*CMFL,* 210, 211). It is this type of "image" that we find in Alberti's political poetry of 1931–33 when the poet of politics attempts to represent reality either as it is or as it should be rather than to portray it subjectively. The voyage from darkness to light experienced in 1932 by Alberti also, therefore, has stylistic manifestations in his poetry of the early thirties. If we compare the "Elegía cívica" with poems such as "Al volver y empezar" (*UFRE*) or "Mitin" (*C*), the hermetically perplexing image has been replaced by an accessible and shareable one accurately reflecting and effectively communicating the social circumstance analyzed by the poet's assumed public voice.

Social reality and the new image used to record and change it are evident in the introductory poem of *Un fantasma recorre Europa,* "Al volver y empezar." The poem is accompanied by the date 1932 and the epigraph "Se les prometen los campos / y al campo van a matarles," lines that serve as the repeated refrain in another of Alberti's poems of the period, "Romance de los campesinos de Zorita" (*C*). The political circumstance described in both poems is the Spain of 1931–32, generally, and the agrarian problems experienced by the Spanish people, particularly, during those years.

The "return" described in Alberti's "Al volver y empezar" is the same "return" analyzed by Louis Aragon in the essays of his 1935 collection *Pour un réalisme socialiste:* "le retour a la realité" of their fellowmen.[5] In Alberti's case, the poet transcribes the situation of the Spanish people and a particular group representing its plight—the peasantry. For Alberti, the Spanish peasantry embodies the dehumanized, "bestias de carga" (l. 16) condition of the entire working class, a condition that he believes is fostered by those controlling the means of production:

```
Vine aquí,                                                          1
Volví,
Volví aquí en el instante en que unas pobres tierras
cambiaban de dueño,
Eran tomadas violentamente por aquellos que hacía                  5
siglos se partían la vida sobre ellas,
Doblados de cintura,
Salpicados los trigos con su sangre.
Llegué aquí,
Volví,                                                            10
Volví cuando eran roturadas por bueyes y por mulos
arrancados,
Cogidos a la fuerza por aquellos que los cuidaron desde
niño,
Que se identificaron con su mansedumbre hasta llegar             15
a ser bestias de carga,
Recibiendo a cambio la pólvora y la cárcel de los mismos
que habían puesto en sus ojos el ansia de los campos.
Vine aquí cuando esto,
Llegué aquí                                                       20
Cuando esta hermosa sangre sucedía.
Volví,
Volví aquí para ponerme de su lado,
Para pedir a mis amigos un adarme siquiera de la suya,
De esa poca que anda por la mano y es aún más caliente          25
al cerrarse entre otra.
Llegué aquí,
Volví
Y vi cadáveres sentados,
Cobardes en las mesas del café y del dinero,                     30
Cuerpos podridos en las sillas,
Amigos preparados a recibir de balde el sueldo de la
muerte de otros.
Vine aquí
Y os escupo.                                                      35
Otro mundo he ganado.
```

In many ways the poem chronicles the age-old agrarian problem in Spain, in general, and the ineffective and inadequate agrarian statute of 1932, in particular. The Agrarian Reform Law that was passed by the Constituent Cortes of the Republic aimed at solving the rural landownership problem. It was, however, a modest proposal and by no means was it a satisfactory remedy for the agrarian problem endemic to the Spain of the early thirties. According to this law, the government expropriated all unworked estates of more than fifty-six acres of the *latifundia* of, primarily, central and southern Spain. The law, however, did not direct itself to the basic questions inherent in the agrarian reform issues of the day: how to divide the expropriated estates and how to redistribute the land so obtained.[6]

According to both the poem and the historical accounts recording social circumstances in Spain in the early thirties, the peasantry was promised land but received instead "la pólvora y la cárcel de los mismos / que habían puesto en sus ojos el ansia de los campos" (ll. 17–18). We are far from the surrealistic landscape described in the "Elegía cívica." In "Al volver y empezar" Alberti has placed both his assumed public voice and his reader squarely in the middle of a genuine social situation, a situation described in concrete terms and from a committed point of view. The poet does not expand the locale where his poem takes place as he did in his political allegory of 1930. Rather, he reduces space to a specific, synecdochical place, "aquí," where three interrelated, completed actions occur simultaneously: "Vine," "Volví," "Llegué." The poem's first-person speaker is "immersed" in a specific locale,[7] the world of the common people, and in a specific process, the "living process" of the collective's social circumstance.

The speaker of "Al volver y empezar" is, however, not merely a witness to the social injustice recorded. He is also an active participant in matters concerning the people, and his actions have a purpose: he aims to criticize and change these matters. Adereth's observations regarding what he has termed "committed realism" can be applied to Alberti's "Al volver y empezar" and the critical attitude adopted by the poem's public voice. Adereth explains: "Committed realism necessarily implies that literature does more than simply mirror the world, it actively intervenes in order to change it. . . . For 'littérature engagée,' the truthful depiction of the world is not an end in itself—it is but the means by which the artist instills in his reader the will to act. To the images which embody the essence of reality, he adds the imaginative vision of what reality could be" (*CMFL,* 177, 178). The "otro mundo" (l. 36), the "imaginative vision of what reality could be," is what Alberti comprehends fully in "Al volver y empezar," throughout *Consignas* and *Un fantasma recorre Europa,* and later in his subsequent collections of political poetry. Still, Alberti's "committed realism" first emerges in these two collections of 1933, when the poet affirms his own active intervention in the world of his fellowmen.

In "Al volver y empezar" Alberti carefully investigates the conflicts existing in Spanish rural society in 1932. He does, however, do more than this. The poet, through his outraged first-person public speaker, offers a declaration of allegiance to that segment of society that he believes has been unjustly treated both in Spain's past and present: "Volví aquí para ponerme de su lado" (l. 23). At the same time, echoing the narrator of the "Elegía cívica," the public voice of "Al volver y empezar" emphatically rejects those whom he believes are responsible for social injustice: "Vine aquí / Y os escupo" (ll. 34–35). The speaker has observed all aspects of the social reality he has set out to evaluate, and his indignation in "Al volver y empezar" is guided by those external aspects that have aroused him and moved him to action. Alberti's own commitment to the people, his newly embraced Marxist creed and his vision of a better world underlie the final proclamation of the poem: "Otro mundo he ganado" (l. 36). It is this concept of the "other world" that all men should seek together with the poet's accurate description of man's concrete world that Alberti will depict throughout his political poetical production.

There is an intimate connection between Alberti's symbolic "return to reality" outlined in "Al volver y empezar" and his use of an accessible, political mode of writing. The symbolic "empezar" of which he writes has a dual significance in 1932 for the young poet. A poem such as "Al volver y empezar" signals the "beginning" of Alberti's "committed realism" while also marking the "beginning" of a new stage in Alberti's poetic production. As Alberti reveals in a letter to José María de Cossío on 11 July 1932, he has begun to write "una poesía revolucionaria, de fondo político, pero sin dejar de ser poesía." Later in the letter he adds, "Creo que por este nuevo camino iré muy lejos."[8] Within Alberti's symbolic "return" to reality, as will be demonstrated, lies the "beginning" of new subject matter in his poetry of the thirties and new political modes of writing that will mold this subject matter into a poem concerned with "the essence of reality" and "the imaginative vision of what reality could be."

Political Modes of Writing

In *Consignas* and *Un fantasma recorre Europa* various political modes of writing are used in order to clarify and, in some cases, alter the social circumstances surveyed by the poems' speakers. These political modalities can be grouped under the general heading of a *socialist conviction mode of writing*. This modality, as I shall demonstrate with specific examples of Alberti's poems of this era, can be broken down further into two other particular types of political writing found not only in these collections of 1933 but also throughout his political poetic production. They are an *agitative mode* and a *reflective mode*.

The socialist conviction political mode of writing is essentially a socialist-realist mode of writing as defined by Maxim Gorky in 1934. Adereth observes:

> The phrase "socialist realism" was coined by Gorky at the first Congress of Soviet Writers in 1934. The Grand Old Man of Soviet letters meant it to describe the essential difference between the critical realism of the nineteenth century and the new realism which draws upon the experience of the first socialist society. Unlike their predecessors, he claimed, contemporary realists need not confine themselves to criticism of bourgeois society, but can depict the birth of a new civilization; and even in their criticism, they are in a position to make use of historical perspective which scientific socialism analyses and outlines. Granted the two basic assumptions that Marxism is the scientific explanation of human history and that the October Revolution of 1917 ushered in a new epoch, the epoch of socialism, there was nothing outrageous in Gorky's new expression. It was merely an assertion of his belief in the superiority of Marxism and of the Soviet system and an appeal to like-minded artists that they should observe and describe reality in the light of the changes taking place around them and of their socialist convictions. (*CMFL,* 196–97)

Rafael Alberti was one "like-minded" artist in attendance at the First Congress of Soviet Writers who obviously heeded Gorky's appeal to "observe and describe reality in the light of the changes taking place" and in the light of the artist's own "socialist convictions," as his poetry written after that date demonstrates.[9] It is, however, important to note that Alberti's poetry of 1931–33 demonstrates a socialist-realist conviction a few years prior to Gorky's public advocation of this mode of expression. The manifestation of this political modality in Alberti's earliest political poems also predates Aragon's series of speeches, given in 1935 and collected in that same year into his *Pour un réalisme socialiste,* where the French poet defines the concept and calls for the need to describe contemporary reality in terms of a socialist outlook. That Alberti's poetry of *Consignas* and *Un fantasma recorre Europa* is, in the thirties, an early manifestation of this tendency in Western thought and art is worthy of our attention. These two collections of 1933 clearly place Alberti, in particular, and Spanish political poetry, in general, at the fore of socialist-realist revolutionary poetry written during the decade under consideration.

During his visit to the Soviet Union, Alberti began to comprehend what his vocation as a poet of politics meant. After being introduced to the works of the members of the *Unión Internacional de Escritores Revolucionarios,* translating the poetry of Blok, Mayakovsky, Imber, Svetlov, and Asseef, meeting Louis Aragon and Elsa Triolet, and hearing various Soviet poets recite passages from both their own works and those of Mayakovsky,[10] Alberti began to write poetry that was firmly implanted in and that took inspiration from contemporary reality and the socialist convictions and aspirations he shared with other like-minded leftists. The October Revolution of 1917, the creation of the first socialist society, his own encounter with such a society while visiting the USSR, his impressions of and admiration for the common people who fostered such a society, his bond with the writers and poets who depicted this new world, and his own conversion to Marxism all serve as the foundation for the poetry of *Consignas, Un fantasma recorre Europa,* and that published in his revolutionary magazine *Octubre,* founded in 1933.[11]

The term *socialist realism,* as coined by Gorky in 1934 and as I use it here, should not be confused with the *policy* of socialist realism as advocated by the Soviet government especially in the late thirties, the forties, and even today. Adereth observes, and I agree with his observations, that the concept as defined by Gorky "was the natural form for commitment to take, and I do not think Gorky ever meant it to amount to the imposition of specific themes, a specific style or a specific method. Soon, however, the concept became one of the unquestioned dogmas of Soviet orthodoxy, and when it was endorsed by no less a person than the great Stalin himself, it acquired the value of a categorical imperative. Socialist realism was no longer considered desirable, it became compulsory, and instead of representing a challenge to the creative artist, it sank to the level of conformist art" (*CMFL,* 197).

The socialist-realist political mode of writing first evident in Alberti's poetry of *Consignas* and *Un fantasma recorre Europa* is not derived from the approved style sanctioned by Soviet authorities. Rather, it draws upon the poet's experience of his contemporary social reality, his observations of the world around him, his own position, as Sartre repeatedly stresses, as a "man among men" (*CMFL,* 27), and his own socialist convictions. The function of the word is, thus, to transcribe and change reality in terms of socialism and the New Socialist Era. Alberti's poetry, both of this period and those that were to follow, has at its foundation, to use David Caute's words, "the truthful, historically concrete representation of reality in its revolutionary development."[12] The poet who uses a socialist conviction mode of writing is, thus, both a contemporary realist and a critical realist engaged in assessing social development and the historical process.

Socialist realism as the method according to which Louis Aragon constructed his novels and as a doctrine, as he explains, applicable to poetry, prose, and art cannot be overlooked here. Aragon's interpretations of this concept are applicable to its early manifestation as a political mode of writing in Alberti's poems of 1931–33. In *J'abats mon jeu,* for example, Aragon explains that socialist realism is "the realism of our time, which takes into account the historical perspective of the future or of the present, according to each country, in other words, of socialism. . . . Socialist realism is the organizing conception of *facts* in literature, of *detail* in art, which interprets the detail, gives it significance and force, and integrates it into the general movement of history."[13] Aragon's views regarding this concept are further illustrated by remarks from his speech given at the University of Prague: "I demand an open realism . . . a non-academic realism . . . which is capable of modifying itself as it goes along . . . a realism which helps to change the world, a realism which is not meant to reassure us, but to rouse us, and which occasionally, because of that very feature, disturbs us."[14] Alberti's political poetry of 1931–33 and the collections that were to follow demonstrate this same advocation of a "realism which helps to change the world."

Throughout *Consignas* and *Un fantasma recorre Europa* Alberti seeks to define both his newfound role as a poet of politics and the new forms he uses to express the now revolutionary context of his verse. Alberti, like other committed writers of the thirties and later decades, demonstrates what Adereth has referred to as "a sense of social responsibility" which, as the critic explains, "should be, according to '*littérature engagée*,' a critical sense, for the aim of commitment is not to foster illusions but rather to destroy them" (*CMFL*, 33). In *Consignas* and *Un fantasma recorre Europa,* Alberti's "critical sense" and the "social responsibility" of his art are conveyed by essentially two specific political modes of writing: the agitative mode and the reflective mode.

Of the year 1933, Alberti writes: "Empiezo a ser poeta en la calle. Escribo multitud de poemas satíricos y de agitación, que recito en los actos políticos, en las bibliotecas obreras y en las plazas públicas. Aparece *Consignas*, librito en que recojo mis primeros poemas revolucionarios" (*PC*, 14). The political poetry of the agitative modality, primarily found in *Consignas* and the poems published in *Octubre* during this period, is militant in tone. Here the poet aims to have his poetry serve a cause, champion and advance a political ideology, influence his audience, persaude his audience to embrace specific political beliefs coincident with his own, and urge his audience to political action. This type of political poetry demonstrates what Sartre has called an "integrated militant function."[15] By examining the public themes and voices found throughout this poetry, the role of the poet as the agitator of the masses and the role of the poem as a political weapon, we can better understand characteristics of this political mode of writing and determine the value of poetry written in this mode.

Alberti's agitative political poetry has, for the most part, been ignored by the critics. On the one hand this is a curious omission, since the agitative mode of writing pervades this early period in Alberti's political poetic production. On the other hand, however, its neglect is readily apparent if it is understood that many critics, when approaching the political work, attempt both to define and to evaluate it in terms of its aesthetic function. When the poem, however, is judged to have an "integrated militant function," rather than a purely aesthetic function, it has often been dismissed. One critic of Alberti's political poetry explains: "el arte, en general, y en particular la poesía, nunca ha sido auténtico cuando es instrumento para expresar algo tendencioso." [16]

Another political mode of writing, however, is also evident in the poetry of this period, especially in the collection *Un fantasma recorre Europa*. In the poetry of the reflective modality the poet's concerns remain political, although to express these concerns Alberti uses figurative language rather than political rhetoric. His poetry of the public event or issue extends beyond the realm of pure politics, leading his reader to a private vision of political matters. In such poetry, as will be shown, Alberti, as a committed poet, demonstrates what Sartre refers to as "the most complete awareness of being involved (*embarqué*)" (*CMFL*, 34). Sartre explains: "Je dirai qu'un écrivain est engagé quand il cherche à prendre la conscience la plus lucide et la plus entière d'être embarqué, c'est à dire quand il fait passer . . . l'engagement de la spontanéite immediate au réfleché." [17]

In the poetry of the agitative political modality of *Consignas* we often find poetry for politics' sake. The speakers of these poems are concerned with practical, political action rather than with reflection on public issues. It seems that, for the public voices of such poems, it is the urgency of the cause and the encouraging of all men to embrace and further this cause that has taken precedence over having the poem's speaker transfer his commitment from the "level of the spontaneous to the level of consciousness." It also seems that the urgency itself together with the "spontaneous" response encourage an agitative political mode of writing. The pressing message, often taking the form of the poem's highly normative thesis, is conveyed by a particular type of speaker heard in the poetry of this period: the politically inflamed, highly dogmatic voice of the belligerent party spokesperson. Poetry of the agitative modality relies on demands, persuasion, political rhetoric, standardized ideas of the party and the speaker's soapbox. It is not inspired in or sustained by the contemplative pause or reflection on public matters. Sartre explains that commitment involves giving "a complete picture of the human condition" and, therefore, not a one-sided, party view of a set of specific political actions that must be engaged in in order to further a particular ideology or champion envisioned social change. [18] In Alberti's political poetry of the early thirties, this "complete picture of the human condition" is more meaningfully rendered in the poetry of the reflective modality in poems such as "Al volver y empezar," "S.O.S." and "Un fantasma recorre Europa."

Public Voices and Themes: Consignas and Un fantasma recorre Europa

In the majority of the poems of *Consignas* and *Un fantasma recorre Europa*, the private voice of the poet is supplanted by various depersonalized public voices. The poet's own *yo*, either as a first-person speaker or as the subject matter of his poetry, appears only once in *Consignas*, in the poem "Salutación al Ejército Rojo," and twice in *Un fantasma recorre Europa*, in "Al volver y empezar" and "Indice de familia burguesa española (mis otros tíos, tías, tías y tíos segundos)." Throughout these collections of 1933, Alberti assumes a public persona as the poet surveys the sociopolitical reality of the people in the early thirties in Spain, Europe, and the Soviet Union. Specifically, the public voices are that of a bellicose party spokesperson whose mandates direct the people to action, the "we" of the people who proclaim the people's cause and struggle, and an omniscient narrator who records various political matters of special interest to the people. The theme of the role of the common people in erecting the new social order, first evident in the "Elegía cívica," merges with the collectivist point of view adopted by these public speakers. The public voices of *Consignas* and *Un fantasma recorre Europa* themselves embody the active role the common man will play in constructing the Socialist Society.

In *Consignas* the party mouthpiece is heard in "¡Abajo la guerra imperialista!" "Juego," "Sequía," "Mitin," and "Salutación al Ejército Rojo." In *Un fantasma recorre Europa* this public voice is heard in "¡Salud, Revolución cubana!" The "we" of the working class is the main voice heard in "La lucha por la tierra" of *Consignas* and "Un fantasma recorre Europa" and "U.R.S.S." of *Un fantasma recorre Europa*. In *Consignas* the omniscient narrative voice is present in "En forma del cuento," "Aquí y allí," "Villancico de Navidad," "Romance de los campesinos de Zorita," and "Balada de los doce leñadores," while in *Un fantasma recorre Europa* it is found in only one poem, "S.O.S."

The Poem as a Political Weapon

In the poem "Juego" (*C*) the militant mouthpiece of the party, in a dialogue with an inquisitive worker, openly instructs the people and a particular representative as to *how* change can be effected in the existing social order:

—¡Quién el mejor forjador?   1
—Quein mejor forje un martillo y una hoz.

—Camarada, ¿y para qué?
—Para el cura y el burgués.
—Camarada, ¿dónde están?   5

—Camarada, bebiéndose el vino,
    camarada, comiéndose el pan.
—¿Quiénes son sus vencedores?
—Los revolucionarios trabajadores.
—Camarada, ¿y dónde están?
—Desunidos, divididos.   10
—¿Pues cómo los vencerán?
—Camarada, ¡TODOS UNIDOS!
—¿Y con qué?
—Con el martillo y la hoz.

—¡Forja, forja, forjador!   15

The ideological and normative thesis of "Juego," the formation of a
"Frente Único," is expressed by the directive, sloganlike commands of the
party spokesperson and is further emphasized by the introductory statement
accompanying the poem in the 1933 edition of *Consignas:* "Camaradas mayores: propagad este juego entre vuestros hijos. Que la consigna del *Frente
Único* se realice en ellos, hijos de proletarios con un solo enemigo en común." According to the party's propagandist, Marxism, revolution, an ideologically unified people, and instructive, persuasive words such as those of
this *juego* will aid in the creation of the envisioned new society.[19]

This thesis is repeated in variation throughout *Consignas* and becomes the
sociopolitical *leit motif* of the collection. In "¡Abajo la guerra imperialista!"
the European workers in factories manufacturing war materials are warned by
the party's mouthpiece that such items will be used against the Soviet Union
and thus impede the progress of the socialist revolution.[20] The speaker
demands:

¡Alerta trabajadores,
no trabajéis en las fábricas!
. . . .
Que nuestra consigna
camaradas, sea:
un único frente
con la roja estrella
y en un rojo Octubre
convertir la guerra.
            (Ll. 24–25; 44–49)

The Spanish peasantry, representing the peninsula's proletariat, is also encouraged to participate in this Frente Único. In the final lines of "Romance de los
campesinos de Zorita" the Marxist spokesperson of *Consignas* proclaims:

¡Campesinos extremeños,
seguid lo que ya otros hacen:

una cadena en la lucha . . .
y senda roja adelante!
                    (Ll. 31–34)

The aim of the belligerent spokesperson heard in the poems previously cited is to agitate and educate the masses in the spirit of solidarity and the goals of the revolution. In this way, the public voice assumed by Alberti both exemplifies and defines the agitative role of the poet of politics. Enthusiastically placing both himself and his poetry at the service of an ideal, Alberti becomes the public mouthpiece of and propagandist for this ideal. Following Vladimir Mayakovsky's definition of the political poet, Alberti is the "agitator / brazen-mouthed ring leader" of the masses.[21] In this way, the poet, his public voice, and his poetry are joined to the people's present and future as together they inspire the collectivity to participate in the revolutionary cause.

Many poems of *Consignas* not only establish Alberti's role as political and public activist, propagandist, and agitator but also they demonstrate the new orientation of the poem conceived as a political weapon. Mayakovsky defines his own politically agitative poetry when he declares:

These bits
    of iron poems
        disinterring,
you'll reverently handle in time
as weapons old,
            but deadly and unerring.[22]

In the poem "Fine!" the Soviet poet further emphasizes that with the "bayonet-gleam / of my poem's words" the masses will "forge ahead" and become active participants in the creation of a new world.[23] Alberti, giving heed to the advice of Mayakovsky and often imitating the Russian poet's style, places the language of the poem in the midst of the revolution.[24] Words thus become weapons in the struggle as they, in themselves, fashion the envisioned new order.

Both the intent and content of much of Alberti's initial political poetry is agitative. Adopting a style of the revolution and a politically agitative mode of writing, the poet often riddles his poetry with the political cliché, political slogans, blatant political rhetoric, and vatic pronunciations designed to incite others to action and/or to persuade them to embrace a particular ideology.

The final moment of the poem "Sequía" serves as an example of the political discourse and rhetoric and the hyperbolical and inflated emotionalism characterizing the agitative mode of writing in *Consignas*.[25] Alberti explains in the introductory summary paragraph accompanying the 1933 publication of the poem: "Trata del desconcierto que produce la falta de lluvia en una aldea.

Los curas, alejándose siempre de toda concepción científica, contribuyendo al adormecimiento del cerebro de los campesinos, y aprovechándose de su ignorancia, pretenden atraer la lluvia con el milagro. Al sentirse engañados, los campesinos, de una manera anárquica, se rebelan contra el cura y la Virgen. Apareciendo, al final, un camarada del Partido que despierta y encauza su conciencia de clase." The combative and aggressive tones of the poem are evident when the enlightened, class-conscious party spokesperson didactically and emphatically declares:

No,
camaradas,
Cerrad las navajas.
¡Muera la anarquía!
Mueran
la sangre, la muerte aisladas.
¡Masas!
Todos los hombres unidos.
Del brazo, el campo y la fábrica,
los soldados, los marinos.
¡Masas!
Contra la anarquía,
¡masas!
Contra la religión,
¡masas!
Contra las camisas negras
en Italia,
contra las camisas pardas
en Alemania,
contra las camisas azules
en España.
¡Masas!
Y el Partido Comunista,
rígido, al frente, guiándolas.
Así,
camaradas.

(Ll. 69–93)

The revolutionary fervor of the language of the closing moment of "Sequía," cited above, points to a problem often associated with agitative political poetry in general: it is ephemeral. When a poem such as "Sequía" is removed from the politically agitated sociohistorical ambience in which it was written and which it reflects, the urgency and impact of the speaker's mandates are lost. Although the poem's linguistic expression does both record and mirror the infectious and exaggerated political emotionalism of the hour, it is difficult to reproduce such a response in an audience removed in time from the public feelings and issues of a bygone era.

The language of "Sequía" is facile and obvious. Familiar soapbox slogans and excessive and repetitive imperatives permeate this poem and others of *Consignas*. These simplified and bellicose "watchwords," serving as both rallying cries and ideologically instructive phrases, were meant to be immediately understood and repeated by the peasants and workers for whom they were intended. For the critical reader demanding more than the obvious, however, these verbal weapons and utilitarian mandates are unimaginative imitations in verse of the jingly propagandistic catchwords of the party, the political rally, and the political placard.

Alberti's title for his first collection of political poetry is aptly chosen. Among the definitions of *watchword* we find: (1) "a preconcerted signal to begin an attack" and also (2) "a word or phrase used as embodying the guiding principle or rule of action of a party or individual."[26] The poetry of this 1933 collection is filled with urgent verbal watchwords designed to incite the people to begin the attack on the existing social order. As poems such as "Juego" and "Sequía" demonstrate, phrases and mandates advocating the principles of the Communist party and cause are also numerous. The epigraph of *Consignas* states: " 'La literatura debe ser una literatura de Partido.' " These words of Lenin, in themselves, remind the reader that what follows are the speakers', the poet's, and the party's watchwords, incorporated into the poem itself.

The form of Alberti's agitative political poems is not strikingly original. Often, the linguistic expression is monotonous and commonplace mainly because the same sloganlike commands are repeated in many poems of this collection. In Mayakovsky's political poetry, form was all-important, and as Alexander Kaun notes, in his poetry the "form in which the revolution could be expressed was to be as fresh and new as the contents of the new life."[27] In much of Alberti's earliest political poetry of the agitative modality, however, form is sacrificed for the sake of politics, and in the final analysis, form itself is often forsaken. For the Spanish poet, the urgent declaration of his theme and thesis takes precedence over his harnessing the political impulse in poetic form.

Poetry for politics' sake is evident in "Mitin."[28] Addressing those who compose the working class with the emotional fervor and sense of urgency characteristic of the speaker of a political rally, the poet's public voice declares:

¡Arriba!
Las guadañas en alto,
segadores,

las hoces a la altura del hervor y la fiebre de la sangre.
¡Arriba!
Los martillos en alto,
trabajadores,
obreros de las fábricas que os derriban y os tumban en provecho del ansia de
   los buitres.
¡Arriba!
Las piquetas en alto,
hombres oscuros que arrojáis los pulmones y los ojos en la mazmorra negra
   de las minas.
¡Arriba!
Los fusiles en alto,
soldados que ignoráis el convenio con Francia para pronto apuntar vuestros
   cañones contra la Unión Soviética.
¡Arriba!
¡FRENTE UNICO!
Los relojes del Kremlin os saludan cantando la Internacional,
las radios de la U.R.S.S. os envían los hurras del Ejército Rojo,
de Madrid a Lisboa una estrella se agranda cubriendo todo el cielo
y silba el primer tren que no conoce las fronteras antiguas.
¡Arriba, camaradas!
¡Viva la Unión de las Repúblicas Soviéticas Iberas!

                                                            (Ll. 14–35)

The party's mouthpiece, in a language filled with the political cliché, political
rhetoric, and political symbols (perhaps symbols would be better suited for
banners and flags than a poetic text), instructs and incites the masses to action.
In the poem "Mitin," Alberti, following the advice of the former Soviet
Commissar of Education Lunacharsky, whose words constitute the epigraph
of Xavier Abril's introduction to Consignas, demonstrates that " 'El arte no
está destinado exclusivamente para producir goce estético' " (p. 1). Rather,
this poem and others of Consignas are intended to be political weapons and in
this way they serve something other than themselves.[29]

   The poetic or aesthetic effect of poems such as "Juego," "Sequía," and
"Mitin" is small, if there is any at all. Much of Alberti's early agitative verse
has little or no poetic effect; it is of instrumental rather than aesthetic value. In
the poetry of Consignas both the poet as agitator of the masses and the poem
as political weapon have been placed, as Alberti declared in 1931, "at the
service of the Spanish revolution and the international proletariat." The language of the agitative political poem becomes the binding force, the adhesive
agent joining the public voice of the poet to the collectivity of whom and for
whom he writes and to whom he speaks. In this way the poet, the people, and
the poem itself participate in and actively construct the anticipated new era.

If the political poet is to serve as the agitator of the masses and if the agitative poem is to serve as a political weapon, then can we criticize the poet for not creating an aesthetically effective poem and can we ask the political poem to do something that it clearly was never meant to do—namely, to be aesthetically effective? Much of Alberti's initial agitative political poetry has been dismissed by the critics precisely because they claim that this poetry has little or no aesthetic value. Alberti's earliest political poetry, however, has not been studied in detail as *agitative* poetry—agitative in intent, content, expression, and effect.

In *Consignas,* Alberti does succeed in his newfound role as the spokesperson of and for the revolution, the party, and the masses. His poetry, in turn, thus serves as an instrument to be brandished by the masses in the revolution for the party. Having a utilitarian purpose and value, the agitative political poem accomplishes its aims. By means of the poem's speakers, the theme of the *pueblo,* and the poet's own revolutionary style, this poetry mobilizes and educates the masses while simultaneously proclaiming and envisioning the aims of the collectivist rather than individualistic society of the future.

The agitative political poetry of *Consignas* and that published in *Octubre* are obvious examples of a committed poetry that expresses its commitment in an extravagant and often boasting manner.[30] The political cliché and slogans in addition to boisterous, theatrical calls to action and revolt often reduce the ideas expressed in the poem to the agitative expression of these ideas. It seems that in *Consignas* it is not *what* is communicated that is of interest to the aggressive party mouthpiece so much as that it be expressed in a manner designed to disturb and persuade the masses.

The agitative mode of writing found in much of Alberti's poetry of this period underscores what Adereth explains as "the greatest danger facing 'littérature engagée' . . . forgetting 'littérature' for the sake of 'engagement.' " Sartre cautioned in *Situations II:* "Dans la littérature engagée *l'engagement* ne dait en aucun cas faire oublier *la littérature.*"[31]

Political poetry of the agitative modality brings us to one further consideration in discerning the aims and the approach of such poetry and in determining its value. The specialized lexicon of a poem such as "Juego" or "Mitin" demands a precisely determined, limited reading of the text. In such a reading, as Roland Barthes explains when analyzing Marxist writing in the essay "Political Modes of Writing," "each word is no longer anything but a narrow reference to the set of principles which tacitly underlie it." The word does not have its "neutral dictionary meaning; it always refers to a precise historical process, and is like an algebraical sign representing a whole bracketed set of previous postulates." Barthes explains: "French revolutionary writing always proclaimed a right founded on bloodshed or moral justification, whereas from the start Marxist writing is presented as the language of knowledge. Here, writing is univocal, because it is meant to maintain cohesion in Nature; it is the lexical identity of the writing which allows it to impose a stability in its explanations and a permanence in its method; it is only in the light of its whole linguistic system that Marxism is perceived in all its political implications."[32]

Deviating from Barthes's ideas here, but nevertheless using them as a point of departure, the reader of the poems of *Consignas,* for example, is faced with, as Barthes puts it, "a language expressing value judgements."[33] The poem is reduced to a Marxist explanation of specific public themes, and therefore the reader must read the poem in this way. Such a reading may, however, pose various problems for the reader. First, the narrow, explanatory reading might run counter to the reader's own political allegiance or persuasion. In other words, the actions called for and the value judgments expressed in the poem might differ from the reading the reader might like to give to what has been defined and appraised in the text. Second, in such poems where words and images refer to specific, well-defined, and often politically clichéd principles and a singular historical process, the interpretation of the word or image has already been given *before* the reader even initiates his or her own reading. The reader of the agitative political poetry of *Consignas* is, therefore, not always able to be a producer of meanings. Rather, the reader often becomes a subrogator of meanings. The process of poetry and the process of reading in *Consignas,* and in Alberti's agitative political poetry of the decades that were to follow, have been reduced to a constrictive, codified process of Marxist transference where the reader merely substitutes the word or image of the poem for the political principle underlying and motivating the text.

When applied to the poetry of *Consignas,* Barthes's observations regarding Marxist writing could lead to a possible explanation for why readers and critics have often rejected politically tendentious literature.[34] It is not that such literature has little or no aesthetic value that might cause the reader-critic to ignore or dismiss it. Rather, such literature might be rejected on the grounds that it is so highly codified within a strict ideological framework and so obviously explanatory and expressive of specified political value judgments that it leaves little or no room for the reader to produce the meaning of the poem.

What has been said of the style, diction, tone, and prosaism of poems such as "Juego," "Sequía," or "Mitin" is also true of another poem of *Consignas,* "La lucha por la tierra." The last poem should, however, be considered here because it is the only work of the collection presented from the unique social perspective of the "we" of the Spanish peasantry. Embracing the whole of the collective and its goals and revolution, this poem reflects the collectivist spirit and purpose of the common man's role in the historical process. Recalling

Vladimir Kirilov's poem "We," Alberti's "La lucha por la tierra" offers an interpretation of a specific public issue—the peasantry's struggle for land—and a general political phenomenon—the social revolution. Alberti's public voice echoes the Soviet poet's own assessment of the peasants' struggle in his own land:

> We have unlearned to pine for heaven.
> We want everyone on earth to have enough to eat.
> No groans and wails for bread shall be heard.[35]

Alberti explains the content of his poem in the introductory note accompanying its publication in *Consignas:* "Aquí se expresa, a gritos, un campesino consciente, después de su transformación antirreligiosa."[36] The poem reads as follows:

> Nos dirigíamos a Dios,
> le suplicábamos a voces
> porque le suponíamos más arriba de los tejados y los palomares,
> más allá de la espalda de la última estrella.
> Nos habían repetido hasta paralizarnos que él era el único creador de todo,
> tanto del piojo negro que se alimenta y cría en la cabeza del pobre
> como del estómago pesado que se hace congestionar la siesta de los ricos.
> El regía los partos de las vacas,
> retiraba la sangre de nuestras mujeres para luego rendir a nuestros hijos,
> consumirlos matándolos.
> Y como cualquier propietario o explotador de hombres
> exigía además que le llamásemos Señor.
> Esto nos enseñaron desde niño los curas,
> el arzobispo en su visita pastoral
> y los dueños del campo que labramos hasta que nos derriba.
> Eramos más que bestias.
> Pero ahora, Señor, una hoz te ha segado la cabeza
> y un martillo de un golpe ha derribado tu trono para siempre.
> Es una estrella roja la que incendía los escombros podridos de tu cielo.
> Ahora trabajamos,
> ahora nos sublevamos hasta ser reprimida nuestra sangre contra la tierra que
>   nos pertenece,
> ahora combatimos diariamente no por esa patria lejana,
> ese salario invisible que es la promesa de tu gloria
> o esos tormentos con que nos amenazas como aliado de la burguesía.
> No es en tí,
> no es aquellos que se venden y negocian contigo
> en quien pensamos cuando de sol a sol las horas y el cansancio nos
>   refuerzan el odio.
> Esa patria lejana no entierra sus cimientos en las nubes,

la pisamos,
la reconocen nuestros pies,
espera y grita bajo ellos:
LA TIERRA.

Xavier Abril's remarks in the introduction to the 1933 edition of *Consignas* shed some light on "La lucha por la tierra" in particular and the collective voice heard both in this poem and in others of *Un fantasma recorre Europa*. Abril observes:

> Es el momento en que principia a desdeñar lo personal, privado y clandestino de la lírica burguesa. El poeta, el hombre social, posee ya, en potencia, la seguridad de su destino, de su meta, que no es una meta "original" sino la misma que persigue la inmensa mayoría de los explotados. En estas condiciones, Alberti viaja por los pueblos de España con una nueva fe, con nuevos ojos sociales. Comprende la grandeza de las luchas de los campesinos por conquistar la tierra, al mismo tiempo que la miseria de los agentes de la burguesía, expresada en la "Reforma Agraria." El hombre y el artista—el sujeto social—se dan cuenta de la terrible realidad de la historia capitalista: los antagonismos irreconciliables de las clases. Más tarde siente apremio de conocer los otros panoramas de Europa donde la lucha revolucionaria de Marx y de Lenin, con el que ha de triunfar la Revolución Mundial, lo hace suyo, descubriendo en aquél, como todos los intelectuales revolucionarios han descubierto, la verdad de la vida y de la historia pasada y, sobre todo, futura. (*C*, 4)

In "La lucha por la tierra" Alberti establishes a series of antitheses underscoring both the theme of the poem and the poet's own fundamental attitude toward the "we" with whom he identifies and for whom he speaks. The main antithetical pairings, past/present, heaven/earth, God/peasantry, rich/poor, not only develop the poem's public theme, the plight of the landless peasants in Spain, but also its normative thesis, what could be done in order to change the peasantry's present condition. The poem itself is constructed on a binary system of opposites and can be divided into two equal sections consisting of sixteen lines. In each moment, the spatial, temporal, concrete reality of the peasants' past and present is identified and scrutinized. This structural division underscores the thesis/antithesis dialectic found both in society and in the poem transcribing this social reality. From the juxtaposition of opposites developed in the poem a synthesis is reached only when Marxism replaces capitalism, a classless society undermines the past and present eras of class distinctions, and "LA TIERRA," as the collectivist voice emphatically proclaims in the poem's closing moment, has become the unique possession of the formerly landless peasantry.

The dogmatic party spokesperson of "Sequía" and "Mitin" has been replaced, in "La lucha por la tierra," by the more pensive yet nevertheless hostilely vocal "we" of the Spanish peasantry. The latter voice attempts to comprehend the historical process and the concrete reality in which it has lived and now lives. In the final analysis, what is apprehended is that these can be changed only by means of social revolution. "La lucha por la tierra" is one further example of the agitative poetry of *Consignas* in that the thematic antitheses developed are directly stated with an often combative and, at times, blasphemously sarcastic tone. The anger demonstrated by this speaker, however, is an authentic anger originating in and caused by the sociopolitical reality experienced by the people whom the "we" of "La lucha por la tierra" embodies. It is this singular emotional response that the collectivist voice attempts to comprehend and that the poet records in this poem. The full and lasting comprehension of the social process, the common man's role in this process, and the collective rage experienced by a particular class are what the public voice of "La lucha por la tierra" assesses.

In this poem it is clear that Alberti has placed not only his poetry in the midst of the sociohistorical reality of the Spanish peasantry but also at the service of its "struggle for the land" and its participation in the social revolution. It is also clear that the poet himself has denounced his Catholic upbringing in favor of his newfound "religion" of Marxism. Lechner observes that in this poem we witness Alberti's "ruptura con el ambiente religioso en que nació y se educó" (*CPE*, 90) and also his "interés por el hombre concreto de este mundo y su vida tangible y un disinterés casi total por lo que no pueda realizarse en este mundo concreto, cuyas condiciones de vida desea cambiar radicalmente" (*CPE*, 70).

In his study of Spanish commitment poetry, Lechner's observations regarding the significance of the motif of the countryside and the role of the peasantry should be considered in any discussion of Alberti's poetry where the peasant becomes the protagonist of his verse and thus plays an important symbolic part. Lechner observes:

> En la poesía comprometida de España . . . ocupa un puesto central el campesino, situado en su natural ambiente del campo, de la tierra que cultiva. No hay—en la poesía comprometida—asomo de rasgos idílicos—salvo quizás en . . . Miguel Hernández—; se describe al campesino en su autenticidad histórica, tanto en lo espiritual como en lo que a su mundo material se refiere . . . la poesía comprometida de la España del siglo XX nos da, mejor que la novela o el teatro, una idea de lo que pasaba en el campo. . . . los poetas centraban su atención, no en el mundo industrial, sino en el agrario, nada idílico, donde vivía la major parte de la población del país. Casi todos los poetas, conscientes de la situación social de su país, fijaron su atención en el problema nacional más grave, en lo que pudo influir acaso la circunstancia de casi todos ellos procedían de regiones tipicamente agrícolas y ninguno de los

grandes centros industriales. En el caso de la poesía comprometida no es éste un tema tradicional, sino nuevo, puesto que se trata de una referencia a la problemática social contemporánea. (*CPE*, 127, 129–30)

Alberti's "Al volver y empezar," "La lucha por la tierra," "Sequía," "Aquí y allí," and "Romance de los campesinos de Zorita," in addition to Emilio Prados's "Hambre en el campo" and "¿Quién, quién ha sido?" are transcriptions of the serious agrarian problem facing Spain in the early thirties.[37] Furthermore, they are also examples of the thematic matter of much of Spain's commitment poetry of that era.

Harnessing the Political Impulse

In "Un fantasma recorre Europa" (*UFRE*) the collectivist voice of Alberti's poetry of the thirties most strikingly and originally reveals the role of the people engaged in constructing the new era. Alberti does not approach his political subject matter and public theme from the point of view of his own feelings and biases, as he did in "La lucha por la tierra." Nor does he approach his overt subject from the point of view of the party spokesperson in the midst of the political rally, as he did in "Juego" or "Mitin." Deeply rooted in social circumstances, "Un fantasma recorre Europa" charts these circumstances and their relation to the collectivity in a reflective and provocative way. Here Alberti has not forgotten literature for the sake of engagement. Rather, both are forcefully combined as the poet effectively uses his craft to express the role of the people in the historical process. This poem serves as our example of Alberti's political poetry of the reflective modality.

In October 1933 "Un fantasma recorre Europa" appeared concurrently in the collection of poems of the same title and in a unique, double issue of *Octubre*.[38] Both publications celebrate, as the introductory editorial of *Octubre* indicates, the sixteenth anniversary of the socialist revolution. The thematic matter of this poem is intimately linked to and inspired by the historical process of that event and its repercussions throughout Europe in the early part of the twentieth century. In this way, the poem both records and commemorates the undertakings, aspirations, and achievements of the social group whom the poet not only represents but also fervently identifies with— the "nosotros" of the international proletariat. "Un fantasma recorre Europa," however, is more than a chronicle in verse of the process it records. This narrative poem impresses its readers as a drama where an intense conflict of forces is vividly portrayed and where the reader-spectator, in turn, experiences a heightened emotional state, a state that he or she shares with both the poem's collective protagonist and also the collectivity's representative, the poet himself.

Various compositional formulas structure the poem, develop its thematic conflicts, sustain its rhythm, contribute to its organic unity, and underscore its emotional intensity. The method of "intellectual montage," a method already evident in the "Elegía cívica," as we have seen, and "lifting an event to the heights of pathos" are two such formulas developed by Alberti in this poem. As will be demonstrated, these methods are poetic adaptations of those used by the Russian film theorist and director Sergei Eisenstein.[39]

The thematic narrative of "Un fantasma recorre Europa" can be divided into three parts according to the content of each.[40] Part 1 (ll. 1–16) tells of the reactions and actions of "las viejas familias" (l. 1) of Europe when their life-style and wealth are threatened by an ominous but as yet unidentified danger. Part 2 (ll. 17–35) recounts the mandates issued by the now outspoken "nosotros" of the ruling class when a menacing specter penetrates all of Europe. Part 3 (ll. 36–47) describes the deeds of the unified, vocal industrial and agricultural European proletariat at the moment in which it openly acknowledges and embraces the symbolic phantasm.

```
. . . y las viejas familias cierran las ventanas,                    1
afianzan las puertas
y el padre corre a oscuras a los bancos
y el pulso se le para en la Bolsa
y sueña por la noche con hogueras,                                  5
con ganados ardiendo,
que en vez de trigos tiene llamas,
en vez de granos chispas,
cajas,
cajas de hierro llenas de pavesas.                                 10
¿Dónde estás,
dónde estás?
Nos persiguen a tiros.
¡Oh!
Los campesinos pasan pisando nuestra sangre.                       15
¿Qué es esto?

Cerremos,
cerremos pronto las fronteras.
Vedlo avanzar de prisa en el viento del Este,
de las estepas rojas del hambre.                                   20
Que su voz no la oigan los obreros,
que su silbido no penetre en las fábricas,
que no divisen su hoz alzada los hombres de los campos.
¡Detenedle!
Porque salta los mares,                                             25
recorriendo toda la geografía,
```

porque se esconde en las bodegas de los barcos
y habla a los fogoneros
y los saca tiznados a cubierta
y hace que el odio y la miseria se subleven   30
y se levanten las tripulaciones.
¡Abrid,
abrid las cárceles!
Su voz se estrellará contra los muros.
¿Qué es esto?   35

Pero nosotros lo seguimos,
lo hacemos descender del viento Este que lo trae,
le preguntamos por las estepas rojas de la paz y del triunfo,
lo sentamos a la mesa del campesino pobre,
presentándolo al dueño de la fábrica,   40
haciéndolo presidir las huelgas y manifestaciones,
hablar con los soldados y con los marineros,
ver en las oficinas a los pequeños empleados
y alzar el puño a gritos en los Parlamentos del oro y de la sangre.
Un fantasma recorre Europa,   45
el mundo.
Nosotros le llamamos camarada.[41]

The three major structural divisions call attention to the thematic, ideological, and dialectical conflict and synthesis of opposites underlying the poem.
Part 1 establishes the *thesis* of class tensions existing in the social order and
the omnipresence and power of the ruling class. Part 2 illustrates the poem's
thematic and ideological *antithesis:* the advancement of the politically symbolic specter throughout the land and sea and the effect it has on those who
suffer "el odio y la miseria" (l. 30). This episode further underscores the
antithetical pairings of the main characters presented in this drama: the
wealthy families/the phantom and the wealthy families/the proletariat. This
dual dramatic confrontation itself demonstrates the social conflict that lies at
the heart of the revolutionary process. Part 3 illustrates the poem's *synthesis:*
the voice of the "we" of the proletariat supplants that of the aristocracy as the
former, united by and in the revolutionary cause, identifies, assists, and cham-
pions the goals of its long-awaited "camarada" (l. 47).

As a Marxist, Eisenstein believed that "the law of the dialectical conflict
and synthesis of opposites could provide principles of dynamic editing."[42]
Eisenstein defines this coordination of shot to shot and image to image in the
following passage, cited earlier in chapter 2: "By what, then, is montage
characterized and, consequently, its cell—the shot? By collision. By the
conflict of two pieces in opposition to each other. By conflict. By collision. . . . From the collision of two given factors arises a concept. . . .
Montage is conflict" (*FF*, 37–38). Applying Eisenstein's concept and method

of cinematic, "intellectual montage" to "Un fantasma recorre Europa," from the "collision" of two aspects of the poem, be they structural, thematic, rhythmic, or tonal, a synthesis is ultimately reached, "the thematic matter," as the Soviet film theorist calls it, "the image of the theme itself."[43] The "thematic matter" of Alberti's poem of 1933, the synthetic, international entente of the common people, is succinctly summarized in the closing lines as the global proletariat acknowledges and welcomes a Marxist future (ll. 45–47).

The entire poem is constructed around the concept of conflict. Social conflict both inspires and motivates the fundamental antithetical pairing of the poem's central voices— "nosotros–las viejas familias"/"nosotros"-*pueblo*. The first two episodes collide in space and time and from this clash a synthesis is obtained only when the haunting, ever-active, personified specter successfully disseminates the revolutionary ideas it embodies and gains the support and allegiance of the people. The form of the poem itself, like Eisenstein's films, is "wholly determined by montage rhythms." In "Un fantasma recorre Europa" rhythm is established by "the building up and the releasing of successive states of tension,"[44] the collision of "montage images" (*FF,* 30) and the juxtaposition and eventual combination of pulsative patterns.

The overall pattern of progression of "Un fantasma recorre Europa" follows the common Eisensteinian formula of tension-action-stasis. This pattern, or formula, structures the poem, provides its rhythmic framework and intensity, reproduces the tempo of the historical and revolutionary process, sustains the dynamic interplay of images and, finally, actively and accurately reflects the thematic matter of the thesis-antithesis-synthesis of socialist evolution.

Within the plot of the poem's three episodes, tension is first established, gathers momentum, bursts into action and, ultimately, subsides. This narrative and developmental unity is as identical in the whole as it is in the parts. Episode 1, or part 1, provides, theatrically speaking, the exposition which introduces an omniscient narrative voice who chronicles particular actions and events occurring throughout Europe, actions and events that are the response to an omnipresent, threatening force. The narrative begins *in medias res* with three suspension points and the conjunction "y." By means of ellipsis and the series of descriptive action verbs introducing the poem, the reader is quickly drawn into an ambience of mounting tension and suspense.

Momentum gathers as the narrator observes and recounts, in a rapid series of anaphorically connected long shots, the actions and reactions of a specific representative of the wealthy class—the father:

> y el padre corre a oscuras a los bancos
> y el pulso se le parra en la Bolsa
> y sueña por la noche con hogueras.
>
> (Ll. 3–5)

Synecdochically, his actions are those of his class, his fate is that of the old families, his fear is that which affects the entire ambience. The actions-reactions retold here, be they those associated with the frenzy of securing wealth or the imagined horrific nightmare where wealth and land disintegrate (ll. 5–12), demonstrate the hysteria and tension infusing the environment as the mysterious phantasm begins its journey.

The alarm reaches its peak when the envisioned social tensions suddenly burst into action:

Nos persiguen a tiros.
¡Oh!
Los campesinos pasan pisando nuestra sangre.
(Ll. 13–15)

The more objective, omniscient narrative voice has been dramatically re-placed by the subjective "we" of the old families as this social group both retells and responds to what has now been identified as the revolution.

The tension-action pattern of the entire first episode abruptly reaches a surprisingly static conclusion when the terror and rebellious explosion sub-sides and the simple, brief, a-rhetorical question "¿Qué es esto?" (l. 16) brings to a halt the once active scene. This line signals the first transition point in the narrative. The same question will be repeated at the end of episode 2 (l. 35), marking the poem's second transition point. These caesurae call attention to the momentary periods of inactivity in the poem's narrative while, at the same time, they thematically underscore the poem's conceptual antithesis: the identity and the omnipresence of the specter who will change the course of social and political events. Many of Eisenstein's films also utilize such caesurae in the narrative's pattern of progression. The director explains their function: "And the remarkable thing about these dividing points is that they mark not merely a transition to a merely different mood, to a merely different rhythm, to a merely different event, but show each time that the transition is to a sharply opposite quality. To say that we have contrasts would not be enough: the image of the same theme is each time presented from the *opposite* point of view, although it *grows out of the theme itself*" (*P,* 10). These observations, when applied to Alberti's "Un fantasma recorre Europa," both clarify and help to illustrate "the sharply opposite quality" signaled by the caesurae closing episodes 1 and 2—the social revolution and the ideology motivating it.

The action of part 1 is temporarily suspended, and white space fills the printed page. This conceptual and ideological respite, however, is brief. When the second moment of the poem begins, the reader once again is immediately plunged into a tempestuous ambience of alarm, action, and reaction as the families fill the silence with their own urgent mandates. The second episode gains impetus by means of the juxtaposition of a series of direct and indirect commands (ll. 17–24, 32–33). The tension and the activity of this episode, however, are derived not from these mandates but rather from the conflict that results as the threatening, revolutionary phantasm disobeys these orders and invades all aspects of society and the environment (ll. 21–31). The tension-action pattern of progression is further intensified by the collision of "montage phrases." The mandates "Cerremos / cerremos pronto las fronteras" (ll. 17–18), for example, are rapidly undermined by the action of the phantom: "avanzar de prisa en el viento del Este" (l. 19). The "families' " command of "¡Detenedle!" (l. 24) collides in time and space with and is dramatically reversed by the advent of the all-powerful, ever-moving specter: "salta los mares, / recorriendo toda la geografía" (ll. 25–26). Once again, the narrative's pattern of tension-action-stasis culminates in the echoing and reverberating refrain "¿Qué es esto?" (l. 35). The reader must establish the conceptual connection between the actions of the personified phantasm and the underlying theme of the revolution it metaphorically embodies. This theme now embraces the globe, socially, geographically, and emotionally at the close of this episode as the thesis-antithesis established in part 1 reaches dramatic and epic proportions in part 2.

In the poem's third episode, the poet slightly alters the tension-action-stasis developmental pattern. The causal tension of the episode is simply referred to by the conjunction "pero" (l. 36), which recalls the events chronicled in parts 1 and 2. The emphasis shifts, thus, from the tension pattern to the significant sociopolitical action pattern as the voice of the "we" of the international proletariat describes its militant reactions (ll. 36–47). The predominant motifs of wealth, bloodlines, class distinction, and "el odio y la miseria" (l. 30) are undermined by the social process in which the common people and the specter are jointly engaged when the outspoken, public voice of the "we" of the working class expresses and explains its activities and dreams. The entire tension-action-stasis pattern culminates in the poem's closing lines when this poetic voice underscores the universal fraternal and revolutionary synthesis that has been brought about by the people unified by the Marxist ideology (ll. 45–47).

In each episode and in the poem conceived as a unified whole, Alberti presents and re-presents, as Eisenstein terms it, the "image of the same theme . . . from the opposite point of view" (P, 10) until finally, in part 3, the collective, resounding voice of the "we" of the universal proletariat both proclaims and actively embodies this theme. Conflicting tensions, actions, events, moods, rhythms, and public voices have been transformed into their opposites when the common man emerges as the catalyst for and the integral and vital participant in the dialectical process.

Eisenstein characterizes this transformation of one element into its opposite as the "leap" (P, 15). He explains: "The decisive elements of composition conform to the formula of the ecstatic: the action always makes a leap into a new quality and this new leap is usually a leap into the opposite direction" (*P*, 15). The pattern of progression of "Un fantasma recorre Europa" corresponds to this Eisensteinian "formula of the ecstatic." This conceptual, thematic, structural, and narrative method, in fact, itself mirrors the ideological underpinnings of and the impetus behind the social revolution. When analyzing *The Battleship Potemkin* the Russian film theorist observes: "We can safely say that there is a third aspect to the organic unity of *Potemkin*. The leap which characterizes the structure of each compositional element and the composition of the entire film is the compositional expression of the most important element of the theme—the revolutionary outburst. And that is one in a series of leaps by means of which social development proceeds uninterruptedly" (*P*, 16). This same thematic, structural, and developmental component not only unifies and sustains Alberti's "Un fantasma recorre Europa" but also joins it to the very social process recorded in and expressed by means of the poem itself.

The "collision" of opposites and the "leap" into the opposite also characterize the poem's verbal expression and rhythmical patterns. The dramatic and significant clash of "montage images" or "montage phrases" is evident if the actions recounted in episode 1 are, for example, contrasted with those of episode 3. The capital, inheritance, livelihood, and power coveted and protected by the wealthy class ("corre a oscuras a los bancos" [l. 3]) have been seized by the proletariat and its spectral leader ("nosotros lo seguimos . . . haciéndolo . . . alzar el puño a gritos en los Parlamentos del oro y de la sangre" [ll. 36, 41, 44]). This collision of "montage phrases" is further highlighted, in parts 2 and 3, when the mandates issued by the families are juxtaposed with the dramatic inversion of these orders achieved by the people:

—Cerremos,
cerremos pronto las fronteras.
Vedlo avanzar de prisa en el viento del Este,
. . . .
Que su voz no la oigan los obreros,
que su silbido no penetre en las fábricas,
que no divisen su hoz alzada los hombres de los campos.
(Ll. 17–19, 21–23)

The *pueblo,* however, responds differently:

Pero nosotros lo seguimos,
lo hacemos descender del viento Este que los trae,
. . . .
lo sentamos a la mesa del campesino pobre,
presentándolo al dueño de la fábrica,
haciéndolo presidir las huelgas y las manifestaciones.
(Ll. 36–37, 39–41)

Both rhythmic montage and free verse vividly reproduce and dramatically emphasize the aggressive, relentless tempo of the sociohistorical process and the "revolutionary outburst" transcribed by the poem. Rhythmic montage is, in fact, a formula of conflict that structures and propels the poem. The hectic actions recorded in episodes 1 and 2, for example, gain momentum as they rhythmically clash both in geographic space and on the printed page. This vibrant opposition is especially evident when, in episode 2, the brief commands of "Cerremos" (l. 17), "¡Detenedle!" (l. 24), "¡Abrid!" (l. 32) are juxtaposed with the longer "montage phrases" charting the course of the specter's revolutionary activity (ll. 25–30). Both anaphora and the omission of punctuation in these lines further sustain the flowing, accelerated course of the personified revolution. When these longer, more fluid "montage images" are juxtaposed with the terse, rigid mandates of the families, the thematic matter of both the dialectical process and uninterrupted social development arises.

As a formula of conflict rhythmic montage is further evident in the two dividing points of the poem's narrative. Each caesurae, as has been explained earlier, is introduced by the concise query "¿Qué es esto?" (ll. 16, 35), which in turn is followed by a rapid series of lengthier "montage phrases" answering this repeated question. The reader, after each pause, suddenly must comprehend the flurry of explanations that gain momentum as they identify and intensify the omnipresence of the mysterious force. After coming to a deliberate and dead halt at the close of parts 1 and 2, the reader is thrown headlong into the act of deciphering and resolving the social conflict transcribed.

The formula of the "leap" into the opposite is also sonorously sustained in the poem. By assonantly linking "cajas" (l. 9) of part 1, for example, to the elusive yet paradoxically ever-present "fantasma" of part 2 and the long-awaited and now welcomed "camarada" (l. 47) of part 3, Alberti not only calls attention to the underlying thesis-antithesis-synthesis of his thematic matter but also lends a resonant quality to it.

In addition to these various montage methods "Un fantasma recorre Europa" also demonstrates the Eisensteinian "pathetic" formula of composition. The Soviet film theorist has noted: "A pathetic work makes us *relive acutely the moments of culmination and substantiation* that are in the canon of all dialectical processes" (*P*, 16). Eisenstein further observes: "Pathos arouses deep emotions and enthusiasm. To achieve this, such a work must be built throughout on strong explosive action and constant qualitative changes. . . . If we wish the spectator to experience a maximun emotional upsurge, to send him into ecstasy, we must offer him a suitable 'formula' which will eventually excite the desirable emotions in him" (*P*, 13). According to the Russian film director, various "pathetic" methods can be used: "The simplest method is to present on the screen a human being in the state of ecstasy, that is, a character who is gripped by some emotion, who is beside himself" (*P,* 13). Alberti employs this, the "simplest" of pathetic formulas, in part 1 of the poem, when, in a rapid series of cinema-inspired, alternating montage close-ups and long shots, the cameralike eyes of the narrator focus on the representative of the old families, the father, who, "gripped" by the emotions of fear and hysteria, frantically attempts to protect his belongings. In part 2, the poet's focus shifts to the outspoken "we" of the families, who, now beside themselves with panic, attempt to protect not their possessions but rather the entire land and all its inhabitants from the invading and threatening force. The force itself, the omniscient phantasm, is also "gripped by some emotion" as it penetrates, changes, and revolutionizes all with which it comes into contact. The "we" of the proletariat is, in part 3, the central, ecstatic, collective being presented in a state of emotional and revolutionary fervor. Alberti's adaptation of this uncompounded, pathetic formula further heightens and maintains the sociopolitical dialectic of the poem because the characters themselves "relive acutely the moments of culmination and substantiation that are the canon of all dialectical processes" and, consequently, cause the reader to do the same.

Both Eisenstein and Alberti, however, recognize a more complex and more effective method of infusing the work of art with pathos. Eisenstein refers to this process as "the constant and qualitative changes in action, not through the medium of one character, but through the entire environment. In other words, when everything around him is also 'beside itself' " (*P,* 13). The poet is able to transpose Eisenstein's pathetic formula to the poem itself in all three episodes. In his adaptation of the director's montage method of the "conflict of scales, spaces, masses, depths, close-ups and long-shots,"[45] Alberti vividly captures the excitement and mounting emotional fever gripping the ambience. This is especially evident when the poet transforms the narrative's action pattern into a series of "montage images" of agitated space: "bancos, Bolsa, hogueras" (part 1), "fronteras, estepas, fábricas, campos, bodegas, mares, geografía, cárceles" (part 2), "estepas, mesa, fábrica, huelgas, oficinas, Parlamentos, Europa, mundo" (part 3). The pathos of the poem, in this way, is intimately linked to and accurately reflects the reaction of those who fear the specter's advance, the progress of this force, and ultimately the qualitative "leap" into the final explosive action reverberating throughout "the world"— the revolutionary eruption of the "we" of the common people when it brings about social change.

Eisenstein has observed: "Living through an historical moment is the culminating point of the pathos of feeling oneself part of the process, of feeling oneself part of the collective waging a fight for a bright future" (*P,* 16). Such a statement, when applied to "Un fantasma recorre Europa," sheds considerable light on the poem if it is recalled when and why it was written.

The "social task," to use Mayakovsky's term,[46] of "Un fantasma recorre Europa" is expressed by the poem itself and also by the introductory editorial of the issue of *Octubre* in which it first appeared:

> Un nuevo año de triunfo y de victoria se ha unido a los que desde 1917 viene celebrando la Unión Soviética. Saludamos en él al valiente proletariado de la construcción socialista. . . . Un hombre ejemplarmente distinto ha sido traído sobre la Tierra por la revolución de Octubre. A las juventudes, a la infancia soviética, a los intelectuales, a los obreros de la ciudad y del campo, a los que han conseguido que sea realidad esa montaña de esfuerzo que es la construcción socialista, a los que la defienden, al Ejército Rojo, los escritores y artistas revolucionarios, desde las tierras removidas por la inquietud revolucionaria de España, envíamos nuestro entusiasmo.[47]

Having "lived through the historical process" and having understood the "social task" of both the effort and the work itself, the poet and his poem record and render meaningful the dialectical pathos of that process.

Linked to the period in which it was written, the event it commemorates, and the magazine and the collection in which it was first published, "Un fantasma recorre Europa" has itself become a vital component of both the historical moment it transcribes and the socialist construction it advocates. Linked also to the poet's own socially committed outlook, the very process of poetry in "Un fantasma recorre Europa" reflects and is transformed into the political, dialectical, and ideological process Alberti so ardently desires. It is in this way that Eisenstein's observations regarding the pathetic and political work of art can be applied to "Un fantasma recorre Europa": "The work of art becomes organic and reaches the heights of genuine pathos only when the theme and content and idea of the work become an organic and continuous whole with the ideas, the feelings, with the very breath of the author" (*P*, 21).

"Un fantasma recorre Europa" is an example of how Alberti can, on occasion, rise above the clichés of propaganda and create, within the discourse of the poem, a pronouncedly new perception of reality. The style of this poem is not pedestrian, nor is its discourse merely a restatement of the standardized ideas of the party, as is evident in the poetry of *Consignas* previously studied. The originality of this poem and the collection in which it first appeared stems from the poet's striking synthesis of politics and poetics in a form that is, at one and the same time, uniquely his own and also an adaptation and transcription of the rhythmic evolution of the socialist process. The fresh and vigorous style of "Un fantasma recorre Europa" is not impaired by an ideology. Rather, it is the essence of Marxism that structures and unifies the poem, conveys both its thematic and pathetic matter, and sustains its dynamic tempo.

Vladimir Mayakovsky, as the critic Alexander Kaun observes, dedicated "all of his resonant power of a poet" to fight for a better future for all mankind. Mayakovsky's poetry, he further explains: "marked a new stage in the development of Russian poetry and a big step forward in world art in general. He glorified the joy of life, the buoyancy of the hardest of marches— the march into communism."[48] "Un fantasma recorre Europa" also captures the progress, the difficulty, and the rhythm of that same "march." It was poetry such as this that marked "a new stage of development" in Spanish poetry.[49] With the publication of *Un fantasma recorre Europa* and *Consignas,* together with the founding of *Octubre* in that same year, Alberti not only brought politics into the discourse of poetry in pre–Civil War Spain but also he brought the revolution itself with its aims, evolution, and ultimate rebellious outburst. In "Un fantasma recorre Europa" the dynamism, the dialectic, and the pathos of the entire revolutionary process are, in all of their epic proportions, most convincingly transcribed.

Poetry's "Social Command"

Three representative poems of Alberti's collections of 1933 illustrate various aspects of the common people observed and evaluated by the final public voice heard in the poetry of this period, the omniscient narrator who lives among and is committed to his fellowmen. "S.O.S." is an analysis of the capitalism/Marxism dichotomy where the poem's narrative voice offers views on and solutions to global economic depression. "Aquí y allí" contrasts the lamentable plight of the poverty-stricken, uneducated peasant children of Spain with the optimism and cheerfulness of the children in the USSR. Recording the very real political incidents occurring in a small Spanish town, "Romance de los campesinos de Zorita" examines the difficulties encountered by the peasantry when it attempts to remedy its deplorable situation. Moving from a worldwide view of the proletariat and its problems to specific manifestations of this class's social situation in Spain, the public voice of the omniscient narrator of these poems retells, and in the retelling comprehends, the reality of the common people he represents.

"S.O.S." was first published in *Un fantasma recorre Europa.*[50] Lechner observes: "Otro testimonio de solidaridad con los que sufren, en este caso fuera de las fronteras nacionales, lo constituye el poema *S.O.S.,* inspirado en el paro forzoso de millones de hombres sanos y deseosos de trabajar, pero que se encuentran condenados al hambre y a la miseria debido a las leyes que rigen la economía capitalista" (*CPE,* 70). The narrator of this poem accurately captures the difficult situation of the unemployed proletariat in the concise paradox "No hay trabajo / y hay manos" (ll. 23–24), which is further intensified by the haunting, rhythmical, underlying motif-in-variation heard throughout the poem (ll. 8–13, 30–34).[51]

"S.O.S." is constructed on a series of synecdochical accumulations where the part for the whole and the whole for the part emphasize the condition of the unemployed common people:

6 millones de hombres,   1
12 de manos muertas,
de ojos descerrajados por la angustia,
la miseria y el hambre que agrandan por las noches la invasión de las horas
   lentas del odio y el insomnio.
Y el cielo se pregunta por el humo   5
y el humo por el fuego
y el fuego por las fábricas por el carbón que espera dejar de ser al fin
   paredón muerto de las minas.
Los parados del mundo se levantan,
crecen,
se empinan los parados como el mar,   10
se derrumban,
se levantan
y crecen.

10 millones de hombres,
20 de brazos tristes,   15
como ramas sin lluvia,
caídos,
secos como ramas.
Y hay un medio planeta sin cultivo
y hay barreras que impiden la posesión común del sol agrario de las granjas   20
y hay ríos que quisieran desviarse,
erugirse hasta regar al lecho de los trigos.
No hay trabajo
y hay manos.

El capital prefiere dar de comer al mar.   25
En Brasil el café se quema y es hundido entre las algas,
el azúcar en Cuba arrojada en las olas se disuelve salada,
las balas del algodón en Norteamérica
y los trenes de harina son volcados en la prisa invasora de los ríos.

Y mientras,   30
ellos crecen,
se empinan,
se derrumban,
se levantan.

15 millones,   35
20,
40 de pies parados en la tierra,
de cuerpos que no duermen,
de hombres que desesperan y muertos que se matan.

Amigos,   40
escuchad.
      ¿Qué?
          Nos llaman.

The narrator chronicles first the personal situation of the unemployed workers and then all that is involved in their collective situation of being unemployed. These masses surge and multiply during the worldwide economic
slump that affects each individual, particularly, and an entire class, generally.
The narrator reports in a straightforward manner the number of unemployed
(ll. 1, 14, 36–37) and eventually, as these statistics continue exponentially to
increase, all reference to mankind disappears from this progression. Underscoring, thus, the numerical figures themselves and the global attention given
to these figures rather than to the people each represents, the speaker of
"S.O.S." emphasizes the cumulative plight of the dehumanized people (l. 4)
in the midst of the worldwide economic depression. The poet's use of synecdoche is further intensified when these mounting statistics of the unemployed
masses are coupled with the individual and the collective each represents:
"manos muertas," "ojos descerrajados por la angustia" (ll. 2–3), "pies parados en la tierra," "cuerpos que no duermen" (ll. 37–38).

Free verse, pulsating combinations of longer and shorter verses, accumulations of synecdochical expressions, asyndeton, and anaphora not only create
and enhance the poem's rhythm but also swiftly bring the reader to the closing
lines and the normative thesis, the social message, underlying Alberti's
"S.O.S." For the narrator, the solution to the working class's problem of
unemployment lies with those who consciously choose to change this condition. The solution, for this committed poet, lies in solidarity and the actions of
the unified "we" of the common people and its direct participation in the
construction of a Marxist-socialist new era (ll. 19–20).

In *How Verses Are Made*, Vladimir Mayakovsky both poses and answers
the question "What, then, are the necessary conditions for getting one's
poetic work started?" (p. 192). His response, in part, sheds considerable light
on Alberti's "S.O.S." Mayakovsky enumerates five general rules regarding
"how verses are made," the first two of which are applicable to the poet, the
matter, and the form of "S.O.S." He believes in "the existence of a social
task that can be accomplished only through poetic work. There must be a

social 'command.' " He also characterizes the poet and the group he represents when he writes: "You must have an exact knowledge of or at least a
feeling for aspirations of the class or group you represent" (p. 192).

The "social task" of "S.O.S." is evident in a letter written by Alberti to
José María de Cossío in 1932. Alberti, in discussing an earlier version of this
same poem, writes: "Es una poesía inspirada en las estadísticas, pero una
poesía . . . . Una poesía revolucionaria, de fondo político, pero sin dejar de
ser poesía."[52] The "social command" of "S.O.S." takes its inspiration from a
significant worldwide social circumstance of the common people of the early
thirties: unemployment. The "statistics" of the unemployed are not only the
catalyst for the poem but also its propelling force, for as the poet mounts
statistic upon statistic the sociopolitical reality underlying these figures gains
momentum and colossal proportions until, finally, the poem itself closes with
five brief words calling attention to the underlying "social command," a
"command" that involves more than the poet, his narrative voice, and his
pueblo-protagonist. This "command" also actively addresses and involves the
reader, especially the reader of the early thirties who could easily identify with
the plight of the common people analyzed in the text. A mere enumeration of
depersonalized statistics could have removed the poet, the narrator, the protagonist, and the reader from the human social reality represented by these
numbers. Alberti, however, as Mayakovsky urges, has both "knowledge of"
and "a feeling for" the unemployed of whom and for whom he writes. His
narrator is committed to this class and therefore urges that the collective both
comprehend and change its condition.

In "S.O.S." Alberti does not concentrate on his own personal response to
the human existential situation of "hombres que desesperan y muertos que se
matan" (l. 39), as he did in "Al volver y empezar" or "La lucha por la tierra,"
nor does he emphasize obvious political rhetoric, heard in a poem such as
"Mitin," where party slogans summarize and even simplify the human condition. Rather, in "S.O.S." the narrator retells the social reality of the unemployed people. In the mold of a journalist listing the facts and figures and, on
occasion, adding analyses of both the cause and the effect of the economic
situation, the omniscient narrative voice of "S.O.S." gives form to the underlying "social command" and social "feeling" inspiring the poem.

The narrator of "Aquí y allí" (*C*) is closely aligned to, at one and the same
time, the exploited peasants of Spain (part 1) and the ideology that will, in his
estimation, change their situation (part 2).[53] When the poem first appeared in
Consignas it was accompanied by the author's introductory note: "En la
Unión Soviética, lo más maravilloso son los niños; limpios, sanos, alegres,
pantinando por el río Moscoba helado, como bolas de pieles. Fuertes: la

verdadera realidad y porvenir de la Unión Soviética. Y no pude olvidarme de los hijos de los trabajadores de España, especialmente de esos que vi a los campesinos pobres de Extremadura."

In the introduction to the 1933 edition of *Consignas,* Xavier Abril observes of Alberti: "En su visita a la Unión de Repúblicas Soviéticas, la fuerza de la revolución, lo gigantesco de la edificación socialista, las posibilidades maravillosas de desarrollo de una nueva *Cultura* y humanidad de trabajadores sin clases, le aclaran el único camino justo a seguir: el de laborar con la propaganda de la poesía revolucionaria . . . por el exterminio de los opresores tradicionales de la clase obrera. . . . El poeta ha sabido interpretar las exigencias de nuestra época, entrando a tomar parte en las luchas por la implantación de un nuevo orden social" (pp. 4–5). This contrast between the present reality of the peasantry of Spain and Alberti's vision of what this reality could be constitute the "social command" underlying not only "Aquí y allí" but also "En forma del cuento," "Juego," "Sequía," "La lucha por la tierra," "Romance de los campesinos de Zorita," and "Balada de los doce leñadores" of *Consignas.* In both "En forma del cuento" and part 1 of "Aquí y allí," the Spanish peasant child represents the condition of his or her class and symbolizes the innocent victim easily exploited and manipulated by social forces that he or she is neither responsible for nor able to control. The omniscient narrator of "Aquí y allí" records the human drama of the situation of the peasantry. In part 1, the narrative voice asks a series of rhetorical questions, emphasizing the effect of the condition of the people while also elliptically implying the causal agent. As in the "Elegía cívica" written a few years earlier, the exploiter is left unnamed and the narrator chooses to focus on the effects of exploitation, needed land reform, and a system of social class distinction, all of which have contributed to the disillusionment and hopelessness inherent in the condition of the Spanish peasantry of the early thirties.

The unadorned and compact narrative of part 1 of "Aquí y allí" records and restates the stark reality of the peasant children, in particular, and the peasantry, in general. The miserable tragedy of their situation is transcribed in heartfelt verse revealing the narrator's own distress when he attempts to record honestly the economic and spiritual impoverishment of the class he represents. The emotional impact of this first section of the poem stems from the narrator's sincere response to the plight of these children. Each child is looked upon as an individual and as a member of an exploited class. The poet's assumed narrative voice responds openly to the existential circumstance of this class by means of his poignant testimony and also his sensitivity to the fears, aspirations, and frustrations of others. The emotional impact of this first part of the poem is further derived from the fact that it lacks a strong degree of closure. The open-ended question concluding this section allows the reader to furnish his or her own answers, comparisons, contrasts, and emotional responses as the reader, like the narrator, first observes and then understands the fate of these innocent children. Even though the narrator has linked the peasant children to a specific locale in Spain, the reader, nevertheless, is able to leap geographically as well as conceptually from this confined space to all of Spain and to the tragedy and fate of the collective Spanish peasantry. By furnishing a private vision of the public event, the narrator of this first moment of "Aquí y allí" underscores the pathos of the sociopolitical situation and also involves the reader in his own pathetic response.[54]

C. M. Bowra has noted: "The more violent the impact of events is on a poet, and the more deeply he is committed to them, the more he needs some uniting idea or mood to master them and bring them to order" (*PP,* 84). In part 2 of "Aquí y allí" Alberti's narrative voice attempts to use "la realidad latente del sueño socialista" (l. 29) as the "uniting idea" that will "order" the events and even rectify and resolve the dilemma presented in part 1. When the "uniting idea" is, however, of an ideological bent and when it is stated in a doctrinaire manner lacking any poetic or imaginative insight then, it seems, the poet, through his narrative voice, becomes removed from the "impact of events" that he analyzed in part 1 of the poem. In the second moment of "Aquí y allí" the narrator becomes the party's mouthpiece, espousing the positive aspects of the cultural revolution and the activities of "los hijos de Octubre . . . la gloria de Lenin" (ll. 28, 32). Overtly political and blatantly propagandistic, the narrator's private vision of the public event both "aquí" and "allí" is now lost among the political platitudes, slogans, and ideas promulgated by the party and not the individual poet in this second moment of Alberti's poem.

The highly normative "uniting idea" and obvious "social command" of part 2 of "Aquí y allí" unfortunately undermine the successful elements of part 1. The narrator's human concern and distress have been replaced by simplistic political pride and admiration, and his former sincerity and frankness are now overshadowed by affectation and exaggeration. Whereas in part 1 the reader could furnish responses to the questions asked, in part 2 nothing is left to the reader's imagination or emotions: the party's spokesperson furnishes all solutions and responses. The compact narrative of part 1 of the poem, ordered by pathos, a sustained mood, and a specific uniting idea gives way to a rambling description that seems to be more of a political appendage than a sustained inquiry into the situation of the Spanish peasantry: "aquí" and "la verdadera realidad y porvenir de la Unión Soviética," "allí." Alberti himself seems to have recognized the inadequacy of this second moment of "Aquí y allí" because when the poem was later republished it consisted only of part 1 and bore a new title, "Los niños de Extremadura."

Like "Al volver y empezar," the "social command" underlying "Romance de los campesinos de Zorita" is the Spanish agrarian problem, peasant unrest, and social, rural instability of the late twenties and thirties. The poem is a dramatic retelling of, as the poet reveals in the introductory passage accompanying the poem's first appearance in *Consignas,* "las luchas heroicas que los campesinos de Extremadura sostienen contra el hambre y por la posesión de las tierras. Sucesos que las clases trabajadores de España nunca olvidan: Castilblanco, Zorita, Fuente de Cantos, Herrera del Duque . . ." (p. 22).[55]

The tragedy of the peasantry's situation culminates in and is expressed by the ballad's refrain that serves as the leit motif of both the poem and the Republic:

> Se les prometen los campos
> y al campo van a matarles.
> Promesa cumplida en sangre.
> . . . .
> Se les prometen las tierras
> y en tierra van a dejarles.
> Promesa pagada en sangre.
>   (Ll. 9–11, 27–29)

As in "Aquí y allí," "La lucha por la tierra," and "Al volver y empezar," for the poet, society is clearly divided between the "have-nots" and the "haves," between "los trabajadores" and "los explotadores," between "los campesinos" and "las autoridades." In "Romance de los campesinos de Zorita," the narrator records a series of events stemming from real incidents occurring in a particular Spanish town. In the process of the poem, these events take on symbolic overtones when the peasants of Zorita come to represent, in general, the plight of the working class ("El que trabaja no es nadie" [l. 17]), the essence of the social struggle ("Promesa cumplida en sangre" [ll. 11, 29]), and the hope for the people's socialist future ("¡una cadena en lucha . . . / senda roja adelante!" [ll. 32–33]). The omniscient narrative voice of this poem, unlike that heard in the first moment of "Aquí y allí," remains more emotionally detached from the events and participants of the story he retells in lines 1–29. The prosaism of his account, together with his objective reporting of the incidents occurring in Zorita, call attention to the essence of the peasantry's circumstance: the events experienced and retold in the ballad are commonplace in the Spain of the early thirties. In this microcosm of Spain, hunger (l. 5), confrontations with "the authorities" (ll. 6–8), an individual's death (ll. 12–14), and the death of unsuspecting and innocent members of the collective (ll. 21–26) are the norm. This knowledge disturbs the observer-narrator of the ballad and causes him to urge change in the existing social condition. The abrupt change in tone of the last four lines of the poem and the narrator's direct intervention and call to action at once signal that the former witness to the peasantry's situation has now realized that only social revolution can bring about social change:

¡Campesinos extremeños,
seguid lo que ya otros hacen:
una cadena en la lucha . . .
y senda roja adelante!
        (Ll. 30–33)

The aggressive tone, revolutionary content, and political rhetoric of these final lines of Alberti's ballad are political echoes of other calls to action heard in *Consignas*. In "Juego" or "Mitin" they are not out of place because the entire poem is a sustained political command. However, in "Romance de los campesinos de Zorita" the intervention of the poet's bellicose public voice as the party spokesperson disrupts the presentation of events and detracts from the gravity of the social situation retold and assessed earlier in the ballad. Once again, whenever Alberti overstates the "social task" of his poetry, calling direct attention to it rather than to the pressing social problems of the common people he represents, the political poem becomes a boisterous pronouncement of its underlying ideology rather than a reflective analysis and critique of social conditions and concerns.

Alberti has described the poetry that he wrote in the early thirties in the following way: "Antes mi poesía estaba al servicio de mí mismo y unos pocos. Hoy no. Lo que me impulsa a ellos es la misma razón que mueve los obreros y a los campesinos; o sea una razón revolucionaria. Creo sinceramente que el nuevo camino de la poesía está allí."[56] In his address before the First Congress of Soviet Writers during this same period Alberti reveals that poets such as he "cantan el momento donde se realiza el ideal de justicia de la revolución española."[57] These observations characterize Alberti's political poetry of *Consignas, Un fantasma recorre Europa,* and that published in *Octubre.* One of the first Spanish poets of this century to incorporate politics and the revolution into the subject matter of his poetry, Alberti accordingly had to face the difficult task of redefining and restating the role of poetry concerned with public events. He, and other revolutionary poets like him, came to view the poem as a vital and important political tool that would express the "razón revolucionaria" and the "social command" that guided and inspired his commitment to the common people. In the thirties in Spain, Rafael Alberti, Luis Cernuda, Emilio Prados, Pascual Plá y Beltrán, and Arturo Serrano Plaja ushered in a new and decisive era in Spanish poetry as each discovered and advocated what Pablo Neruda later called "la utilidad pública de la poesía." Rafael Alberti was, however, as Cano-Ballesta indicates, "el indiscutible iniciador de la poesía revolucionaria en España . . . el jefe visible de esta nueva orientación de las letras" (*PEPR*, 195). Decades later, this new orientation would find repercussions in the socially committed poetry of Blas de Otero, Gabriel Celaya, and others of the first generation of postwar poets in Spain.

In the introduction to the 1933 publication of *Consignas*, Xavier Abril states: "La obra de Rafael Alberti señala una fecha histórica en la literatura destinada al servicio de la causa proletariada. Ella corresponde, en la justeza de su línea, al grado de desenvolvimiento de la revolución. . . . Camaradas de la tierra y de la fábrica: saludemos en la actitud de Alberti, un triunfo auténtico de vuestra fuerza en marcha. Ya sólo la dialéctica de la revolución es capaz de transformar a aquellos escritores que se encuentran libres de compromiso con la nefasta sociedad burguesa" (pp. 5–6). Cano-Ballesta affirms of *Consignas:* "Alberti pone la poesía española por los cauces que la conducirán a la revolución poética más honda que tiene lugar desde el romanticismo" (*PEPR*, 119). And of *Un fantasma recorre Europa* the same critic observes: "Abre desconocidas rutas y una temática nueva en la creación lírica. Rafael Alberti adopta un tono combativo, enérgico, agresivo; levanta su voz de denuncia ante la opresión de los campesinos por el mismo gobierno de la República. El acontecer de la vida política española, en sus continuas revueltas y la represión subsiguiente, hechos históricos recién ocurridos, arrancan al poeta su canto de protesta" (*PEPR*, 116–17).

Other critics, however, are not as generous as these in assessing the "social command" underlying *Consignas* and *Un fantasma recorre Europa*. Cano-Ballesta points out that many critics and poets alike often rejected Alberti's earliest revolutionary poetry. Juan Domenchina, for example, appraised Alberti's political verse in this way: "Pero en trance de poetizar, tan descabellado, absurdo y cómico resulta improvisar un ditirambo a la Unión de las Repúblicas Soviética Iberas como componer concienzudamente una oda a las virtudes políticas del Sr. Pildáin."[58] Such criticism, however, as Cano-Ballesta accurately points out, was written "desde la vertiente de la poesía pura, que denuncia con vigor nuevas orientaciones de la lírica, y refleja el grado de escándalo que suscitaron" (*PEPR*, 119).

As readers of *Consignas* and *Un fantasma recorre Europa* we must, as Bowra urges, take the collections "as we find them" (*PP*, 33) and see just what the poet was trying to do and how well he succeeded in doing it. The two collections are landmarks in the development of modern poetry and in the course of art and ideas in Spain precisely because they brought both politics and the revolution into the once-sacred domain of poetic discourse and, at the same time, urged the reader to approach, participate in, and evaluate the sociopolitical reality recorded in and by the poem itself. The collections placed both the poet and his poetry at the service of an ideology, thereby displacing the poetic muse and substituting in her place the inspiration of a sociopolitical cause, the "razón revolucionaria" of the poet and the people. *Consignas* and *Un fantasma recorre Europa* offer the reader willing to explore their matter, form, and worth insight into not only a specific type of poetry, poetry of a socialist conviction, but also the role of poetic discourse in assessing social concerns.

The Voice of Protest

The public voices heard in *Consignas* and *Un fantasma recorre Europa* of 1933 echo throughout other poems Alberti wrote between 1931 and 1935 and published in various collections. *El burro explosivo,* begun in 1934 but not published until during the Spanish Civil War, *Nuestra diaria palabra* (1936), and *13 bandas y 48 estrellas* (1936) consist of poems written during 1934–35. In 1937, Alberti published *De un momento a otro (poesía e historia) (1932–1937),* which incorporated selected poems of *Consignas, Un fantasma recorre Europa, Nuestra diaria palabra, 13 bandas y 48 estrellas,* and various poems on the Spanish Civil War gathered under the title *Capital de la gloria.* In 1938, *Poesía: 1924–1937* was published and it included those poems that had previously appeared in *Poesía: 1924–1930* along with those of *Verte y no verte, El poeta en la calle (1931–1936), Homenaje popular a Lope de Vega* (1935), *El burro explosivo* (1934–35), *Romances de la Guerra de España* (1936), and the poems gathered earlier in *De un momento a otro (poesía e historia) (1932–1937).*[59]

Many of the initial political problems examined in Alberti's collections of 1933 are developed further in the poems he wrote in the mid-thirties and later published in his collections of 1936–38. The thematic matter of the poems of these later collections is essentially an extension of that already studied in detail in the analyses of representative poems of *Consignas* and *Un fantasma recorre Europa.* One is thus able to summarize and categorize the thematic matter of Alberti's poetry of the thirties published after 1933 in terms of the public themes and tones first presented and developed in his two earliest collections of political verse.

Excluding momentarily the poems of *Capital de la gloria,* which will be examined separately in chapter 4, the theme of the role of the common people in the new era, the unifying idea of the collections of 1933, continues to motivate the poems published after that date. One poem in particular, "Siervos" of *De un momento a otro (poesía e historia),* succinctly summarizes and reiterates this central theme of Alberti's political poetry of the thirties:

> Siervos
> viejos criados de mi infancia vinícola y pesquera
> con grandes portalones de bodegas abiertos a la playa,
> amigos,
> perros fieles,
> jardineros,
> cocheros,
> pobres arrumbadores,
> desde este hoy en marcha hacia la hora de estrenar vuestro pie la nueva era
>   del mundo,
> yo os envío un saludo
> y os llamo camaradas.
>
> (Ll. 1–11)

The miners of the Asturian region of Spain emerge, in 1934, as the poet's specific representative of the common man and the common man's struggle for freedom and dignity. "El alterta del minero" and "Libertaria la fuente" are extensions of "Al volver y empezar" and "La lucha por la tierra" and thus further develop Alberti's central theme of the role of the people in public matters. The theme of the united international proletariat, evident in, for example, "S.O.S." and "Un fantasma recorre Europa," receives an added dimension in the poems "Cargadores," "Bakú," and "Mar Negro" and throughout *13 bandas y 48 estrellas.* The theme and thesis of revolution are developed in "Dialoguillo de la revolución y el poeta," "Si Lope resucitara," and "La Revolución y la Guerra," poems that use as their point of departure the sociopolitical ideas and social conviction first manifest in "Juego," "Mitin," and "Un fantasma recorre Europa." The poet's repudiation of his own bourgeois upbringing, a theme first found in embryo in "Indice de familia burguesa española" of *Consignas,* is developed more fully and in a less caustic manner in "Colegio (S.J.)," "Hermana," "Balada de los dos hermanos," "Siervos," and "Os marcháis, viejos padres." The division in society between the "haves" and the "have-nots" assessed by the public voices of "Aquí y allí," "Juego," and "La lucha por la tierra" is developed in terms of Alberti's vision of a classless society in "Colegio (S.J.)," "Siervos," and the poems composing *13 bandas y 48 estrellas.* Lastly, the "enemy" of the people's cause, first sketched in "Sequía" and "La lucha por la tierra," is developed more fully and with sustained and bitter condemnation in many of the poems of *El burro explosivo,* especially "A Gil crucificado" and "La iglesia marcha sobre la cuerda floja." The public themes and voices first manifested in *Consignas* and *Un fantasma recorre Europa* are thus seminal to those that Alberti would explore and utilize throughout his poetry of the mid-thirties.

Much of the poetry in *El poeta en la calle* and *De un momento a otro,* in particular, is discussed insightfully by both Lechner and Cano-Ballesta in their studies of Spanish commitment poetry. A few of their observations are worthy of our attention here. Cano-Ballesta remarks:

> Rafael Alberti está convencido de consagrar su inspiración a una causa noble. El compromiso con la sociedad es llevado a cabo con todas sus consecuencias a pesar de las reacciones que llega a provocar. Numerosos amigos se distancian de él, críticos lamentan la pérdida de un poeta protestando que no es ése el fin de la poesía. Pero si ésta ha cambiado los temas, la orientación y el tono, nadie puede negarles fuerza, intensidad y extraordinaria calidad. . . . Esta 'poesía de urgenica' ha invertido el ideal lírico de años atrás. Lo que pretende primaria-mente es servir a una causa, hallar eco en la masa, despertar los ánimos e inyectarles una sana indignación contra la injusticia. (*PEPR,* 200)

Lechner adds that the poetry of these two collections was written in order to speak directly to the people: "Esta voluntad se echa de ver en el uso frecuente de formas poéticas populares, de un vocabulario sencillo y de frecuentes apóstrofes, preguntas e incitaciones dirigidas al lector; la sintáxis—el eje de los problemas de 'oscuridad' en la poesía—suele ser poco complicada" (*CPE,* 125). In his appraisal of the revolutionary poetry of Alberti and Prados, in particular, and that first appearing in *Octubre,* in general, Lechner concludes:

> Cuando estos poetas del siglo veinte protestan, no lo hacen, ni quieren hacerlo, desde un sector privilegiado de la sociedad y en beneficio de él; al contrario, elevan su voz en beneficio de los demás, de los que sufren y concretamente en pro de la emancipación de una capa social más 'baja' que aquélla de la que ellos mismos proceden. . . . Quieren ser políticamente conscientes y estar integrados en la sociedad, que no ven como una colección de estamentos, sino como un conjunto de hermanos entrañablemente unidos: fueron al pueblo sin esperar que el pueblo viniera a ellos. . . . Casi todos estos poetas se oponían mediante su poesía a la estructura básica de una sociedad que repudiaban. . . . Lo que sí fomentaron fue la reflexión sobre el papel del escritor en la sociedad y un acercamiento a lo que constituye la base de cualquier arte: el hombre. (*CPE,* 138)[60]

In surveying the poems appearing in *El poeta en la calle* and *De un momento a otro* and the public themes and voices these collections share with those of *Consignas* and *Un fantasma recorre Europa,* two changes in emphasis are apparent. The tone of protest first evident in "Sequía" and "La lucha por la tierra," for example, is more malicious and openly belligerent in Alberti's poetry written during and after 1934 than in his poetry written prior to that date. Provoked by the series of tragic events that occurred in the Asturias in the fall of 1934, Alberti's public voice of indignation and outrage would stridently condemn, with vicious verbal attacks, those who tried to impede the people's struggle. Another striking difference between the poetry of 1933 and that appraising social affairs written after that date is that the underlying "razón revolucionaria" of *Consignas* and *Un fantasma recorre Europa* is now directly translated into specific, practical political action. The poems included in *El poeta en la calle* and *De un momento a otro,* for example, it should be remembered, appeared as a grouping during the Spanish Civil War, a public event that in itself prompted immediate political involvement. It is thus significant that Alberti's public voices are now directed to the people in the midst of the people's war, the people whom the poet hopes will be motivated by the collective "razón revolucionaria" of the struggle and inspired by the "poesía revolucionaria" recording this struggle.

In many of the poems of *El poeta en la calle* and *De un momento a otro,* revolution is not a hypothetical event pertaining to the speaker's vision of bringing about the socialist era, as it was in "Juego" or "Mitin" of *Consignas.* In "El alerta del minero" of *El poeta en la calle,* which will serve as our representative poem, revolution pertains to the present circumstance of the everyday reality of the miner-comrade-spokesperson who actively protests any attempts to thwart the collective aims of the people. This poem records and appraises the events that Alberti hoped would not be forgotten by the people during the Spanish Civil War:

> De la mina salgo, amigo,   1
> de la mina, compañero.
> Soy minero barrenero.
> Ven conmigo.
>
> Al álamo aquel que baja   5
> lento, por el monte, dile
> que se dé prisa y vigile
> tu pobre choza de paja.
> También cuidará del trigo
> que te hurtaron los señores.   10
> Ven conmigo.
> ¡Venid todos los pastores!
> ¡Eh, muchacho! ¡Los corderos!
> los apacienten los pinos,
> ¡y vengan los campesinos   15
> que llegan los ingenieros!
> ¡Eh, los carros!

(Quien se interpone lo quita
a golpe de dinamita
la lumbre de los cigarros.)   20

De la mina salgo, amigo,
Ven conmigo.

Hoy cuide el pez de los remos
de la barca pescadora,
que ya nos llegó la hora   25
de ser lo que ser debemos.
¡Cargadores, descarguemos
de su carga al enemigo!
¡Eh, pescador, ven conmigo!

—¡Voy contigo!   30

Vengan las mozas viriles
y sufra enterrado el miedo,
que ya las torres de Oviedo
tiemblan de ver los fusiles
en las manos de nuestra gente.   35
¡Corre y vente!
¡Hasta el viento está conmigo!
¡Sigue la roja corriente!

—¡Voy contigo!
—De la mina salgo, amigo.   40

The conversational tone and colloquial language of "El alerta del minero" directly link the poem to the people of whom and for whom it was written. The essence of the struggle (ll. 34–36) is simply stated and rendered meaningful by the miner-spokesperson who informs his fellow miners of the solidarity he knows to exist among the working class (ll. 12–18, 24–30) and of his own knowledge of the collective identity and "social task" of this class (ll. 26–27). The peasants of Alberti's "Romance de los campesinos de Zorita" comprehended only that "el que trabaja no es nadie" and those of "Al volver y empezar" knew only their identity as "bestias de carga." The miner in Alberti's poem commemorating the Asturian revolt of 1934, however, according to the poem's rebellious and politically revolutionized public voice, does not dream; rather he acts. He does not envision a future, rather he actively engages in the struggle of the present. The public voice echoing throughout "El alerta del minero" speaks not only for those miners involved in the October revolution in the northern mining region but also on behalf of his "proletarian brothers" during this stage of the social revolution in Spain.[61]

The envisioned solidarity and full-scale working class revolution proclaimed by the "we" of the people in "Un fantasma recorre Europa" has now become the cornerstone of the "new society" being created by the Asturian miners during October 1934.[62]

When writing of Alberti's poetry of 1934 Lechner observes: "La revolución de Asturias fue, sin duda, la experiencia más honda, más determinante en su actitud posterior, así como lo fue para la mayoría de los artistas e intelectuales españoles de aquellos días" (*CPE*, 68). Alberti, when recalling the year 1934 in his "Indice autobiográfico," writes of the impact of this experience on his life and work and his personal and political response: "Cuando estalla la revolución de los mineros de Asturias, me encuentro en Moscú. . . . No pudiendo regresar a España, quedo nuevamente en París, de donde salgo rumbo a América para dar conferencias y recitales en socorro de las víctimas de la revolución asturiana" (*PC*, 14).

Despite the optimism of the Asturian October revolution recounted in "El alerta del minero," the incident ended in violence, death, imprisonment and, ultimately, the dissolution of the "new society" to which the miners, in particular, and the proletariat, in general, were dedicated.[63] This tragedy is retold in two companion poems published in *El poeta en la calle*, "Libertaria la fuente" and "El Gil, Gil." The former poem tells of the death of the symbolic figure of "la madre" in whom lies, as the repeated refrain suggests ("La quiero desenterrar" [l. 1]) both the hope for and the memory of the political freedom embodied in the participants of the "el Octubre asturiano" (l. 25). In the latter poem, the bitter and sarcastic public narrative voice blames the Asturian tragedy, "la sangre de cinco mil" (l. 34), on the parliamentary crisis precipitated by Gil Robles and the CEDA (Confederación Española de Derechas Autónomas), the hated "enemies" of the Left-Republicans in October of 1934.[64] "El Gil, Gil" first appeared in Alberti's *El burro explosivo*, and in the introduction to this collection Alberti states that what follows will consist of "poemas político-burlescos de la historia de España . . . poemas, cargados de dinamita" (p. 2). "El Gil, Gil" along with "Epitafio a un presidente," "Al nuncio de S.S. en España," "In memoriam," "Gil en campaña," and "A Gil crucificado" are examples of poems of the agitative political mode of writing. Here Alberti viciously attacks those whom he believed were responsible for

> . . . la sangre pura
> de cinco mil heroicos asturianos
> para ganarse el prometido cielo.[65]

Such vituperative verse serves as an audible protest and a way for the poet to release his anger and indignation concerning a public event. In "El Gil, Gil," for example, the outraged public voice, assessing the manner in which the Asturian revolt was quelled, declares:

¡Qué son el de sus tacones,
llenos de clavos mortales,
sellando en los hospitales
la muerte de las prisiones!
Todo con aire monjil.
¡Oh qué bien que baila Gil!

¡Qué figura
pisando en la sepultura
la sangre de cinco mil!
Para lavarle las manos,
dos ángeles vaticanos
le dan un aguamanil.
¡Oh qué bien que baila Gil!
                    (Ll. 26–38)

Personal, malicious verbal assaults such as those cited above or those pronounced by the riled public voice of "In memoriam" are not directed to the public issue so much as to the public figure whom the poet personally despises and holds responsible for the public event. The poem degenerates into a prosaic, uninspired harangue where Alberti uses the printed page for the purpose of expressing his own anger. The "social command" of the political poem thus erroneously stems from an unrestrained personal emotion rather than from the public issue and the social class the poet represents. "El alerta del minero," although written in a monotonous, pedestrian, and even mundane style filled with political clichés and hyperbolic commands, nevertheless does not lose sight of the public event with which it is concerned nor does it ignore the "social command" underlying the inception of the poem.

During the first three weeks of October 1934, "multiple events" were occurring in Spain, events which, according to Gabriel Jackson, form the "three main strands . . . to an understanding of the Spanish Civil War: the general strike, the regional revolt in Catalonia and the revolutionary commune in the Asturias."[66] Jackson observes:

While these multiple events were occurring, the Spanish public could not know in detail what was transpiring in widely separated parts of the peninsula. But certain things were very clear, and very frightening. The President and the Cortes had been unable to maintain parliamentary government. An attempted general strike had led to the declaration of a national emergency, with consequent censorship and police rule. Two armed uprisings had occurred, one in the name of Catalan regional liberty and one in the name of proletarian revolution. The specter of revolutionary violence, and the counter-use of Moorish troops,

had horrified Spaniards of all persuasions. These things had taken place against a
background of heavy-handed police action against strikers, rising peasant agita-
tion, rising Catalan nationalism, the radicalization of a large proportion of the
Socialists and the strident advances of German and Austrian Fascism. Luckily
the general strike and the Catalan rising had been contained with a minimum of
violence. But the Asturian rising had challenged the entire basis of the parliamentary Republic, and the government had suppressed it with troops whom the
great majority of Spaniards considered to be both foreigners and savages.[67]

These events are the backdrop for many of Alberti's poems published in *El
burro explosivo, El poeta en la calle,* and *De un momento a otro.* These
collections chronicle particular sociopolitical events in Spain during 1934–36,
events that are, as the title of Salvador Dalí's painting of 1936 so aptly
reveals, a "Premonition of Civil War."[68]

In his "Indice autobiográfico" Alberti recalls the year 1935: "Conferencias
y recitales en Nueva York y La Habana. Aquí conozco a Nicolás Guillén y, en la
cárcel, a Juan Marinello. Permanezco en México (capital) durante casi un año,
relacionandome con los escritores y grandes pintores de ese país: Orozco,
Siquieros, Diego Rivera . . . Al regresar a Europa, paso ante las cosas [*sic*] de
Venezuela, escribiendo algunas poesías, que incluyo luego en *13 bandas y 48
estrellas,* poema contra el imperialismo yanki" (*PC,* 14). The thirteen poems
collected in *13 bandas y 48 estrellas,* first published in 1936 and later recollected in part 3 of *De un momento a otro,* are songs of protest against and critical
evaluations of the role of "el imperialismo yanki," (*PC,* 14), "la diplomacia
del horror," and "la intervención armada" in the Americas, their effects on the
people, and the limitations they place on freedom.[69] As in "Un fantasma
recorre Europa" and "S.O.S.," written a few years earlier, the poems of *13
bandas y 48 estrellas* are international in focus and content. The poet's assumed
public voices appraise the present situation of the limited freedom experienced
by the American common people in general and envision the construction of a
new social order of justice, equality, and human solidarity. According to the
poem's speakers, in the new era the dual "crimen" of imperialism and capitalism will be abolished in "ese sacudimiento que destruya / la intervención
armada de los dólares."[70] From this destruction the new future of the Americas
will emerge, as the closing poem "Yo también canto a América" reveals:[71]

Tu venidera órbita asegures
con la expulsión total de tu presente.
Aire libre, mar libre, tierra libre.
Yo también canto a América futura.
(Ll. 73–76)

Aligned to the international common man in both his present circumstance
and his future aspirations, the public voices of *13 bandas y 48 estrellas*

express, as Lechner observes, "el compromiso de Alberti frente al nuevo mundo" (*CPE*, 73).

Summarizing the content of the third section of *De un momento a otro*, Lechner remarks:

> Ataca al capitalismo yanqui dondequiera que lo vea, ya en su forma más espectacular e impresionante—los rascacielos de Nueva York vistos desde el barco—, ya en sus manifestaciones dispersas por el continente entero: esclavitud económica y consiguiente esclavitud real de indios y negros, presidentes dictatoriales y crueles mantenidos en su puesto por los intereses económicos de más allá de las fronteras hispanoamericanas. . . . Poesía de urgencia . . . escrita a cada instante, que no aspira a servir la causa, no ya mediante un examen de conciencia y la presentación de sus resultados, sino mediante la denuncia de cuantos males encuentra dentro de su país y fuera de él. (*CPE*, 73)

The voices of protest and tones of indignation and denouncement resounding in Alberti's poems of this collection will be heard years later in *Signos del día* (1945–55) and in the poem "Un soneto para terminar: Vietnam" (1965) when Alberti once again evaluates and responds to many of the same social problems that the public voices of *13 bandas y 48 estrellas* first explored.[72]

The poetry of *13 bandas y 48 estrellas* reveals, on the one hand, additional globally inspired preoccupations of the politically active Alberti of the early thirties. On the other hand, however, the preoccupations evident in this collection are intimately linked to and stem from those that had already surfaced in *Consignas* and *Un fantasma recorre Europa,* concerns that were immediately associated with the sociopolitical circumstance of the First Spanish Republic. Whether Alberti's public voices chronicle the exploited "negro" in "Casi son," "El indio" of the poem of the same title, or the collective "campesinos de Zorita" or the peasants of "La lucha por la tierra," they speak on behalf of and in unison with the people and their struggle.

In the "Elegía cívica" Alberti's personal poetic voice resonates with rage as it retells the horrifying encroachment of death on life, injustice on justice, and restriction on liberty in the Spain of the late twenties. Free of the surrealist rhetoric and the oneiric fantasies of Alberti's first political poem, "New-York," the introductory poem of *13 bandas y 48 estrellas,* explores a similar ambience of death, destruction, injustice, and obstructed freedom where

> Alguien se despertaba pensando que la niebla
> ponía un especial cuidado en ocultar el crimen.
>
> (Ll. 1–2)

Here, the clairvoyant, first-person speaker, firmly grounded in the political reality in which he finds himself, observes:

> Era yo quien entraba ya despierto, asomado a la niebla,
> viendo cómo aquel crimen disfrazado de piedras con ventanas

se agrandaba, ensanchándose,
perdiéndose la idea de su altura,
viéndole intervenir hasta en las nubes.
Y era yo quien veía, quien oía, ya despierto.
(Ll. 27–33)

Multiple aspects of the pervasive "crimen" are disclosed throughout the poem's first moment (ll. 1–60). The ubiquitous nature of this menacing force is reflected in the free-verse form used in the poem's first section. Pertaining, at first, to the past, this threatening, ominous force encroaches on the present where its identity is finally discerned and disclosed. In the poem's second moment (ll. 61–84), the meaning of the "crimen" is finally known, and its cause and effect are studied in the self-contained, unrhymed, hendecasyllabic quartets of the poem's second section. The first quartet of this second moment defines this force and clarifies its location and effects:

Nueva York. Wall Street, Banca de sangre,
aureo pulmón comido de gangrena,
araña de tentaciones que hilan
fríamente la muerte de otros pueblos.
(Ll. 61–64)

The figurative and fatal "alba de las náuseas / . . . de la consunción de la parálisis progresiva del mundo / y la arterioesclerosis del cielo" (ll. 29–30) of the "Elegía cívica" has been replaced by a particularized locale, "Nueva York. Wall Street," and a particularized, identifiable agent of destruction, "Banca de sangre," as the speaker studies the terrible results of the policies of the United States:

Tu diplomacia del horror quisiera
la intervención armada en los astros;
zonas de sangre, dónde sólo ahora
ruedan minas celestes, lluvias vírgines.
(Ll. 73–76)

The speaker's apocalyptic vision of "New-York," his symbolic microcosm for the United States in general, is not limited to this particular cityscape and its inhabitants (ll. 3–26) but rather it extends beyond "aquel amanecer de rascacielos" (l. 16) and "oscuros, explotados / desamparados hombres macilentos" (ll. 12–13) and finally encompasses all of the Americas. For the speaker of "New-York," these two continents are dominated by "el imperialismo yanki" and, within the prophecy of this poem, the life and freedom of the common people are menaced by "hombres mercenarios con fusiles" (l. 38), and "todo envuelto siempre en un tremendo vaho de petróleo" (l. 57). According to the speaker, whenever the United States pursues its policies of armed intervention and endless quests for oil throughout the Americas, the freedom of the people is jeopardized. This quest is summarized in the repeated refrain of "New-York," a refrain succinctly summarizing both the speaker's vision of the congested scenario of the city and the destructive profit-motivated interests of Wall Street:

y todo envuelto siempre en un tremendo vaho de petróleo,
en un abrasador contagio de petróleo,
en una inabarcable marea de petróleo
(Ll. 24–26, 57–59)

As in the "Elegía cívica," in the apocalypse envisioned by the public speaker of "New-York" lies the genesis of the new era of freedom and social justice for the people. This theme of apocalypse-genesis, underlying all of the poems of *13 bandas y 48 estrellas,* unifies the closing moment of the introductory poem to this collection:

Mas aún por América arde el pulso
de agónicas naciones que me gritan
con mi mismo lenguaje entre la niebla.
tramando tu mortal sacudimiento.

Así un día tus trece horizontales
y tus cuarenta y ocho estrellas blancas
verán desvanecerse en una justa,
libertadora llama de petróleo.
(Ll. 77–84)

Although *13 bandas y 48 estrellas* further delineates aspects of social change and proletarian solidarity that Alberti's public voices of *Consignas* and *Un fantasma recorre Europa* first imagined and proclaimed, the expression of these themes and theses is distinct. One striking difference is that in the collection recording the situation of the common people of the Americas, the raucous public voice of a party spokesperson, Marxist rhetoric, political slogans, and blatant political indoctrination are missing. The public voice of *13 bandas y 48 estrellas* echoes the social concerns of the people to whom he sings and not the political discourse and tactical aims of the party. The public voice of *13 bandas y 48 estrellas,* directing his poetry to the common man he serves, urges and predicts:

Despiértate, y de un salto reconquista
tu subterránea sangre de petróleo,
brazos de plata, pies de oro macizos,
que tu existencia propia vivifiquen.

Va a sonar, va a sonar, yo quiero verlo,
quiero oirlo, tocarlo, ser su impulso,

ese sacudimiento que destruya
la intervención armada de los dólares.
                    (Ll. 45–52)

The tone of protest and the prophetic vision expressed in *13 bandas y 48 estrellas* leads to one further observation. In retrospect, Alberti's early assessment of and response to politics in the Americas of 1935 are indeed revealing. The political and figurative "crimen" witnessed by the poet's public voices and transcribed in poems such as "New-York," "Casi son," "El indio," "El Salvador," "Panamá," "Costas de Venezuela" and "Yo también canto a América" has haunted and continues to haunt the Americas today. The public voices of Pablo Neruda, Ernesto Cardenal, Carlos Germán Belli, Robert Bly, and Daniel Berrigan echo that of Rafael Alberti as each attempts to shape in verse his vision of and response to the people's role in determining the future of the Americas.

"A New Human History"

Maxwell Adereth has observed in *Commitment in Modern French Literature:* "The committed writer knows that in modern society he must side *with* certain social forces against *injustice*. He refuses to compromise with the Establishment, but his rebellion is part of a wider movement" (*CMFL,* 34). This observation is certainly true of and applicable to Rafael Alberti as a committed political poet in the thirties. As early as 1931, Alberti sided with the common man of his contemporary reality, both nationally and internationally, believing him to be the "social force" from which would originate the new society. This social alignment and commitment is evident in the poetry chronicling the common people's participation in the construction of that society, most specifically that of *Consignas* and *Un fantasma recorre Europa* and later in many of the poems of *El burro explosivo, Nuestra diaria palabra, 13 bandas y 48 estrellas, De un momento a otro,* and *El poeta en la calle.* Throughout his poetry of 1931–35, Alberti "refuses to compromise with" social forces promoting injustice and undermining the people's efforts to erect the new era. In fact, in his agitative verse of the early thirties, as has been demonstrated, Alberti's strident and belligerent public voice often harshly condemns such forces and the social inequities these advance.

A study of Alberti's poetry of the early thirties reveals that his verse, be it of the agitative or the reflective modality, is set in motion and guided by a dual "razón revolucionaria": the poet's commitment to the people and their new era and also the poet's theme of liberty for the people. According to Jean-Paul Sartre, as Adereth has noted in his study of French commitment literature, "because he speaks to free men, the committed writer . . . can have only one theme—Liberty. Not Liberty in general (which is a meaningless abstraction), but the concrete liberties which men try to win and preserve at each stage of their historical development" (*CMFL*, 36). Alberti himself echoes these words of Sartre in 1962 when he writes, "He exaltado en mi verso la liberación de los hombres y el amor y la fraternidad y la paz. Creo que mi mano puede estrechar la de todos los hombres" (*PEC*, 618).

Rafael Alberti, as a committed poet in the early thirties and throughout his lifetime, has dedicated his work and his life to securing liberty for the common people. His work and his life have, for over half a century, remained intimately committed to the history and the freedom of the people. On 24 May 1965, in Moscow, upon receiving the Lenin Peace Prize, Alberti summarized this dual commitment:

Los poetas sabemos desde hace siglos que hemos de decir en nuestros versos cosas que lleguen al corazón humano. Desde Dante, Petrarca, Byron, Miczkievich, Víctor Hugo, Whitman, Pushkin, Petófi, Maiakovski y tantos más, hasta el poeta vietnamita que hoy se duele junto a su arroz amargo, todos han estado al lado de los pueblos, junto a su libertad. Porque los poetas hemos de ser, como quería Antonio Machado, poetas del tiempo. Ese es nuestro compromiso: ser, existir, dar universalidad a un momento, volver ecuménico lo intensamente sentido y válido, aceptar lo humano, rehacerlo, no retroceder, equivocarse y seguir, hacer unas veces arma del verso y otras flores, puesto que nos ha tocado, vivir entre el clavel y la espada. . . . Mi vida . . . [está] comprometida con la historia de mi pueblo. (*PEC*, 626)

Sergei Eisenstein's observations regarding the collective's role in social development and social change, recorded at the outset of this chapter, are pertinent here: "Of all living beings on earth we alone are privileged to experience and relive, one after another, the moments of substantiation of the most important achievements in social development. More. We have the privilege of participating collectively in making a new human history" (*P*, 16). Rafael Alberti comprehends this public social and collective task and privilege so well and with such conviction that his political poetry of the last fifty years never ceases to record the success and failure of this noble endeavor.

A product of a feverish political climate, a politically inspired poet and an urgent and consuming political dream, the poetry of *Consignas* and *Un fantasma recorre Europa, El burro explosivo, Nuestra diaria palabra, 13 bandas y 48 estrellas, De un momento a otro,* and *El poeta en la calle* is external, social, and collectivist. Alberti is no longer concerned with portraying the afflictions plaguing his inner self as he was in *Sobre los ángeles, Sermones y moradas, Yo era un tonto,* and even, to a certain extent, the "Elegía cívica." His revolutionary poetry of the early thirties cannot be characterized as internal, personal, and individualistic, as were his poems written prior to that decade. In his poetry of 1931–35, and that which he would write during the Spanish Civil War and in political exile after the war, what is of interest to Alberti is the collectivity and his own relationship, both as poet and member, to the collective. The poet is concerned with the public domain of the collective and the public matters affecting this collective. His poetry is a poetry of social themes and public voices as he surveys, transcribes, and often critiques the everyday, concrete reality of the people he represents.

In *Poetry and Politics,* C. M. Bowra summarizes the contemporary reality surrounding the poet in the thirties and the evolution that many of these poets underwent as they abandoned the introspective and cryptic poetry many of them had written in the twenties in favor of a poetry allowing each to communicate with and speak on behalf of his fellowmen. Bowra observes:

> The political turmoil of the thirties, with its bloated tyrannies and their menace to the whole civilised world, confronted poets with a hard decision. The art in which most of them had been brought up was not well equipped for dealing with large emotions and wide horizons, but they could not always escape from prevalent movements in politics or fail to take up a position with regard to them and sometimes this had the urgency of religious conversion. Once they had embraced a cause there was nothing they would not dedicate to it, including their own precious and carefully nurtured art. If poets were expected to have a message, they were prepared to provide it. For some the change was especially difficult because they had been brought up in poetical techniques, such as Dadaism and Surrealism, which could hardly be expected to have any popular appeal and did not aim at clarity of expression. Yet they felt that they must get into closer touch with their fellow-men and find a sense of unity with them, and for this their art was ill-equipped. A poet may wish to sink his personality in that of others, whose sufferings he shares or would like to share, and to speak both for them and with them, in the simplicity of natural man faced by hideous dangers and driven back on his basic human state. His change of mood calls for a change of style, for a manner which will enable him to identify himself with others on issues which none can escape. But such an adjustment is never easy, and at times it may cost more than it is worth. The problem is to find a new manner which is as poetically effective as the old but which speaks for a wider range of experience to a larger audience. The challenge has been taken by some highly gifted poets, and in their responses we can see what is gained and what is lost. (*PP,* 123–24)

This "challenge" and Rafael Alberti's "response" to such a challenge are manifested in the public themes, public voices, and the political modes of writing evident in his poetry written during the early thirties. By closely examining the poet's verbalized "response," the poem itself, we are now better able to comprehend and assess what has been "gained" and "lost" in adopting a political and public mode of writing and in placing poetry, to use Alberti's own words, "at the service of the Spanish Revolution and the international proletariat."

In *Consignas, Un fantasma recorre Europa,* and later in *El burro explosivo, Nuestra diaria palabra, 13 bandas y 48 estrellas, De un momento a otro,* and *El poeta en la calle,* Alberti addresses and eventually answers the three difficult questions that Sartre would later raise and also answer in *What Is Literature?:* What is writing? Why write? and For whom does one write?[73] These same questions have been addressed by many committed artists since the thirties as each attempted to isolate and define the problems of art, the role of the artist in society, the artist's involvement in his or her own sociopolitico-historical reality, and the meaning, to borrow Adereth's observation, of "commitment as a valid and challenging method of approaching artistic creation" (*CMFL,* 34). In analyzing the specific public themes, voices, and modalities that first surfaced in *Consignas* and *Un fantasma recorre Europa,* we, as readers, are in a better position to address the questions posed by Sartre and other committed writers. Alberti's earliest collections of political poetry clearly mark his first attempts at creating and communicating new and distinct political modes of writing, his comprehension of the socialist conviction and social command underlying and motivating these modes, and his awareness of and commitment to the people for whom he writes. The collections of political verse that Alberti wrote in the early and mid-thirties demonstrate that his "approach to artistic creation" is and would thereafter be one of analyzing the pressing public matters of his time and reflecting and expressing these in the public themes of his poetry of "a new human history."

The Poet
and the Spanish Civil War

Para muchos España era el enigma y la revelación
de aquella época de la historia.

Pablo Neruda, *Confieso que he vivido*

Yesterday the belief in the absolute value of Greece,
The fall of the curtain upon the death of a hero;
    Yesterday the prayer to the sunset
And the adoration of madmen. But to-day the struggle.

W. H. Auden, *Spain*

*I*n the history of Spain, no single event precipitated the eventual *golpe del estado* of 18 July 1936, when the Insurgents rose against the Popular Front government of the Republic, an action initiating the three-year conflict of the Spanish Civil War.[1] Numerous newspaper accounts, historical investigations, memoirs, biographies, poems, novels, plays, and films have been concerned with this war and its consequences. One need only to glance through Hugh Thomas's bibliography in *The Spanish Civil War* (pp. 805–32) to discover, for example, the extent to which this conflict has been examined and remembered.[2] Gabriel Jackson indicated in *A Concise History of the Spanish Civil War* the possible underlying reasons for such widespread and lasting interest in this particular moment of Spain's history when, in 1974, he wrote: "More than thirty years after the triumph of General Franco the Spanish Civil War remains fascinating and controversial both within Spain and internationally. There are several reasons for this: The background of intense ideological struggle; the coincidence of the war with the international confrontation of Fascism, Communism and Democracy; the occurrence of revolution and counter-revolution; the ferocity, the commitment and at times the nobility of the participants; and the permanent human interest of the spiritual issues involved" (p. 7).

"But To-day the Struggle"

With the aid of historical hindsight we are, perhaps, better able to comprehend that the Spanish Civil War was more than a confrontation between Nationalist and Republican forces. It was a multifaceted struggle in an ideologically divided Spain, a conflict whose origin and circumstance are intimately connected with both the history of Spain, particularly, and Europe, generally, and the overall sociopolitical context of the thirties. The Spanish Civil War was essentially a struggle to establish the Just Society for the common people of Spain. The Spanish Civil War was therefore nurtured by the will of a people who resisted threats to individual and collective liberty. In that struggle personal and collective involvement in and commitment to the goals of the Popular Front were essential to the defeat of fascism and the consequent erection of the people's new era.

The Spanish Civil War provoked famous and influential artists of the thirties to examine the cause, effect, and meaning of the people's war in their works and impelled some of them to go to Spain and commit themselves to the struggle.[3] In *The Thirties and After,* Stephen Spender offers a glimpse of this historical interval in world politics:

> It was the Spanish Civil War which produced the greatest manifestations of unity on the anti-fascist left, resulting in the meetings and demonstrations of the Front Populaire. An article written by Auden in the *New Statesman,* written when he was in Valencia, strikes very much the same note as I do in my journalism during the civil war:
>
>> For a *revolution* is really taking place, not an old shuffle or two in cabinet appointments. In the last six months these people have been learning what it is to *inherit their own country,* and once a man has tasted *freedom* he will not lightly give it up; freedom to choose for himself and to organise his life, freedom not to depend for good fortune on a clever and outrageous piece of overcharging or a windfall of drunken charity. (*TA,* 28)

In "Heroes in Spain," which first appeared in the *New Statesman* and the *Nation* in May of 1937, Spender writes:

> I went to Barcelona, Valencia, Madrid, Morata, Albacete and Tartosa (where thousands of people had camped out on the hills at night for fear of an air raid);

and I travelled a good deal between these places, going in trains, lorries and private cars. My first and last impressions were not of the struggle for power amongst the heads of committees in the large towns, nor inefficiency and bureaucracy, common as they are during a revolution which is also a war; but the courage of the people in Madrid, the enthusiasm of eighty percent of the people everywhere for the social revolution, the generosity of the workers wherever I met them, in the streets, in the trains, in lorries; the marked difference between the awakening younger generation of Spanish workers and the stupified older ones. Every observer who stays in Republican Spain comes back again and again to a realization that it is the people of Spain who count. . . . I returned from Spain feeling more strongly than I have ever felt before that I support the Spanish social revolution. Since the war must be won if the revolution is to be retained, there is nothing to do but accept it as a terrible necessity. (*TA*, 68–69)

For Spender and other poets, artists, writers, and filmmakers of the thirties, the Spanish Civil War had a specific and significant political purpose: it was, above all, a war of the people and for the people. As Spender writes in "Tangiers and Gilbraltar *Now*": "It is not often in the history of a nation that the phrase 'the people' has any meaning: but there are moments when suddenly the masses acquire a conscious will. Such moments occurred during the French and the Russian Revolutions; and are now in Spain."[4]

This "conscious will" of the masses is recorded in the film *The Spanish Earth* by Joris Ivens. According to the critic Thomas Waugh, "*Spanish Earth* was the first film to formulate the concept of the people's war . . . and to insert this concept into main stream public discourse."[5] Ivens's image of the Spanish Civil War and civil revolution not only chronicled the people's struggle but also would forever be an inspiration to all viewers who believed in and were committed to the goals of that particular struggle in history and any struggle of the people that might still lie ahead. Thomas Waugh observes: "In countering images of victimization with images of resistance and revolution, *Spanish Earth* articulates a world view that sees people as agents of history, not its casualties. The final word is given not to the airborne mercenaries and their bombs, but to the people rooted in the central symbol of the film, the earth."[6]

Those who fought for or supported the Republic hoped to achieve, in the words of José Bergamín, "libertad . . . verdad . . . justicia" for the people. Bergamín further explains that "esta sangre viva de nuestro pueblo, que manos fratricidas están vertiendo ante nuestros ojos," has revealed in war, "la verdad del pueblo que guerrea: la más pura verdad de nuestra España, nuestra, solo nuestra: porque popular, porque humana; porque liberadora, verdadera, justiciera."[7]

The meaning of the fratricidal conflict is also probed by many poets of the era. The following lines written by three of the most significant Hispanic poets of the Spanish Civil War offer further transcriptions and interpretations of the people's struggle and the meaning it had for those who witnessed the combat and envisioned the "people as the agents of history." Rafael Alberti's "18 de Julio" discloses:

Sufre el mapa de España, grita, llora,
se descentra del mar y su mejilla
tanto se decolora,
que se pierde de grana en amarilla.
Se retuerce su entraña en tal manera,
que lo que va a parir ya está en la aurora:
18 de Julio: Nueva Era.

(Ll. 27–33)

In the brief "La victoria de las armas del pueblo" of *España en el corazón,* Pablo Neruda envisions:

Mas, como el recuerdo de la tierra, como el pétreo
esplendor del meta y el silencio,
pueblo, patria y avena, es tu victoria.

Avanza tu bandera agujerlada
como tu pecho sobre las cicatrices
de tiempo y tierra.[8]

The war poetry of Spain's soldier-poet Miguel Hernández is inspired by the "viento del pueblo" of his fellowmen. These verses from "Recoged esta voz" summarize the role of the poet and the people in the struggle:

Hombres, mundos, naciones,
atended, escuchad mi sangrante sonido
recoged mis latidos de quebranto
en vuestros espaciosos corazones,
porque yo empuño el alma cuando canto.

Cantando me defiendo
y defiendo mi pueblo cuando en mi pueblo imprimen
su herradura de pólvora estruendo
los bárbaros del crimen.

(Ll. 13–21)[9]

"No sois la muerte, sois las nuevas juventudes"

Of the year 1936 Rafael Alberti has written: "Días de pasión, de alegría de heroísmo, de 'paraíso a la sombra de espadas.' . . . En medio de un Madrid casi cercado, escribo celebrando su inmortal defensa, numerosos poemas que agrupo bajo el titulo de *Capital de la gloria* (*PC,* 14–15). *Capital de la gloria* is Alberti's intimate poetic diary of the Spanish Civil War.[10] The underlying theme of these poems is death as a source of life; specifically, death in the conflict is not merely death, but rather it is a form of new life, since from the "catastrophe" of war will emerge the "glory" of the revitalized Spanish people.[11] The opposing forces of death and life in the struggle, their symbolic and metaphoric manifestations in the poetry of this period, and their paradoxical union within the anticipated new political era provide an inherent thematic structure for Alberti's poems of the Spanish Civil War. The role the people are to assume in both the conflict and in the resulting era "de alegría, de aurora, de libertad y sueño" is sketched throughout the poems of this collection.[12] In this way, Alberti further establishes and refines features of the complex *pueblo*-protagonist already evident in the "Elegía cívica," *Consignas, Un fantasma recorre Europa,* and other poems of the thirties. The role of the poem itself as both a personal expression of the public event and as a means, to use Alberti's own words, of harnessing the "desorden impuesto" of war is also an essential feature of *Capital de la gloria.*[13]

The intertwined themes of death and resurrection and the role of the people in the present and future eras in Alberti's poetry of the Spanish Civil War is also prevalent in that of Miguel Hernández, Pablo Neruda, and Emilio Prados. This theme is perhaps most effectively presented in Alberti's long poem "Madrid-Otoño." Written in the fall of 1936, it is the introductory poem of *Capital de la gloria* and originally gave title to the collection.[14] By examining this particular poem in detail we can better appreciate the essential theme not only of Alberti's collection but also of much of the poetry written on behalf of the Republic during the war. In addition, many of the prevalent motifs, cluster images, and intrinsic tones that first emerge in this poem are later developed throughout Alberti's poetry of the Spanish Civil War.

In the fall of 1936 an intensive siege of the capital began. Repeated bombings, artillery fire, and hand-to-hand combat occurred daily as the Insurgents battled the Republicans for Madrid. Hugh Thomas records: "No great city in history had been so tested, though the attack was a foretaste of what was to happen in a few years to London, Hamburg, Tokyo and Leningrad."[15] This ambience of the capital "madura para los bombardeos" (l. 17) is the setting of "Madrid-Otoño:"

1

Ciudad de los más turbios siniestros provocados,   1
de la angustia nocturna que ordena hundirse al miedo
en los sótanos lívidos con ojos desvelados,
yo quisiera furiosa, pero impasiblemente

arrancarme de cuajo la voz, pero no puedo,   5
para pisarte toda tan silenciosamente,
que la sangre tirada
mordiera, sin protesta, mi llanto y mi pisada.

Por tus desnivelados terrenos y arrabales,
ciudad, por tus lluviosas y ateridas afueras   10
voy las hojas difuntas pisando entre trincheras,
charcos y barrizales.
Los árboles acodan, desprovistos, las ramas
por bardas y tapiales
donde con ojos fijos espían las troneras   15
un cielo temeroso de explosiones y llamas.

Capital ya madura para los bombardeos,
avenidas de escombros y barrios en ruinas,
corre un escalofrío al pensar tus museos
tras de las barricadas que impiden las esquinas.   20

Hay casas cuyos muros humildes, levantados
a la escena del aire, representan la escena
del mantel y los lechos todavía ordenados,
el drama silencioso de los trajes vacíos,
sin nadie, en la alacena   25
que los biseles fríos
de la menguada luna de los pobres roperos
recogen y barajan con los sacos terreros.

Más que nunca mirada,
como ciudad que en tierra reposa al descubierto,   30
la frente de tu frente se alza tiroteada,
tus costados de árboles y llanuras, heridos;
pero tu corazón no lo taparán muerto,
aunque montes de escombros le paren sus latidos.

Ciudad, ciudad presente,   35
guardas en tus entrañas de catástrofe y gloria
el germen más hermoso de tu vida futura.
Bajo la dinamita de tus cielos, crujiente,
se oye el nacer del nuevo hijo de la victoria.
Gritando y a empujones la tierra lo inaugura.   40

2

¡Palacios, bibliotecas! Estos libros tirados
que la yerba arrasada recibe y no comprende,
estos descoloridos sofás desvencijados
que ya tan sólo el frío los usa y los defiende;
estos inesperados   45

retratos familiares
en donde los varones de la casa, vestidos
los más innecesarios jaeces militares,
nos contemplan, partidos,
sucios, pisoteados,   50
con ese inexpresable gesto fijo y oscuro
del que al nacer ya lleva contra su espalda el muro
de los ejecutados;
este cuadro, este libro, este furor que ahora
me arranca lo que tienes para mí de elegía   55
son pedazos de sangre de tu terrible aurora.
Ciudad, quiero ayudarte a dar a luz tu día.

The contemplation of autumn, the cycles of nature, the juxtaposition of death with life in both nature and war, and the poet's private vision of the public event develop the central theme of resurrection. "Madrid-Otoño" has been divided by the poet into two sections. In the first part (ll. 1–40), the poem's first-person speaker wanders among the skeletal remains of the shelled city, pondering its present reality and envisioning its future. In the second part (ll. 41–57), the poem focuses on a particular aspect of the capital, its palaces, and the state of these as a result of war.

Rebirth is dramatized throughout the poem's first moment by the imagery of ruin and rejuvenation, the juxtaposition of the present with the future, and the contrapuntal tones of sadness and hope. In this way, the first section of "Madrid-Otoño" can itself be divided into two antithetical yet complementary moments. The speaker first witnesses the shattered aspects of the once-vibrant city and then envisions its future revitalization. In the apostrophe to the palaces, and the libraries found within them, the poet momentarily suspends these thematic, temporal and tonal pairings as he reflects on elements of the city that, for him, have assumed important political significance during the Civil War. Although this brief political interlude alters the tone and texture of the poem, death as the germ of new life is the thematic thread joining the two distinct sections.

The opening apostrophe, constituting the first sixteen lines, establishes the ambience of the city, the speaker's response to the scene witnessed, and finally, the cause of the capital's "angustia nocturna" (l. 2). The collectivity, poetically portrayed by the synecdoche "con ojos desvelados," has become a single vigilant spectator of the cause and consequence of the destruction. In contrast, the individual speaker, metaphorically represented by his "furiosa . . . voz" (ll. 4–5), is not merely a vocal observer. He wanders through the remains of the shelled city and as he walks his thoughts become both "mi llanto y mi pisada" (l. 8), both his response to and impressions of war.

The speaker's solitary journey begins in the outskirts of the capital (ll. 9–12). Images of decay, deadening, chilling cold and bare trees develop the motif of autumn and the death accompanying this season. The autumnal scene is itself a metaphor as each element of the moribund ambience reflects the absence of life in "Madrid-Otoño." However, within the suburbs "trenches" are found. At first their presence is surprising to the reader, since these are normally neither a part of nor associated with a fall landscape. By sonorously linking two apparently disparate elements, "afueras" and "trincheras" (ll. 10, 11), Alberti underscores his speaker's double vision of the ubiquity of death in both nature and war. By anthropomorphizing the landscape, the poet transfers elements associated with the corpses in the trenches to the environment itself. In this way, the cold, stiff, recumbent outskirts, the withered leaves, and the stark trees now deprived of life share the fate of the dead soldiers.

The opening apostrophe of the poem's third stanza, "Capital ya madura para los bombardeos" (l. 17), names the agent of destruction. The ordeal of fire and bombings portrayed in the initial stanza of "Madrid-Otoño" is now intensified when the actual cause of the city's "nocturnal anguish," of the omnipresence of death, and of the elegiac lament is revealed as the poet's assumed persona watches the illuminated sky.

The cameralike eye of the speaker moves from a panorama of the city's outskirts in the second stanza to a close-up of the cityscape in stanzas 3 and 4. His footsteps and thoughts take him into "las avenidas de escombros y barrios en ruinas" (l. 18). Alberti skillfully draws attention to the struggle between the opposing forces of death and life by juxtaposing images of the bombardment with those of the hearth: "la escena del aire . . . la escena / del mantel y los lechos todavía ordenados" (ll. 22–23). Careful examination of the poet's diction in this fourth stanza reveals that "escena" denotes the backdrop of the war while also referring to a part of a play. In this way, the "drama silencioso" (l. 24) encountered by the poem's speaker as he wanders among the city's empty homes is both the ambience and the outcome of war. Within this single word "escena," Alberti not only unites cause and effect but also underscores the confrontation of death and life inherent in war.

In each of the four initial stanzas of "Madrid-Otoño" there is an upward and downward movement as the poem's speaker first surveys the flaming sky and then witnesses the resultant destruction below in the city and its environs. This movement culminates in the metaphors sketching the vision and interpretation of the "silent drama" following the bombings. The walls of the hollow, devastated dwellings remain upright, lifting the speaker's eyes to their new roof: the exploding sky. At the same time, these walls enclose and form the setting for the "drama" enacted below.

Alberti's multiple metaphors of "los biseles fríos / de la menguada luna" (ll. 26–27) brilliantly sustain the ascending-descending focus of the poem's

speaker while also capturing and intensifying his perception of the consequences of war. Literally "la menguada luna" means the waning moon. This
celestial body in "the scene in the air" (l. 22) is seen by the speaker as he
looks through the now open-air roofs. However, *luna* also means mirror and
so is associated with the abandoned closets in the "scene" below. Curiously, it
is the lone "lunar looking glass" (l. 27) that reflects and profiles the moon
above and the pallid light it casts on the empty theater in the drama of war.

The stark, chilling ambience evoked by the presence of the celestial moon
permeates the eerie terrestrial "scene" of the lifeless dwellings. Sadly
enough, there are no actors in the "silent drama" originating in and resulting
from war. The only trace of man is the diminished form of his "trajes vacíos"
(l. 24) lingering in the wardrobe mirror on the deserted stage.[16] The artistic
and complex imagery of the fourth stanza reveals the cruelest reality of all: in
war, man cannot escape death. Metaphors of death, ruin, and emptiness
culminate in this poetic portrayal of the absence of human life in the aftermath
of the conflict. Perhaps here, more than in any of the other passages of the
poem, we most intensely experience the speaker's deep-seated anguish as he
witnesses the fierce inhumanity of war.

Within the morbid ambience of "Madrid-Otoño," the very body of the
personified city is itself threatened by death in the conflict (ll. 29–34). As the
first-person speaker inspects the recumbent capital, he perceives its "shelled
forehead" (l. 31) and "flanking, wounded trees and plains" (l. 32). Skillfully
uniting these features of the human body with the "vanguard" and "flanks" of
its battle lines ("frente . . . costados" [ll. 31–32]), Alberti portrays Madrid
as a living citadel. Realizing this, the poem's speaker says: "tu corazón no lo
taparán muerto, / aunque montes de escombros le paren sus latidos" (ll. 33–
34). Beneath the rubble, within the empty houses, among the withered leaves
that line the trenches, the figurative heart of Madrid pulsates. Although the
heartbeat may not be heard through the din of war, this city of "Madrid-
Otoño" is a poetically personified, symbolic, living force refusing to succumb
to death.

Throughout the first five stanzas, the speaker calls attention to the reality of
war in Madrid in the autumn of 1936. In the closing moment of the poem's
first section, his attention shifts to the capital's future era:

> Ciudad, ciudad presente,
> guardas en tus entrañas de catástrofe y gloria
> el germen más hermoso de tu vida futura.
> (Ll. 35–37)

Within the ruins of the city, beneath its exploding, flaming skies, in the midst
of its atmosphere of death and destruction there exists its figurative future life:

the era that will emerge after the war has been won. The presence of this new life within the conflict is dramatized by the poetic personification of the city as earth-mother. Implanted within its womb is the symbolic embryo of Spain's future life. From the city's fertile "entrañas" will one day be born the "nuevo hijo de la victoria" (l. 39).

The speaker's faith in the anticipated era, emerging like the phoenix from the ashes of war, gives him a newfound hope. Paradoxically, within the "catastrophe" lies the "glory" (l. 36), for in death the resurrection of the Spanish people originates. The sixth stanza counters the preceding lines of "Madrid-Otoño." The imagery of disintegration, ruin, and absence of life, which developed the morbid ambience of the capital, is now juxtaposed with that of regeneration, rejuvenation, and birth. Marking the climax of the poem, this passage expresses the contrapuntal tone of hope underlying the vision of the war-torn capital. The barren outskirts covered with both the dead leaves of autumn and the trenches of war and the lifeless homes through which the speaker initially journeyed will be transformed one day. The death-life cycle inherent in nature is also found to be an integral part of the capital of "catastrophe and glory," of present death and future life.

In his closing apostrophe to the city of the present and future, Alberti introduces the fundamental theme of not only "Madrid-Otoño" in particular, but also of all of his war poetry: death as a source of new life. His somber meditation on war and autumn and on the death found in each ends with a jubilant proclamation of a vision of the future. The elegiac tone (l. 8) of the poem's first moment has been replaced by that of newfound hope in these closing lines of the sixth stanza as the witness to the city of the war envisions the "capital of glory."

As mentioned earlier, Alberti's apostrophe to the capital's palaces constitutes the second moment of "Madrid-Otoño" (ll. 41–57). The speaker abruptly turns from his complex view of the city and unexpectedly focuses on its palatial residences. The melancholy description of autumn in the war-torn city and the presence of death in each passing day have been left behind as the first-person speaker directs his thoughts to an aspect of Madrid that has a sociopolitical significance. For centuries, these palaces have belonged to wealthy families of Spanish society and on their walls portraits formerly hung depicting "los varones de la casa, vestidos / los más innecesarios jaeces militares" (ll. 47–48). These are the "retratos familiares" (l. 46) of those who, for this poet and his assumed persona, represent and incarnate the enemy. At this moment in Spain's history, however, these portraits are "cut, soiled" (ll. 49–50). They have not been destroyed by the bombings. Rather, they have been "trampled" (l. 50) by the Spanish people now inhabiting the palaces.

In another early poem of the war, "El último duque de Alba," Alberti recalls the seizing of such palaces by "Las Milicias comunistas" during the fall of 1936. In this ballad, the poem's speaker encourages the duke, who in this poem symbolizes the enemy, to look into his now occupied palace, for there:

> verás cómo tus ojos
> ven lo que jamás pensaran:
> palacio más limpio nunca
> lo conservó el pueblo en armas.
> Las Milicias comunistas
> son el orgullo de España.
>   (Ll. 55–60)[17]

These verses of both "El último duque de Alba" and "Madrid-Otoño" therefore record the poet's perceptions of a very real event of the early months of the war: the seizure of palaces and estates by the workers' trade unions and militiamen.[18]

Unfortunately, the meditation on death in war and the elegiac lament to the capital of the "catastrophe" have been briefly interrupted. Alberti's assumed poetic voice, a "raging voice" (ll. 4–5), is no longer directed to the figurative cause of death and destruction, as it was in the first section of the poem. Rather, his wrath falls upon the public figures who symbolize the antagonist of the conflict. In the poet's vision, the seizing of such palaces, his own anger, and the people's participation in the struggle become figurative, vital "traces of blood" (l. 56) diffused throughout the "dawn" (l. 56) of Spain's nascent political era.

In the closing apostrophe the poem's speaker declares: "Ciudad, quiero ayudarte a dar a luz tu día" (l. 57). Expressing his desire to serve as midwife in the "birth of the new child of victory" (l. 39), the speaker openly proclaims and vividly underscores his firm commitment to Madrid and the *pueblo* it represents. The wandering, saddened speaker of the poem's opening stanzas now triumphantly voices his optimistic desire to be an active participant in Madrid's present struggle and future epoch.

Although Alberti's apostrophe to the palaces seems to be a disruptive appendage to an otherwise artistically unified tribute to Madrid, there is a thematic correspondence between the last line of this apostrophe (l. 57) and the final stanza of the first part of the poem (ll. 35–40). In both passages imagery of birth develops the theme of death as a source of life. The speaker's initial desire to uproot his "raging voice" (ll. 4–5) is at last fulfilled (ll. 54–55), for his emotions have been vented in the poetic word, the means by which he assists in the birth of Madrid's new "day" (l. 57).

The figurative "new child of victory" of Alberti's *Capital de la gloria* is, in

Miguel Hernández's war poetry, a child that is at one and the same time a child of the poet's own flesh and blood born during the war and also a symbolic child incarnating the hope and the future of the Spanish people. In his stirring poem "Canción del esposo soldado" Hernández explains why he, as a soldier-poet-husband, participates in the war. He writes to his wife:

> Escríbeme a la lucha, siénteme en la trinchera:
> aquí con el fusil tu nombre evoco y fijo,
> y defiendo tu vientre de pobre que me espera,
> y defiendo tu hijo.
>
> Nacerá nuestro hijo con el puño cerrado,
> envuelto en un clamor de victoria y guitarras,
> y dejaré a tu puerta mi vida de soldado
> sin colmillos ni garras.
>
> Es preciso matar para seguir viviendo
> . . . .
> Para el hijo será la paz que estoy forjando.
>
> (Ll. 25–33, 41)

In "Hijo de la luz y de la sombra" this both real and symbolic child of Hernández's life and poetry is portrayed as a luminous, vital force in whom lies the origin of the future *pueblo:*

> Haremos de este hijo generador sustento,
> y hará de nuestra carne materia decisiva:
> donde sienten su alma las manos y el aliento
> las hélices circulen, la agricultura viva.
>
> El hará que esta vida no caiga derribada,
> pedazo desprendido de nuestros dos pedazos,
> que de nuestras dos bocas hará una sola espada
> y dos brazos eternos de nuestros cuatro brazos.
> No te quiero a ti sola: te quiero en tu ascendencia
> y en cuanto de tu vientre descenderá mañana.
> Porque la especie humana me han dado por herencia
> la familia del hijo será la especie humana.
>
> Con el amor a cuestas, dormidos y despiertos,
> seguiremos besándonos en el hijo profundo.
> Besándonos tú y yo se besan nuestros muertos,
> se besan los primeros pobladores del mundo.
>
> (Ll. 25–40)

In other poems of *Capital de la gloria* the theme of death and resurrection is sustained and developed through the imagery of genesis, germination, and growth and the symbolic motifs of autumn and spring. The symbolic seed of

Spain's future life, initially found beneath the ruins in "Madrid-Otoño," receives an epic dimension in the poem "Vosotros no caísteis." Addressing the dead soldiers, the poem's speaker eulogizes: "No sois la muerte, sois las nuevas juventudes" (l. 20), and thus, paradoxically, these dead soldiers incarnate life, for in death they have become the fructifying seed of Spain's future era, firmly implanted in the furrow-trenches of the war-torn land. They are the collective "semilla de los surcos que la guerra os abriera" (l. 8), and even in the apocalypse of war this spokesperson for the people envisions the anticipated genesis of the new generations. In the poem "Aniversario," death is the origin of life and from the dead the revitalized nation will spring forth "de los terrones de tierra / con la misma razón sencilla de los trigos" (ll. 7–8). The recurrent metaphor of the seed of life originating in death concisely captures the fundamental theme of Alberti's war poetry, is symbolic of the role of the people in the anticipated era, and underscores the tone of hope pervading *Capital de la gloria*.

The arrival of spring to the war-torn land is the poet's point of departure for his meditation on the resurrection of life in the sonnet "Abril, 1938." The poet's cosmic interpretation of nature's death-life cycle aids him in comprehending the omnipresence of death in the "tremenda sacudida" (l. 4) that is war. The emergence of spring throughout the countryside mirrors the future rejuvenation of the "patria ensangrentada" (l. 13) after the conflict has been won. As his oxymoron so accurately expresses, the future Spain will be enriched and revitalized by the "vida muerta y nueva vida" (l. 8) originating in and resulting from war:

¿Otra vez tú, si esta venida   1
más que imposible me parece,
puesto que sube y reverdece
en tan tremenda sacudida?

¿Otra vez tú, tan sin medida   5
tu corazón, que estalla y crece,
mientras la tierra lo enriquece
de vida muerta y nueva vida?

¿Otra vez tú poniendo flores
sobre la tumba improvisada,   10
sobre el terrón de la trinchera

y esa apariencia de colores
en esta patria ensangrentada?
¿Otra vez tú, la Primavera?

Of the poem "Abril, 1938," Díez de Revenga has accurately observed: "El poema . . . tiene la forma estrófica del soneto. El eneasílabo realiza aquí la función de lo que en un soneto sería el endécasilabo. . . . Rítmicamente el verso es muy interesante porque todos ellos son eneasílabos trocaicos. . . . Esto da homogeneidad al ritmo del poema. . . . Rafael Alberti ha cantado un momento de España en este soneto eneasílabo, dando al verso toda la capacidad del tradicional y culto endecasílabo."[19] The anaphoric repetition of the rhetorical question "¿Otra vez tú?" not only further enhances the sonnet's rhythm but also evokes the presence of its personified, mysterious protagonist, "Primavera" (l. 14). The entire poem is really a single, extended rhetorical question directed to the season of the year incarnating life and hope and, for the poet in the war, symbolizing the "nueva vida" (l. 8) which will emerge after "tan tremenda sacudida" (l. 4). The fusion of these thematic opposites with both nature and war, further underscored by the sonorous linking of these symbolic dualities, is what is observed as the speaker of "Abril, 1938" surveys the result of the conflict and envisions a positive, future effect.

The arrival of spring (l. 1) to the barren and war-torn land is presented in an entirely new way in this sonnet. Spring, in the midst of war, becomes a participant in the natural conflict of death/life. Spring not only mourns the dead combatants of the struggle and places flowers on their graves but also, at the same time, continues to fulfill its role within nature as the harbinger of new life. For the poet of the war, this season itself assumes a heroic dimension as it participates in the struggle between two forces in opposition, death and life, and helps to further the triumph of vitality and growth over death and ruin.

"Abril, 1938" is, however, an extended rhetorical question and thus the poem's speaker could simply be asking his question-in-variation in order to affirm simply and clearly his own belief in and hope for the nascent era of the people. However, could not this question also indicate the speaker's own doubt in the resurrection of life originating in war? Line 2 of the sonnet, "más que imposible me parece," seems to signal wonderment, even confusion, as the first-person speaker witnesses the actions of the harbinger of life to the death-filled land ("venida," "sube," "reverdece"). Yet, at the same time, this statement-question seems to indicate disbelief in the likelihood that such an action could eventually occur. Spring, as a symbol of pulsating new life ("tu corazón, que estalla y crece / mientras la tierra lo enriquece" [ll. 6–7]), nevertheless, within the natural cycle, at least, never ceases to replenish the moribund countryside. In that particular vision of natural resurrection and regeneration the speaker of "Abril, 1938" believes, finds hope, and seeks solace.

Antonio Sánchez Barbudo, in November of 1937, soon after the first publication of the grouping of poems entitled *Capital de la gloria,* wrote: "Aparte de la calidad magnífica del verso, de su rigor absoluto, lo que más impresiona sin duda en estos poemas es el tono, la calidad opaca de lumbre en rescoldo, el apagado viento que campea en ellos. Tienen color de otoño, diríamos, Madrid-Otoño se llama el primer poema de esta serie. Color de tristeza y muerte, de esperanza oculta levantada sólo por amor, color de siglos, color de invierno que llega, de dolor que no vencer a la alegría."[20] This "color de tristeza y muerte, de esperanza oculta" characterizes the tone of such poems as "Abril, 1938," "Madrid-Otoño," "Vosotros no caísteis," "Los soldados no duermen," and "El otoño y el Ebro" and also underscores the most prevalent theme of *Capital de la gloria,* death and resurrection. With his "voz de mañana / voz de aire nuevo entre espantos nacida," Rafael Alberti records the paradox that is war.[21] From this paradox will emerge, as presented in the poetry of *Capital de la gloria,* both the unifying tone of the collection and also its unifying idea. The poet's own elegiac voice and hope-filled voice are fused in this extended homage to the "capital of glory" when from the "tremenda sacudida" (l. 4) that is war emerges "la vida muerta y nueva vida" (l. 8), as Alberti so accurately records in "Abril, 1938." This poet, "en medio de un Madrid casi cercado" (*PC,* 15), has witnessed the destructive nature of war and the omnipresence of death in the conflict. Nevertheless, his "faith" in the people's struggle and the resulting new era remain steadfast, as he tells his companion in "A 'Niebla,' mi perro":

> Niebla, mi camarada,
> aunque tú no lo sabes, nos queda todavía
> en medio de esta heroica pena bombardeada,
> la fe, que es alegría, alegría, alegría.
>
> (Ll. 17–20)

Thus, as Sánchez Barbudo accurately observed in 1937, it is in *Capital de la gloria* where Alberti "canta el color de la muerte . . . que dentro de esa muerte él ve, latiendo, una vida."[22]

Lechner has further noted: "Alberti insiste en que la muerte en esta guerra no es muerte sino vida: vida para las ideas de los que siguen combatiendo, vida para generaciones futuras, un ejemplo en que todos beben fuerzas para continuar por su camino. Muerte que fecunda, que prepara la vida del porvenir, base de la futura España, o, como dice el propio poeta en una composición que resume esta idea: 'No sois la muerte, sois las nuevas juventudes,' verso que forma parte del poema *Vosotros no caísteis*" (*CPE,* 162–63). "La muerte fecundante" is, as Lechner indicates in his study of twentieth-century Spanish commitment poetry (*CPE,* 150), a *topos* of the *Romanceros de la guerra civil* of the era under consideration.[23] It is found, however, not only in much of the poetry of the Civil War but also in essays published in various magazines during the conflict. José Bergamín, for example, in the first issue of *El Mono Azul,* writes: "el que da su vida por el mono azul con el mono azul como expresión humana de su cuerpo, como alma de su vida, de su verdad de hombre, de su integridad total de pueblo, ése no tiene el mono azul sudario desesperado de los muertos, sino la veste luminosa y humilde de una inmortalidad definitiva, gloriosa: la de la libertad, la verdad y la justicia de su pueblo: la del porvenir que le redime."[24] Two years later in the article "El Mono Azul, tercera vida" we find: "Camaradas: EL MONO AZUL comienza su tercera etapa. . . . Apiñaba en sus filas a muchos jóvenes escritores. Hoy trae luto por algunos de sus artistas, que dejó sembrada la muerte para el futuro glorioso de España."[25] This topos, for example, also underlies a slogan of Dr. Negrín, the last wartime prime minister of the Popular Front government: "La sangre que embebe nuestro suelo fructificará—No se perderá—No será estéril."[26]

In Alberti's poetry of the Spanish Civil War, the theme of death as a source of new life receives an epic dimension in such poems as "Vosotros no caísteis" and "Los campesinos." In these two poems, and in others of *Capital de la gloria,* the theme of death and resurrection is intimately linked to that of the role of the common people in the present and future Spain. As an active participant in both the war and the anticipated new era that would emerge after the conflict has been won, the people continue to be the symbolic protagonist of Alberti's poetry of the late thirties. The theme of the people's role in the new political era, as we have seen, is constantly evolving throughout his political poetry of this period. It is, however, in his poetry of the Civil War that this theme assumes its most significant, heroic dimension. For the poet, as his poetry of the thirties reveals, the common man is the source of the future life of the Spanish nation. During the Spanish Civil War, the exemplary participation of the common man in the conflict, even if this participation entailed his death, is needed if the revitalized collective of the future is to emerge.

"Vosotros no caísteis" first appeared in *Hora de España* and was written, as the parenthetical note accompanying it indicates, in Madrid, December 1936.[27] The predominantly alexandrine quartets underscore the deliberate and triumphant cadence of Alberti's hymn of and to life. Imagery of birth and growth blend with that of sound and song as the poet celebrates, rather than mourns, those who died in the struggle:

¡Muertos al sol, al frío, a la lluvia, a la helada,   1
junto a los grandes hoyos que abre la artilería,
o bien sobre la yerba que de puro delgada
y al son de vuestra sangre se vuelve melodía!

Siembra de cuerpos jóvenes, tan necesariamente   5
descuajados del triste terrón que los pariera,

otra vez y tan pronto y tan naturalmente,
semilla de los surcos que la guerra os abriera.

Se oye vuestro nacer, vuestra lenta fatiga,
vuestro empujar de nuevo bajo la tapa dura   10
de la tierra que al daros la forma de una espiga
siente en la flor del trigo su juventud futura.

¿Quién dijo que estáis muertos? Se escucha entre el silbido
que abre el vertiginoso sendero de las balas,
un rumor, que ya es canto, gloria recién nacido,   15
lejos de las piquetas y funerales palas.

A los vivos, hermanos, nunca se les olvida.
Cantad ya con nosotros, con nuestras multitudes
de cara al viento libre a la mar a la vida.
No sois la muerte, sois las nuevas juventudes.   20

The future life of the people in the anticipated era is expressed by means of images of germination and bloom. The poem's speaker both witnesses and envisions the symbolic implantation of the soldier-seed in the furrow-trenches (ll. 5–8), the resulting "forma de una espiga" (l. 11) as this symbol of life penetrates the earth above the grave, and finally the development of this seed as the "flor del trigo" (l. 12) blossom in the new era. Alberti merges images of germination with those of genesis as the speaker of his poem celebrates the figurative labor of the symbolic earth-mother and the resulting birth of her infant sons, her "juventud futura" (ll. 9–12). The death of these soldiers thus signals the collective beginning of the future generation and is, in itself, a symbolic resurrection in the midst of war. The dead soldiers incarnate a vibrant, reverberating canticle of life heard throughout the war-torn land. Paradoxically, they constitute a living chorus, a perpetual, pulsating song of life because their death in the conflict is essentially a sonorous rebirth, a "rumor, que ya es canto, gloria recién nacido" (l. 15).

Alberti's song to the people in "Vosotros no caísteis" recalls especially two poems of César Vallejo's *España, aparta de mí este cáliz*, written while the Peruvian poet was in Spain during the fall of 1937. In the poem "Himno a los voluntarios de la República,"[28] for example, Vallejo eulogizes the militia man of the conflict who, for this poet, incarnates not only the essence of the people's struggle for freedom but also and above all, the personal and collective ideology of brotherhood and love to which the poet subscribes. Of this poem James Higgins observes that the militia man, for Vallejo, "is not simply a soldier fulfilling his duty: he is a volunteer who kills and embraces death in the cause of humanity. It is his heart that marches to the front: he fights for love . . . the *miliciano* is the architect of a new world, a Christ whose falls will redeem mankind."[29] Toward the end of Vallejo's long "hymn" to the soldiers of the Republican cause, he envisions a united front of all volunteer soldiers who have fought on behalf of the Republic and who have come from all corners of the world (ll. 119–39) in order to further and help preserve the people's right to determine the future. Higgins points out: "The column of combatants sings a song of death which paradoxically is a song of the dawn, since the death towards which they are marching will open up a new world. . . . These volunteers who carry with them the climate of their region, heroes from every part of the globe, are at once victims and victors: as individuals they are victims, but as a mass they are triumphant."[30] Vallejo writes:

¡Voluntario fajado de zona fría,
templada o tórrida,
héroes a la redonda,
víctima en columna de vencedores:
en España, en Madrid, están llamando
a matar, voluntarios de la vida!
                    (Ll. 134–39)

In "Masa," another poem of *España, aparta de mí este cáliz,* the poet's vision of death in war and the new era of life is remarkably similar to that of Alberti's in "Vosotros no caísteis." Higgins suggests that in "Masa" this new era will be achieved only when all men "adopt the values" of the Republican soldier, that is, when all men are united in and motivated by fraternal love. The critic observes: "La resurrección del combatiente muerto simboliza el dominio futuro del hombre sobre la naturaleza y el destino. Sin embargo, es de subrayar que Vallejo no está pensando en ningún milagro deslumbrante obrado por el amor: está pensando en un futuro lejano en que el mundo habrá sido transformado por la ciencia y la tecnología empleados por una humanidad unida el servicio del hombre."[31] The closing lines of Vallejo's poem "Masa" demonstrate this profound belief in and hope for the emergence of this new era of love and life engendered by a death that will be a resurrection:

Le rodearon millones de individuos,
con el ruego común: ¡Quédate hermano!
Pero el cadáver ¡ay! siguió muriendo.

Entonces, todos los hombres de la tierra
le rodearon; les vió el cadáver triste, emocionado;
incorporóse lentamente,
abrazó al primer hombre; echóse a andar . . .
                    (Ll. 11–17)

The theme of death and resurrection of the people in the war is also evident in Pablo Neruda's *España en el corazón: Himno a las glorias del pueblo en la guerra (1936–1937).* Neruda's own canticle to life, "Canto a las madres de los milicianos muertos" celebrates the efforts of those who have died in the struggle and the victory that will come about because of their valiant efforts. The poem also simultaneously proclaims, as does Alberti's "Vosotros no caísteis," that the death of the soldiers is not death but rather unified, triumphant, fertile new life:

¡No han muerto! ¡Están en medio
de la pólvora,
de pie, como mechas ardiendo!

Sus sombras puras se han unido
en la pradera de color de cobre
como una cortina de viento blindado,
como una barrera de color de furia,
como el mismo invisible pecho del cielo.

¡Madres! ¡Ellos están de pie en el trigo,
altos como el profundo mediodía,
dominando las grandes llanuras!
Son una companada de voz negra
que a través de los cuerpos de acero asesinado
repica la victoria.
                    ¡Hermanas como el polvo
cadó, corazones
quebrantados,
tened fe en vuestros muertos!
No sólo son raíces
bajo las piedras teñidas de sangre,
no sólo sus pobres huesos derribados
definitivamente trabajan en la tierra,
sino que aun sus bocas muerden pólvora seca
y atacan como océanos de hierro, y aun
sus puños levantados contradicen la muerte.
Porque de tantos cuerpos una vida invisible
se levanta. ¡Madres, banderas, hijos!
¡Un solo cuerpo vivo como la vida:
un rostro de ojos rotos vigila las tinieblas
con una espada llena de esperanzas terrestres!
. . . .
madres atravesadas por la angustia y la muerte,
mirad el corazón del noble día que nace,
y sabed que vuestros muertos sonríen desde la tierra
levantando los puños sobre el trigo.
                                (Ll. 1–30, 58–61)[32]

In Emilio Prados's poetry of the Spanish Civil War this same theme is evident in "Fragmento de carta" of the "Romances (1936–1937)" section of *Destino fiel:*[33]

Y cerca ya de Madrid,
aquí en Castilla la grande,
hay más hermanos conmigo
que estrellas tras de la tarde.
Ni ellos conocen mi nombre
ni yo sé cómo nombrarles;
sólo el nombre del que muere
entre nosotros se sabe,
no por llorar su recuerdo,
pero sí por imitarle,
que el que por nosotros muere,
no muere, sino que nace;
no tengo hermano que caiga
que una espiga no levante.

(Ll. 29–42)

Prados's "Primero de Mayo de 1937" is a further extension of the sustained song to new life found in Alberti's "Vosotros no caísteis" and Vallejo's "Himno a los voluntarios de la República." The poetic voice heard in Prados's ballad of death and resurrection envisions the role of "la Juventud" in both the present conflict and the imminent future era:

Se enciende la Juventud:
bajo la red de sus venas,
toda su sangre prepara
la edad futura que empieza.
Muere Abril; comienza Mayo
y entre surcos y trincheras
el trigo y la juventud
confunde bajo la guerra;
cuando más se agrande el sol
y estén los frutos más cerca,
¡qué gozo sentirá Mayo
al ver sus dobles cosechas!

(Ll. 7–18)

For Alberti, Vallejo, Neruda, and Prados, as their similar views of the role of death in the struggle reveal, war held the promise of the people's future life, and thus death in war, each reasoned, had a life-giving and life-renewing function and meaning. The closing lines of Emilio Prados's "Tránsito (Poema dialogado)" summarize this view:

Lento cruzará el tiempo; lentas irán sus horas
reponiendo los días. . . Pero, ¡mirad, hermanos!:
lentas se van las sombras. . . Dejadlas, que en el suelo
la guerra ya ha sembrado la verdad que germina.

(Ll. 107–10)

This theme is also echoed in Miguel Hernández's "Andaluzas," written during the same period:

Sembrada está la simiente
y vuestros vientres darán
cuerpos de triunfante frente
y bocas de puro pan.

(Ll. 9–12)

Here, however, new life for the people is equated both with a specific type of victory and with what this victory will bring to the poverty-stricken and hungry people—bread. Hernández, like Prados, often focuses on the pressing social problems of the common people in the war and the reason for their struggle: to alter their present condition, chronicled in poems such as "El niño yuntero" and "El hambre," and thereby secure a new era of freedom. As Hernández's assumed public voice of "Nuestra juventud no muere" declares:

No hay nada negro en estas muertes claras.
Pasiones y tambores detengan los sollozos.
Mirad, madres y novias, sus transparentes caras:
la juventud verdea para siempre en sus bozos.

(Ll. 29–32)

Alberti's song to the people's new life is not limited to a particular period in Spanish history. The closing lines of "Vosotros no caísteis" harmoniously fuse the chorus of the dead combatants of the war with that of the living. The soldier-seed of the conflict is thereby joined in his song of birth with his own offspring as the poet's canticle of celebration is projected to the future choruses of Spain's new era. Fifty years after the shelling has ceased, Alberti's hymn has prophetically proclaimed the role of "las nuevas juventudes" (l. 20) in the new social epoch.

In the poetry of *Consignas* and *Un fantasma recorre Europa* especially, the peasantry symbolizes the essence of the common man's struggle to attain freedom, social justice, and a more dignified, noble, and enriching future life. In Alberti's poetry of the Spanish Civil War this portrait of a specific representative of the common people is vividly presented in "Los campesinos":

Se ven marchando duros, color de la corteza   1
que la agresión del hacha repele y no se inmuta.
Como los pedernales, sombría la cabeza,
pero lumbre en su sueño de cáscara de fruta.

Huelen los capotones a corderos mojados,   5
que forra un mal sabor a sacos de patatas,
uncido a los estiercoles y fangales pegados
en las cansinas botas más rígidas que patas.

Sonando a oscura tropa de mulos insistentes,
que rebasan las calles e impiden las aceras,   10
van los hombres del campo como inmensas simientes
a sembrarse en los hondos surcos de las trincheras.

Muchos no saben nada. Mas con la certidumbre
del que corre al asalto de una estrella ofrecida,
de sol a sol trabajan en la nueva constumbre   15
de matar a la muerte, para ganar la vida.

This poem first appeared in both *El Mono Azul* and *Hora de España*.[34] "Los campesinos," along with "Quinto Cuerpo de ejército,"[35] is a tribute to the combatants who formed, according to Alberti, the backbone of the struggle. The predominant trochaic meter of the former poem and the use of the alexandrine verse form establish the methodical, deliberate pace of the soldier-peasants as they march through the battlefields of the war:

Se ven marchando duros, color de la corteza
que la agresión del hacha repele y no se inmuta.
                          (Ll. 1–2)

First calling attention to the visual impression left on the speaker by these peasants in the struggle, the poem's narrative voice describes these "hombres del campo" (l. 11) in terms of the land from which they have come (ll. 1–2, 5–8). Each peasant-soldier is viewed singularly as a robust, sturdy figure, personifying the firmness and formidable qualities of the tree of nature to which he is compared (ll. 1–2). With his metaphor of the soldier-tree, Alberti figuratively captures both the outer physical characteristics and the inner spiritual strength of this combatant in the war. Viewed collectively, the entire troop of peasants forms a living, united front, a vital and impenetrable forest able to thwart the figurative agent of death and destruction, "la agresión del hacha" (l. 2). With this latter image Alberti not only personifies the figurative cause of death in war but also further develops the subject and analogue of the symbolic soldier-tree while dramatizing and intensifying the invincible qualities embodied by the collective in the war.

These men form a unified force so large and so powerful in the struggle that it cannot be contained within limits. Their presence in the defense contributes additional indefatigable strength to the living fortress of Madrid. The "hombres del campo" (l. 11) figuratively incarnate the firmness, the unbending strength and the unyielding persistence of the trees of nature, the animals of the fields, and the resolute defenders of the people. Further characterizing them in terms of the land, the narrator adds yet another dimension to the presence of the peasants in the conflict: each soldier-peasant is a symbolic source of new life, a soldier-seed in the conflict:

van los hombres del campo como inmensas simientes
a sembrarse en los hondos surcos de las trincheras.

(Ll. 11–12)

Images of cultivation and birth dramatize and develop the role of the soldier-peasant in both the present conflict and the anticipated era. Each hemistich of the lines cited above establishes the subject and analogue of the simile of the soldier-seed of the war and its dispersal throughout the furrow-trenches of the battlegrounds. Both the streets of the capital and the trenches in its environs are thus figuratively portrayed as the graves of death that are, paradoxically, the furrows harboring the new life incarnated by the symbolic soldier-seed. Within the paradox that is war, from the felled soldier-tree will spring the new embryonic life of the participants in the conflict.

Miguel Hernández's "Memoria del 5.° Regimiento" and Alberti's "Los campesinos" provide detailed and important glimpses of the soldier-hero so often celebrated in the Republican poetry of the Spanish Civil War. Since Hernández himself was a soldier-peasant-poet, his description of the members of his class and their role in the people's struggle gives an additional dimension to the "men of the fields" admired by Alberti in "Los campesinos." Hernández writes:

Campesinos: segadores,
la fama de los yunteros,
la historia de los herreros
y la flor de los sudores:
albañiles y pastores,
los hombres del sufrimiento,
ante el fatal movimiento
que atropellarlos quería,
fueron a dar su energía
en el 5.° Regimiento.

. . . .

¡Qué largamente seguros
lucharon bajo sus ceños,
qué oscuramente risueños
y qué claramente oscuros!
Eran como errantes muros
generosos de cimiento,
y si llegaba el momento
de morir daban su vida
como una luz encendida
para el 5.° Regimiento.

¡Cuántos quedaron allí
donde cuántos no quedaron

y cuántos se recostaron
donde cuántos de pie vi!
Así cayeron, así:
como gigantes lucientes,
enarboladas las frentes
con un orgullo de lanza,
y una expresión de venganza
alrededor de los dientes.

España será de España
y español el español
que lleva en la sangre un sol
y en cada gota una hazaña.
No seremos de Alemania
en ningún negro momento
porque el puro sentimiento
que nutre a los españoles
seguirá dando sus soles
para el 5.° Regimiento.
                    (Ll. 41–50, 61–90)

"Haciendo de mi voz pulmón de todo un pueblo"

Alberti's poetry of the Spanish Civil War reveals that the poet is a portraitist profiling various features of the hero of this poetry. The numerous poetic sketches of *Capital de la gloria* both delineate distinctive traits of Alberti's multifaceted protagonist and reveal the role this hero is to assume in death in war and resurrection in the future era. Various poems of the collection, as we have seen in our discussion of the common people as the source of new life, eulogize the collective representatives of the people in the struggle. The subjects of these panegyrics include the citizens of Madrid, in "Madrid-Otoño" and "Defensa de Madrid," the dead combatants of the conflict immortalized in "Vosotros no caísteis," "El otoño y el Ebro," "Los soldados se duermen," "Aniversario," and "Madrid por Cataluña," the Spanish peasantry of "Los campesinos," and the soldiers who came from abroad in order to participate in the people's war in "A las Brigadas Internacionales." These poems of the collective hero of the war are not, properly speaking, individualized poem-portraits. They do, however, form a subgrouping within the gallery of heroes profiled throughout *Capital de la gloria* because each further contributes to Alberti's depiction of the complex *pueblo*-protagonist of his war verse.

Specific singular heroes of the conflict are sketched in many of the poems of *Capital de la gloria.* "¡Soy del Quinto del Regimiento!", "Al General Kleber," "A Hans Beimler, Defensor de Madrid," and "Al nuevo Coronel Juan Modesto Guilloto, lejano compañero de colegio en la Bahía de Cádiz" are tributes to important individuals who fought in the struggle.[36] *Capital de la gloria* could be considered an extensive, heartfelt elegy commemorating the dead heroes of the Republican cause, be they, for example, the citizens of Madrid ("Madrid-Otoño"), the soldiers in the trenches ("Vosotros no caísteis"), or Hans Beimler, the Communist leader of the Thaelmann Battalion of the International Brigades.[37] One other poem, "Elegía a un poeta que no tuvo su muerte," laments the death of not a particular combatant in the war but rather of a personal friend and fellow poet, Federico García Lorca, who was murdered at the beginning of the struggle and whose death, for Alberti and other poets in the thirties, assumed a symbolic role.[38] This tribute, however, interrupts the thematic unity of *Capital de la gloria,* since it is the only poem of the collection that does not directly treat the intimately connected themes of the people and death as a source of new life in war.

One last series of poem-portraits is found in *Capital de la gloria.* In three poems first published in *El Mono Azul* and later collected in *El burro explosivo,* Alberti profiles various features of figures incarnating aspects of the perceived antagonist of the conflict. In such poems as "El último duque de Alba," "Radio Sevilla," and "La última voluntad del duque de Alba," Alberti's vituperative pen attacks those whom he believes have in the past impeded and presently continue to impede the people's efforts to secure social justice and freedom. These ballads do not form a part of *Capital de la gloria,* and perhaps the poet recognized that their polemical and agitative content would disrupt his otherwise unified and reflective examination of the public event of war and the impact that this event has on the individual and the collective. These three poems, however, are worthy of our attention not only because they highlight, by means of contrast, additional features of the protagonist of Alberti's war poetry but also because they are linked in content, intent, and expression to his more aggressive political poetry written before the war, most notably *Consignas,* and also that following the war, especially *Coplas de Juan Panadero* (1949).

The citizens of Madrid and their important contribution to the struggle are sketched in the ballad "Defensa de Madrid," which first appeared in the *Romancero de la guerra civil* of *El Mono Azul.*[39] This poem finds its basis in the *romance histórico-nacional* tradition of Spain. According to Ramón Menéndez Pidal and also Manuel García Blanco, these ballads "derivan de hechos coetáneos . . . se inspiran no en un texto histórico, sino en el hecho mismo."[40] Alberti's ballad is inspired by the immediate past, the initial weeks of October 1936, and a specific political event, the city of Madrid under attack by the Insurgent forces. Within the tradition of the *romance histórico-nacional*, "Defensa de Madrid" is intimately linked to the *romances fronterizos* and, in a sense, could be considered as a modernized version of these traditional ballads of Spain. Of this type of ballad García Blanco observes: "No se inspiran tampoco en las gestas ni en las crónicas, sino que derivan de un hecho histórico cuya impresión es todavía reciente. . . . Su tema lo constituyen los episodios bélicos, de área local y generalmente adscritos a un protagonista heroico."[41]

The "episodio bélico" recorded in "Defensa de Madrid" is the early artillery and air attacks on the capital in the fall of 1936. Jackson recounts in *A Concise History of the Spanish Civil War*:

> In October the Insurgent armies converged toward Madrid on a long arc from north-west to the south-west. They were advancing more slowly than they had during August and September. The Army of Africa had suffered heavy casualties and needed rest after the swift march from Seville to Talavera and Toledo. The attack on a city of over a million population would demand far more supplies, and more coordinated maneuvering, than anything which had been required in the Andalusian and Extremaduran battles. Nevertheless, the Insurgent leadership was supremely confident of taking the city early in November. . . . The first minor air strikes against the capital occurred on 7 October. By the middle of the month troops had occupied all the towns within fifteen miles of Madrid. (Pp. 88–89)

"Defensa de Madrid" is directed to the exemplary city and its people and their attempt to resist the assault menacing this "corazón de España" (l. 1). The capital is also metaphorically portrayed as a living, human fortress where each individual citizen represents and incarnates a figurative obstacle that will thwart the advance of the enemy. Both individually and collectively the *madrileños* become the vital front, the animated bulwark of the defense:

> Los hombres como castillos;
> igual que almenas sus frentes,
> grandes murallas sus brazos,
> puertas que nadie penetre.
> . . . .
> Madrid sabe defenderse
> con uñas, con pies, con codos,
> con empujones, con dientes.
>   (Ll. 29–32, 36–38)

By transferring the characteristics of impenetrability and resistance of the formidable architectural structures to features of the human body, captured by synecdoches enumerated in the lines cited above, the citizens are figuratively portrayed as a living fortification whose pulsating vitality cannot be destroyed by death. In this ballad, the *pueblo*-protagonist receives the added dimension of a human citadel, a collective obstacle symbolizing the role of the "brava gente" (l. 16) in the war in this "capital de la gloria."

This sustained apostrophe to Madrid sketches the features of the protagonist of *Capital de la gloria:* the human bastion that refuses to become a living tomb to be conquered by the enemy. It is with prophetic hope that the poem's narrative voice declares in the final lines:

> Madrid, corazón de España,
> que es de tierra, dentro tiene,
> si se le escarba, un gran hoyo,
> profundo, grande, imponente,
> como un barranco que aguarda . . .
> Sólo en él cabe la muerte.
>
> (Ll. 45–50)

When reading this ballad of the Madrid defense, one cannot help but recall that only a few weeks after Alberti published this poem an intensified siege of the capital began. It was during the early days of the assault on Madrid in November 1936 that the city came to represent for Spain and all of Europe the eventual "tomb of fascism." Posters and banners present in the city and people chanting resistance choruses at demonstrations and during the battles nobly declared: "¡No pasarán! El fascismo quiere conquistar Madrid. Madrid será la tumba del fascismo."[42] The city of "catastrophe and glory" came to symbolize the heroic and exemplary efforts of the Republic in its attempt to resist fascism and promote freedom. As Lechner accurately observes of this city: "Se considera la cuna donde nació la resistencia europea contra el fascismo. . . . Desde el día 19 de julio de 1936, Madrid cobró valor simbólico ante los ojos de todos los que creían en la libertad del hombre y en el derecho a elegir un pueblo su propio gobierno—tanto dentro como fuera de España" (*CPE,* 169, 172).

In his poem-portraits of the *pueblo*-protagonist of the conflict, Alberti does not solely limit his attention to Madrid. The poet considers the defense of the capital to be a united effort in which the people of both Spain and other countries participate. The support offered by Cataluña, for example, is celebrated in "Defensa de Cataluña" a ballad that also first appeared in the *Romancero* of *El Mono Azul.*[43] This tribute is really a companion piece of "Defensa de Madrid" and in his *Poesías completas* Alberti published these two ballads as a single poem, thereby underscoring the collective's unity of purpose in the defense of the capital. Lechner observes: "El hecho de que Madrid fuese considerado el centro—material e ideal—de la lucha, no hay chauvinismo: los poetas castellanos cantan igualmente el esfuerzo de los catalanes" (*CPE,* 173). In "Defensa de Cataluña," the "pueblo catalán" (l. 1) assumes an exemplary role during the early months of the war. The independence inherent in the autonomous regional Catalán government is what is desired, on a national scale, by the supporters of the Republican cause.

Throughout *Capital de la gloria* Alberti, "haciendo de mi voz pulmón de todo un pueblo," praises those who fought on behalf of the people in the war.[44] Often he celebrates specific heroes of the Republic and his panegyrics accordingly are both personal and public decorations of honor commemorating specific public figures whom he believes represent the goals of the Spanish people. In "Al nuevo Coronel Juan Modesto Guilloto,"[45] Alberti explains the role of such poems in the war:

> Que . . . también te condecoren con estos versos míos
> Madrid que no te olvida.
>
> (Ll. 19–20)

One such proclamation and "decoration" of honor is the apostrophe "Al General Kleber," where Alberti's public voice pays homage to the commander of the International Brigades in Spain.[46] Encouraging General Kleber to listen to the "voice" (l. 2) of the first-person speaker, the latter records his dual vision of the present circumstance of war (ll. 1–15) and the anticipated political epoch (ll. 16–24). The poem's speaker openly salutes the general in the closing section of the poem (ll. 25–34) when he prophetically proclaims the role that Kleber will have in inaugurating Spain's future era. Blending the distinct tones first of sadness, then of hope, and finally of triumph, the poet not only marks the three moments of the poem but also calls attention to his own personal perception of Spain's present and future while at the same time publicly heralding Kleber's contribution to each.

Having witnessed death throughout the war-torn land, the poem's speaker urges the military leader, intimately addressed as "mi general" throughout the poem, to hear "lo que hoy mi voz tiene de elegía" (l. 2) as he recounts and together they view the grim reality of the conflict:

> Mira, para llorar, los principales
> pueblos con sus palacios y tesoros,
> los castillos, las cosas naturales;
>
> lo que era un hombre, ser hueco frío;
> lo que era un campo, una desierta herida,
> y una vertiginosa tumba el río.
>
> (Ll. 10–15)

Both the formidable citadels of Spain's past and the elemental forces of life of her present have been ravaged by war. Metaphors capturing the resulting omnipresent void together with the *ubi sunt* motif underscore the sorrowful tone of this elegy and the speaker's subjectivized portrayal of the consequences of war. Man, the land, and the river, symbols of life and fertility, experience the pervasive chill of death, a death that the poet transfers from one element of this morbid scene to another by means of the rhyming pair "frío-río." In this vast wasteland even the personified battlefield manifests the wounds afflicting the combatants. Field and soldier become one in death as both reveal the absence of life in war.

Despite the shroud of death enveloping the land, the speaker foresees and urges Kleber to witness "la mañana" (l. 21) of the new era that is about to begin:

> Es el momento en que se cambia todo,
> en que conmocionada y conmovida
> quiere girar la tierra de otro modo.
> (Ll. 16–18)

With men such as this Hungarian general coming to defend the Spanish people the anticipated era will be able to come about as both the Spanish nation and its heroic representative rejuvenate the "desierta herida" (l. 14) left by war and initiate a new life cycle.

In the closing sustained apostrophe, the speaker's voice of triumph and victory replaces his "voz de elegía" of the initial five tercets. Speaking on behalf of the supporters of the Republic, this singular public voice now reechos that of the collectivity. Hailing the military leader, the participation of the people, and the envisioned victory that both will achieve, the speaker proclaims:

> Kleber, mi general, las populares
> gentes de mi país, con sus sembrados,
> sus aldeas, sus bueyes, sus pajares,
>
> con el inmerecido sufrimiento
> de sus mejores hombres derrumbados
> o desaparecidos en el viento,
>
> con mi voz, que es su sangre y su memoria,
> bien alto el puño de la mano diestra,
> por Madrid y tu nombre de victoria,
>
> te saludan: ¡Salud! España es nuestra.
> (Ll. 25–34)

Another heroic personage of the Republic incarnating the theme of the people and celebrated in Alberti's war poetry is Hans Beimler. The poem-portrait "A Hans Beimler, Defensor de Madrid" applauds, in general, the deeds of the "Frente Rojo" during the siege of the capital and, in particular, the heroism of an important figure of the Red Front. Hans Beimler and the soldiers of the International Brigade came to the capital in order to assist in the struggle. The initial lines of Alberti's ballad to the exemplary and famous "Defender of Madrid" establish that those participating in the city's defense were an integral part of and came to symbolize an international front, a European bulwark, intent on impeding the spread of fascism. This international aspect of the Spanish conflict is evident throughout the poem when the narrative-voice repeatedly stresses that not only the Spanish people but also that of Europe hears and responds to the dying cry of a celebrated hero of the Madrid defense.

For the poet, the unifying element of the international defense of the capital is the rallying cry of the dying Beimler, "¡Frente Rojo!" Heard eleven times in the poem, the Republican leader's shout underscores the ideological bond uniting the international, collective front of the Madrid defense, while at the same time it serves as both a structural and thematic device in the ballad.

Beimler's cry initially resounds throughout the peninsula and the divisions of the International Brigade:

¡Frente Rojo!, dijo el héros.
Y cayó en tierra Hans Beimler.
Lo oyeron los españoles,
lo oyeron sus alemanes,
franceses e italianos,
lo oyó Madrid, lo oyó el aire,
lo oyó, temblando, la bala
nacida para matarle.
(Ll. 1–8)

For the public voice recounting the deeds of this hero, the death of the military leader is not an ordinary one. Paradoxically, Beimler's death, like that of the *pueblo* he represents, is looked upon as a source of new life, for his blood figuratively has been "sown" in the furrow-graves of the trenches of war:

¡Frente Rojo!, y cayó en tierra
castellana, de leales,
quien vino desde muy lejos
a sembrar aquí su sangre.
(Ll. 9–12)

Beimler's death and final, sustained cry assume epic proportion reverberating throughout not only the peninsula but also the entire cosmos:

¡Frente Rojo! Suene, silbe,
cruce como bala, estalle

por mar, por tierra, por cielo,
por astros, por todas partes,
vertiginoso, este grito.
                    (Ll. 19–23)

Focusing on the terrestrial elements participating in and reechoing the fallen
leader's cry, the speaker reveals that the all-encompassing, ubiquitous shout
penetrates the whistle of a train, the ambience of villages and cities of the
peninsula, and the orchards and vineyards of the countryside:

¡Frente Rojo! Silba el tren,
campo de España adelante.
Se descubren las aldeas,
los pueblos y las ciudades.
Entre huertos y jardines,
banderas y naranjales,
Valencia saluda el cuerpo
—¡Frente Rojo!—de Hans Beimler.
Los mares de Cataluña,
sus viñas, sus olivares,
las ramblas de Barcelona
—¡Frente Rojo!—de Hans Beimler.
                    (Ll. 33–44)

In the lines cited above, Alberti not only captures the spreading nature of the
hero's cry and the response of the Spanish people to it but also draws attention
to the actual rhythmic advance of the train that carried the corpse of the
"Defender of Madrid" to Barcelona. By recreating in verse the movement of
Beimler's cortege in its journey across the peninsula from one Republican
stronghold to another, the poem's speaker emphasizes the symbolic and unifying role of this hero and the Red Front he incarnates in the overall Republican
defense of Spain.

Imagining the euphoric response of the French capital as the Parisian workers salute and applaud Beimler's advancing funeral procession and reecho his
resounding cry, the poet shifts his attention from the peninsula to France.
There he hears and sees:

¡París, París! Tus obreros,
cantando, en hombros lo traen,
llevándolo hacia los barcos
que se llevan a Hans Beimler.
                    (Ll. 45–48)

The final destination of the cortege is Moscow. It is there that the dead hero
remains, for, as Alberti points out, Beimler's native Germany refused him
burial:

Ya que su patria alemana
caminos no quiere darle.
¡Frente Rojo! Por Moscú,
por la plaza Roja, grandes
cortejos y multitudes
y cantos van a enterrarle,
¡Frente Rojo! Junto a Lenin,
allí, tranquilo, descanse.
                    (Ll. 49–50)

Hans Beimler is not only an exemplary representative of the Madrid defense and the Spanish people he leads in the struggle, but also, due to his contribution, he is honored by the proletariat of other nations. The reecho of Beimler's final cry by each new geographical locale and people introduced in the poem underscores not only the international dimension of the cause the hero represents but also, in the final analysis, the ultimate diffusion of the Marxist ideology inherent in the Red Front. In the poet's vision, with men such as Beimler representing and leading the people in the Spanish Civil War, this diffusion and the resulting political era will one day be secured.

Despite its unifying idea and its intent to bestow praise on a hero of the Republic, a poem such as "A Hans Beimler, Defensor de Madrid" is a prosaic, hyberbolic, and ideologically dogmatic portrait of the *pueblo*-protagonist of the war. In "Madrid-Otoño," Alberti also seeks to salute the efforts of the people in the conflict. There, however, he neither overstates nor simplifies his theme. Rather, his subject of the paradox inherent in war is turned inside out and viewed in a new way: a "catastrophe" that is a "glory," a death that is new life. From the poet's elegy is born his song of hope as he envisions the people's future resurrection. In "A Hans Beimler, Defensor de Madrid," on the other hand, Alberti momentarily loses sight of his personal vision of the paradox and the meaning of war and instead publicly proclaims aspects of the life and deeds of a particular combatant of the conflict. This results in a facile, exaggerated, Marxist sermon rather than a more complex and less doctrinaire disclosure of the central theme and thesis of *Capital de la gloria*.

In *Poetry and Politics* C. M. Bowra observes that in Alberti's poetry of the Civil War the poet "is at his best when he relaxes his desire to make everything clear and allows himself a more generous indulgence in his usual imagery, and then, though he is certainly less complex than in his earlier work, he looks on the events of the Civil War with a momentary detachment and speaks of his own feelings because he must and not because it may help others" (p. 125). When Alberti abandons his soapbox, and thus his persona as the "ringleader" of the masses and his view of the poem as an instrument of persuasion, then the public voice of the poet, speaking on behalf of the people but with a personal insight into the war and its consequences, is an authentic expression of and response to what underlies "la vida muerta y nueva vida" of the Spanish Civil War.

Emilio Prados's panegyric "A Hans Beimler" is a more inspiring tribute to the "defender of Madrid" than Alberti's poem to this Republican hero precisely because the narrator of Prados's poem does not present his audience with a political harangue. Prados draws attention to the role of the people in the struggle by focusing on a particular heroic representative of the collective. Beimler's death, according to Prados's poem, paradoxically incarnates the birth of the future *patria:*

> No es esto morir, hermano,
> sino dar vida y hallarla,
> que la muerte, cuando es muerte,
> de la tierra nos separa
> y tú te quedas con ella,
> roja semilla que aguardas
> para crecer con la espiga
> que hoy defienden nuestras balas.
> Naciste lejos, hermano,
> pero la muerte, en España,
> te hizo nacer en su tierra
> para ganarte a su patria.
>
> (Ll. 23–34)

Not all of Alberti's poem-portraits are panegyrics honoring representatives of the Republican cause. Three ballad-cameos, in particular, sketch aspects of the perceived enemy. These poems were published during the early months of the conflict, and each reflects the initial anger, hostility, and hatred experienced by supporters of the Republic as they engaged in judging the "enemy." In the style of Francisco de Quevedo's *romances satíricos* and *romances burlescos,* Alberti ridicules figures whom he personally believes represent the negative features of the Nationalists in "El último duque de Alba" and its companion piece "La última voluntad del duque de Alba." General Queipo de Llano, the leader of the Army of the South, is the poet's object of derision in "Radio Sevilla."[47] I shall study here one of these ballads addressing the antagonist of the conflict, "El último duque de Alba," in order to have it serve not only as an obvious contrast to the eulogies honoring Kleber and Beimler that have already been examined but also as a poem-portrait further highlighting features of the *pueblo*-protagonist of Alberti's war poetry. In addition, a poem such as "El último duque de Alba," or any other member of Alberti's trilogy depicting the enemy, serves to delineate further the role of the poem as a political weapon, an agitative tool, a means of urging and aiding in the implementation of social change.

Thematically, Alberti's three satirical war ballads are very much allied with the purpose of the magazine in which they first appeared. The first issue of *El Mono Azul* states clearly its aims: "Es una hoja volandera que quiere llevar a los frentes y traer de ellos el sentido claro, vivaz y fuerte de nuestra lucha antifascista."[48] Another statement of purpose also underscores the utilitarian rather than the aesthetic value of many of the works published in the magazine:

"El Mono Azul," cuando empezó a publicarse en los primeros meses de la guerra, y después, ahora mismo, nunca ha tenido el carácter de una "hoja literaria" en el sentido que siempre se les ha dado a estas palabras. No es sólo que no ha querido ser en ningún instante una especie de torneo de los selectos ni vedado de ésta o la otra capillita literaria, sino que ni siquiera ha querido contar únicamente con el concurso de los profesionales de la pluma. Para su misión de hoja volandera de la calle, o en las trincheras, "El Mono Azul" ha unido en todo momento a las voces de nuestros primeros poetas y escritores las de los combatientes, los trabajadores, quienes espontáneamente han sentido el deseo de contar o relatar las hazañas de nuestro pueblo en su lucha contra el fascismo.[49]

In *El burro explosivo,* published by the Fifth Regiment during the war, Alberti describes his three ballads depicting the antagonist of the conflict and also the other poems that were incorporated into that collection. For the poet these ballads are "poemas político-burlescos de la historia de España." He adds: "Estos poemas, cargados de dinamita, continuadores de un camino señalado por nuestros grandes poetas del siglo XVII, creo que merecen el título bajo el cual aparecen recogidos. El 5° REGIMIENTO, dando una prueba de audacia y entusiasmo por la poesía, inaugura hoy con este cuaderno una serie de publicaciones, en prosa y verso, relacionadas con el momento presente de la historia de España" (p. 2).

The central figure of two of these "poemas cargados de dinamita" is the seventeenth duke of Alba, don Jacobo Stuart Fitzjames y Falcó, the Nationalist representative to Great Britain during the war.[50] In the ballad "El último duque de Alba," Alberti, by means of his assumed public persona, records and responds to a very real event that took place in the fall of 1936, in "el momento presente de la historia de España." In November of that year the town house of the duke of Alba, the palace of Liria, was bombed during the air raids on Madrid. The militiamen of the Workers' Committees seized and occupied the duke's former residence after the bombings.[51] In the opening lines, the speaker plays on the name and significance of "Alba" as he illustrates the ballad's central theme: the duke of Alba, his social class, his lineage, and the Nationalist forces he represents have been eclipsed by the dawn of the new political order initiated by the people at war and symbolized by the takeover of the palace. Thus, it is because of the role of the *pueblo-*

protagonist in the conflict that the duke of Alba is, as the speaker describes him:

Señor duque, señor duque
último duque de Alba,
mejor duque del Ocaso,
ya sin albor, sin mañana.
(Ll. 1–4)

After the introductory section of the poem, which will be reechoed and intensified in the last eight verses of the ballad's closing moment, the public narrative voice contrasts the present duke to his grandfather. In the past: "Si tu abuelo, cruel, ilustre / lustró de gloria tu casa" (ll. 9–10). In the present:

tú lustraste los zapatos,
las zapatillas, las bragas
de algún torero fascista
que siempre te toreara.
(Ll. 11–14)

The first section of the ballad (ll. 1–34) demonstrates the obvious hyperbolic inflation of the admirable figure worthy of the audience's attention while it simultaneously, by means of comparison, contrast, and satire, calls attention to the deflation of this same personage who has now become an object of ridicule. In the mold of many of Quevedo's satirical ballads, Alberti's iconoclastic attitude is further illustrated when he compares Titian's painting of the first duke of Alba with that of his own poem-portrait of the present:

Si tu abuelo, el primer duque,
Ticiano lo retratara,
tú mereciste la pena
de serlo por Zuloaga.
Un pincel se bañó en oro,
el otro se mojó en caca.
(Ll. 23–28)

Turning from satire to philosophical reflection in the poem's second moment (ll. 35–68), the speaker contemplates the ephemeral nature of fame, glory, and wealth:

Talento heredado, duque,
fortuna y gloria heredadas,
son cosas que el mejor día,
de un golpe, las lleva el agua.
(Ll. 35–38)

The role of the dawn of the new political order, introduced in the ballad's opening moment, is intensified in the lines cited above as the narrative voice stresses that the new dawn of "el mejor día" is the assailant of the inheritance, both material and spiritual, of the duke of Alba.

The poem's narrator shifts to the present as he directly addresses the duke and urges him to return from London in order to see what the "pueblo en armas" (l. 58) has accomplished:

Vuélvete de Londres, deja,
si te atreves a dejarlas,
la triste flor marchita,
muerta, de tu aristocracia,
y asoma por un momento
los ojos por las ventanas
de tu palacio encantado,
el tuyo, el que tú habitaras;
súbeles las escaleras,
paséalos por las salas,
por los salones bordados
de victoriosas batallas,
bájalos a los jardines,
a las cocheras y cuadras,
páralos en los lugares
más mínimos de tu infancia,
y verás como tus ojos
ven lo que jamás pensaran;
palacio más limpio nunca
lo conservó el pueblo en armas.
                    (Ll. 39–58)

By intensifying the motif of the ephemeral nature of glory and wealth of lines 35–38 with the *ubi sunt* motif found in the verses cited above, Alberti further emphasizes that the old has been replaced by the new and that what once was will never again be. The poet creates in verse a very visual description of the numerous, familiar objects that at one time constituted the regal splendor of the palace. We follow the cameralike eye of the narrator as he focuses on the multiple aspects of the duke's "fortuna y gloria heredadas" (l. 36). In these verses, Alberti not only blends the past and present temporal planes but also those of the present and future. The fleeting and fading elements that formerly symbolized the duke's aristocracy will be, and in fact are, in the hands of and well cared for by the people in the new political era that has begun.

In the final moment of the poem, a contrast is established between the antagonist and the protagonist of Alberti's war poetry:

Señor duque, señor duque,
último duque de Alba:
los comunistas sabemos

que la aurora no se para,
que el Alba sigue naciendo,
de pie, todas las mañanas.
Si un alba muerta se muere,
otra mejor se levanta.
                    (Ll. 69–76)

The duke and all he symbolizes is now "un alba muerta," for "las Milicias comunistas" (1.59) have initiated a new "dawn." One symbolic "alba" has replaced another as "the last duke of Alba" witnesses the people's contribution to the present and future. Reiterating the opening lines of the ballad, the narrative voice not only names the protagonist but also clearly emphasizes its role in the symbolic dawn of the new political era.

Alberti's pen becomes excessively abusive and malicious in "La última voluntad del duque de Alba" and "Radio Sevilla." In the former ballad the public voice proclaims:

Duque de Alba, duque de Alba,
en todo mi idioma encuentro
insultos con que clavarte,
palabras que echarte al cuello
como nudos corredizos
que estrangularan tu aliento.
                    (Ll. 17–22)

In the latter ballad, a grotesque caricature of General Queipo de Llano is presented:

quien ladra,
quien muge, quien gargajea,
quien rebuzna a cuatro patas.
                    (Ll. 2–4)[52]

These figures have been stripped of any heroic or admirable qualities they might have possessed. Alberti's romances burlescos of the war are coarse, shocking, and often savage declarations of contempt in which poetry serves not a political cause but rather a personal cause that the poet claims to be political. That Alberti hates the "enemy" is obvious from these distorted and crude cameos of figures allied with the Insurgent cause. However, the informed and sophisticated reader, demanding more from a romance burlesco than a series of brutish, verbal invectives, will question the instrumental value of verse whose sole purpose is to debase the enemy in order to elevate the *pueblo*-protagonist of these poems to a morally admirable level.

Lechner points out that in the early months of the conflict many poems first published in the *Romancero de la guerra civil* attacked the enemy with vehemence and scorn: "Estos poetas de primera hora reflejan en su poesía la confusión de los primeros meses de la guerra: hechos de armas, ataques satíricos contra el enemigo, celebración de los primeros héroes caídos constituyen la materia prima que elaboran estos artistas" (*CPE,* 167). Once again, in the course of Alberti's political poetic production, the closer he is to an event or political situation that pricks his social conscience, be it the dictatorship of Miguel Primo de Rivera, the massacre of the Asturian miners, or the military coup marking the beginning of the Spanish Civil War, the more agitative and bellicose is his verse and the more instrumental is its value. Only when the political event is viewed with detachment and as an issue or circumstance reflecting larger social and human concerns does Alberti's poetry of public matters become meditative in nature, leading to a more illuminative, penetrating, and meaningful vision of the individual's existential situation joined to the destiny of the collective.

In *Consignas* and *El burro explosivo* and later in *Coplas de Juan Panadero,* when Alberti simplifies the complex public issue or event with iconoclastic portraits, Marxist rhetoric, and vatic public mandates delivered by a party spokesperson, the significance of the public event is lost in the elementary translation. Watchwords and soapbox slogans become more important than the public issue under scrutiny, and both the impact of the poet's theme and the manner in which he expresses this theme are far from forceful, much less inspiring. C. M. Bowra observes:

> Once a poet has been stung into song by some public event, his task is to present it as forcefully as he can from his own understanding of it, and this is where the poetry of our times differs from that of the last century. It is his business to correct the *standard* forms which events take in the public mind and to give new, illuminating versions of them. If newspapers and common talk choose salient points and give an *obvious* interpretation of them, the picture so formed is accepted as correct and complete. But the poet must brush this aside and say something true and new and enlightening. (*PP,* 22–23)

Alberti, in his tripartite portrait of the enemy during the Spanish Civil War, in his scathing poems to Gil Robles in 1934, and in his vindictive verse deriding Franco, written while in political exile, does not make it, as Bowra has urged above, "his business to correct the standard forms which events take in the public mind," nor does he offer "new and illuminating versions of them." Personal attacks on the "enemy" of the people are hardly any more than these. In such poems Alberti has not said anything "new and enlightening," as Bowra advocates, but rather he offers a banal treatment of the multifaceted antagonist of his political poetry.

Alberti's ballads of the duke of Alba and General Queipo de Llano, together with the other satirical portraits of the enemy of the people sketched in

El burro explosivo and later in *Coplas de Juan Panadero,* cannot compare in style, content, treatment, or expression of thematic matter to "Madrid-Otoño" of *Capital de la gloria* or "Al volver y empezar" of *Consignas.* Alberti is at his best as a draftsman of words when he uses the medium of his craft in order to provide his reader with a contemplative, thought-provoking analysis of his external subject. Overstated harangues depicting the antagonist of his verse are not refined investigations of the underlying reasons for prevailing social conditions. Agitative poems such as those of this trilogy do not express the external circumstance so much as they provide the poet with an outlet for venting his own deeply felt animosities and frustrations, thereby momentarily losing sight of the collective for whom he is the self-proclaimed poet of the people.

When Alberti's eloquent "voz de elegía" (l. 2) laments the ubiquitous death and destruction in war in "Al General Kleber" and his "voz de mañana" (l. 5) exults the triumph of the collective's new life in the new era in "Madrid por Cataluña," the poet's public voice effectively discloses the meaning of the people's experience in the conflict. In "Madrid-Otoño," "Vosotros no caísteis," "El otoño y el Ebro," and "Monte de El Pardo," public affairs are rendered personally significant when the poet contemplates and seeks to comprehend the meaning of war rather than deride and verbally abuse those who have caused this war to come about. When Alberti is able to draw upon the experience of the people in the struggle and analyze what it means in relation not only to himself but also to future generations, then his poetry of the public event is an inspiring and effective expression of the event and its significance.

In "El otoño y el Ebro," first published in October 1938 in *Hora de España,* Alberti once again probes the enigma of the war and the role the people assume in the daily death/life struggle that the conflict intensifies. Two years have passed since the poet's witness walked among the ruins of the shelled capital and the barren outskirts of "Madrid-Otoño." The season of death has returned to the peninsula and is itself a metaphoric extension of the omnipresent destruction of life in the continuing war. The deliberate, methodical, predominantly trochaic alexandrine verses initiating the poem underscore the monotonous duration of the struggle:

El otoño, otra vez. Sigue la guerra, fría,   1
insensible al periódico descenso de las hojas.
Como el hombre del Ebro bajo la artillería,
los despoblados troncos junto a las aguas rojas.

Resistencia del árbol, tan dura, tan humana,   5
como la del soldado que entre los vendavales
de la muerte nocturna ve crecer la mañana,
florida nuevamente de lauros inmortales.

Miro las hojas, miro cuán provisionalmente
se desnuda la tierra del bosque más querido   10
y de qué modo el hombre de esta España se siente,
como los troncos, firme, ya desnudo o vestido.

El otoño, otra vez. Luego, el invierno. Sea.
Caiga el traje del árbol, el sol no nos recuerde.
Pero como los troncos, el hombre en la pelea,   15
seco, amarillo, frío, mas por debajo, verde.

In "El otoño y el Ebro," war has become a personified, callous observer of
the pervasive ruin it has caused and the death it finds repeated in and intensified by each passing autumn day. The robust trees of the Ebro valley,
however, refuse to succumb to death. They figuratively incarnate the *élan
vital* and the unyielding strength and durability inherent in nature. These same
qualities are transferred to the combatant in the struggle (ll. 5–6) as each
metaphoric soldier-tree embodies the will to resist and confront the figurative
destructive forces of "los vendavales / de la muerte nocturna" (ll. 6–7). Because of this strength of will the symbolic soldier-tree of the Ebro campaign
will witness the emergence of life in "la mañana florida" (ll. 7–8) of the
anticipated political era. Just as new shoots and leaves sprout from the tree in
spring and sap flows within the tree's vascular system, the soldier incarnates
new life, and he himself represents the vitality of the present and future
people: "Pero como los troncos, el hombre en la pelea, / seco, amarillo, frío,
mas por debajo, verde" (ll. 15–16).

In the midst of the cycles of nature and the artillery contest of war, the
poet's assumed persona contemplates both events, intermingling the two, and
attempts to understand man's role in the struggle. In Alberti's poem-portrait,
"el hombre del Ebro" (l. 3), "el hombre en la pelea" (l. 15) have come to
symbolize, in the poem's closing moment, "el hombre de esta España" (l.
11), the admirable, formidable representative of the people in the conflict. By
the means of asyndeton, the reader quickly moves from a description of death
in nature and war to the final word, "verde." Succinctly expressing the
poem's underlying theme and tone, "verde" is the thematic, connective link
between Alberti's visionary description of death in the people's struggle and
his own belief in the nascent era of the people.

During the summer of 1938, the Republic launched a massive offensive
along the Ebro River.[53] The Republican Army began to cross the Ebro on 24
July 1938, completely surprising the Nationalist forces. Colonel Juan Modesto Guilloto was commander-in-chief of the Army of the Ebro, and Enrique
Lister led the Fifth Army Corps. Alberti celebrates Modesto's role in this
battle in his panegyric "Al nuevo Coronel Juan Modesto Guilloto," where
Modesto receives the epithet "general de ríos" (l. 17); "El otoño y el Ebro" is

dedicated to Lister. The success of the initial crossing of the Ebro during the early stages of the battle raised the prestige of Prime Minister Negrín and the morale of the Republic. Thomas observes that the Republican Ebro offensive in the summer of 1938 was "a moment of hope" for the supporters of the Popular Front government.[54] Influenced by the optimistic spirit of the early months of the Republican campaign, Alberti published "El otoño y el Ebro" in October of 1938, before the Nationalist counteroffensive began. By mid-November, however, the battle of the Ebro, one of the longest and most intense of the war, was over and the fate of the Republican forces decided. Since the Republic had lost nearly all of its army in the north of Spain, its defeat was now imminent. This battle crippled the Republican forces and was decisive in their eventual collapse. The closing lines of Alberti's "El otoño y el Ebro" are even more poignant when read with the aid of historical hindsight, since they reveal confidence, faith, and optimism in the midst of a campaign that ultimately was a sobering experience for the soon to be devastated Republic. "El otoño y el Ebro" thus marks the tragic climax of Alberti's prophetic vision of the public events of the Spanish Civil War chronicled in *Capital de la gloria.* Despite the hope, aspirations, and political ideals of the poet and other supporters of the Popular Front the "glory" of the people's resurrection never came, and the "catastrophe" and aftermath of the Civil War impeded the construction of the Just Society.

"Todo esto me remuerde"

The gravity of the events of 1936–39 in Spain, analyzed in the poetry of *Capital de la gloria,* called for a new expression of the enigma of war. The contradictions inherent in the struggle were to be resolved on an ideological and metaphoric level in poems such as "Madrid-Otoño," "Vosotros no caísteis," and "El otoño el Ebro." An underlying Marxist view of the people's struggle and new era gave a unity of vision to these poems. Metaphor allowed the poet conceptually to penetrate the death/life dialectic clearly manifested in war and also to go beyond this antithetical duality and its manifestation in the public event and imagine its synthetic result—a new destiny for the people. "Monte de El Pardo" offers a new approach and conclusion regarding the enigma of war.[55] This poem reveals that the metaphysical dualities of death/life are exaggerated in and by war and are, consequently, more acutely perceived and completely known by the sensitive, observant individual who, having witnessed the wanton and never-ending destruction of life comes to comprehend the meaning of death. In this poem Alberti offers unique insight into the figurative battlefield of human experience by rendering the political personal.

In *Poetry and Politics,* C. M. Bowra, writing of "Monte de El Pardo," observes that "this is the authentic reflection of a poet who so absorbs his strange surroundings that he is able to present both them and himself from a new angle and to snatch a moment of illumination from the mechanised monotony of war" (p. 126). In the alexandrine quartets of alternately rhymed consonantal verses, Alberti records with precision and emotion the vivid impressions of the conflagration to which his speaker is a witness. Contemplation of the vast, emblazoned ambience leads the poem's speaker to reflect on and attempt to comprehend "este desentenderse de la muerte" (1.5) that is war:

Tanto sol en la guerra, de pronto, tanta lumbre   1
desparramada a carros por valles y colinas;
tan rabioso silencio, tan fiera mansedumbre
bajando como un crimen del cielo a las encinas;

este desentenderse de la muerte que intenta,   5
de acuerdo con el campo, tanta luz deslumbrada;
la nieve que a lo lejos en éxtasis se ausenta,
las horas que pasando no les preocupa nada;

todo esto me remuerde, me socava, me quita
ligereza a los ojos, me los nubla y me pone   10
la conciencia cargada de llanto y dinamita.
La soledad retumba y el sol se descompone.

The setting of the poem, the landscape in which the ordeal of fire and bomb occurs, is itself a metaphor for the illuminated, apocalyptic battlefield where death destroys all forms of life. The speaker's attention is first drawn to the celestial conflagration that knows no bounds as it quickly engulfs the countryside below (ll. 1–4), a countryside that has been ignited by and is now a gigantic, blazing extension of "tanta lumbre / desparramada" (ll. 1–2), "tanta luz deslumbrada" (l. 6), in the inferno of war. The repetition of "tanto" in the poem's opening line together with the use of enjambment not only intensifies the immensity of the holocaust but also the spreading and all-encompassing nature of the destruction caused by "un crimen del cielo" (l. 4).

The holocaust observed by this speaker is not limited to a single locale or temporal moment. Rather, it repeats in space "de acuerdo con el campo" (l. 6) and in time "las horas que pasando" (l. 8) as the ordeal of fire endlessly devastates all forms of life until finally even the most powerful of life-giving forces, the sun itself, cannot withstand the incessant fiery assault permeating the sky (l. 12) and transforming it into a deadly, inflamed infernal dome.

To this speaker, war is a baffling contradiction, an absurd event of death ("este desentenderse de la muerte" [l. 5]). The figures of paradox and oxymoron serve the poet well as he attempts to capture the nature of this contradiction. In "Monte de El Pardo," both paradox and oxymoron are particularly effective in evoking concepts, emotions, and responses that go beyond the reach of human sense and somehow make sense only when understood in terms of their opposites. In "Monte de El Pardo," accumulations of the paradoxical intensify the effects of the ordeal of war on both nature and the populace: "tan rabíoso silencio, tan fiera mansedumbre . . . La soledad retumba y el sol se descompone" (ll. 3, 12). Life is conspicuously absent in the aftermath of the bombings, shellings, and artillery fires of war described in this poem, and mankind itself has been reduced to one lone, observant witness moved by the cause and effect of war. Four verbs of detriment, "remuerde," "socava," "quita," and "nubla" (ll. 9–10), coupled with the single, repeated indirect and direct object pronouns of detriment, "me" (ll. 9–10), emphasize the sufferings and anguish experienced by a singular human being, the poem's first-person speaker, during and after the inflamed scene he has witnessed. This speaker has comprehended the significance of the conflagration of life in war and what he has said in "Monte de El Pardo" is relevant not only to his own personal agony and dilemma but also to those experienced by all participants in the struggle, regardless of their political allegiance and on which side of the battlefield they are found.

"Monte de El Pardo" and "Madrid-Otoño" express not only the paradoxical nature of war but also the impact war has on the individual. In poems such as these, Alberti's poetic voices witness a significant moment in Spain's history and attempt to record how this public event affects the human being in war. These poems offer a glimpse of what the Spanish Civil War meant to Rafael Alberti personally as a man in the midst of the ruin and devastation of the conflict. The politics of the public event has been pushed to the background as the personal, individual human response to the enigma of war is experienced. In "Monte de El Pardo" and "Madrid-Otoño," Alberti does not reflect the attitudes of the party spokesperson or the energized, revolutionary leader of the masses, as he did in "A Hans Beimler, Defensor de Madrid" or "El último duque de Alba." Nor does this poem give voice to the aims of the Marxist-socialist era heralded by the public voices of "18 de Julio" and "1° de Mayo en la España Leal de 1938." In "Monte de El Pardo," Alberti writes from the point of view of his own experience in and response to war. This, in turn, enables the poet to decipher and render personally meaningful the paradox of war.

This personal treatment of a public theme also figures in Pablo Neruda's probing analysis of war in "Paisaje después de una batalla" of *España en el corazón*. Both "Monte de El Pardo" and Neruda's poem offer descriptions of the infernal destruction of war and also personal responses to the destruction of life. Neruda writes: "Guarde mi sangre este sabor de sombra / para que no haya olvido" (ll. 20–21). The closing lines of Emilio Prados's "Destino fiel" also, in many ways, recall Alberti's description of and reaction to war in "Monte de El Pardo." In Prados's poem, however, the first-person speaker comprehends that his heartfelt "song" is sung by a voice of pain and suffering of the present circumstance and also a voice of new life and peace of the future era. Prados's "Destino fiel" closes with an optimistic response to the holocaust of war. In this way, Prados's expression and response fill the ominous and pervasive silence found in Alberti's "Monte de El Pardo" as Prados's jubilant poem celebrates the end of the war:

> ¿Qué tengo yo que en medio de esta hoguera
> ni muerto estoy ni vivo soy aurora?
>
> Sólo tengo mi voz y aquí la pongo.
> Mi canto dejo, igual que sus espumas
> deja el mar por la arena que visita:
> así mi voz derramo por mi pluma.
>
> Así dejo mi voz mojada en llanto,
> porque apartado de la muerte vivo.
> Quisiera desprenderme de mi cuerpo
> por ver más pronto lo que tanto ansío.
>
> Mas si nada merezco y con mi sombra
> he de acabar las horas que aún me quedan
> cumpla mi voz lo que mi vida pierde,
> lo que la muerte de mi vida espera.
>
> Que cuando al fin la guerra esté en su término
> y se pierda en los tiempos la ceniza
> de esta terrible llama en que nos prende,
> mi voz, bajo la paz, se oirá más viva.
>
> (Ll. 107–20)

When Alberti writes about war as he individually experienced and responded to it, as he does in "Monte de El Pardo," we find a reflectively personal and not an agitatively public analysis and evaluation of public matters. When pressing public concerns are rendered personal in *Capital de la gloria,* the reader is able both to learn from the poet's own search for truth and also to experience and share the moment of illumination that comes when the individual deciphers the enigma of war and comprehends the impact of this public event on human life. This "personal treatment of public themes," as Bowra calls it (*PP,* 17), is not peculiar to the thirties; rather, it was an outgrowth of the pressing problems the poet encountered when recording and assessing the nature of war. Of the poets of the First World War, for example, Bowra observes that "what engaged them was not abstract ideas and vague sentiments which propaganda had smeared over it [the war] but its unusual moments and sudden surprises in an isolated and fantastic world. They saw that they could not grasp its whole character, and they concentrated on limited effects which they understood from their own experience. Their response was indeed various, but all agreed that, if poetry was to be written about war, it must be about war as the poet knew it" (*PP*, 16). In "Monte de El Pardo" Alberti does not attempt to grasp the entire, baffling enigma of war but rather to probe its "limited effects" and analyze his own experience in and reaction to war.

"Después de este desorden impuesto"

Bowra observes, as quoted earlier, "The more violent the impact of events is on a poet, and the more deeply he is committed to them, the more he needs some uniting idea or mood to master them and bring them to order" (*PP*, 87). The theme of the people and their participation in death as a source of new life for future generations is, as we have seen, the uniting idea of *Capital de la gloria,* the idea that imposes order on the "disorder" that is war. Rafael Alberti explains this need for order in the experience of war in this way in "Para luego":

> Después de este desorden impuesto, de esta prisa,   1
> de esta urgente gramática necesaria en que vivo,
> vuelva a mí toda virgen la palabra precisa,
> virgen el verbo exacto con el justo adjetivo.
>
> Que cuando califique de verde al monte, al prado,   5
> repitiéndole al cielo su azul como a la mar,
> mi corazón se sienta recién inaugurado
> y mi lengua el inédito asombro de crear.

We have seen in our discussion of *Consignas* and *Un fantasma recorre Europa* that when the "uniting idea" is the party's dogma and not the poet's private interpretation of the public circumstance, the result is often a highly dogmatic portrayal of the human existential condition sketched in terms of the party's aims. We witnessed this in "Mitin," "La lucha por la tierra," the second moment of "Aquí y allí," and especially "Sequía." However, when this "uniting idea" originates in the poet, in his personal interpretation of the political event, then the poet is able to recreate the public issue from the perspective of his own original insight into and experience of public concerns, as evident in many of the poems of *Capital de la gloria.*

Bowra, when characterizing the patterns he sees at work in the development of twentieth-century poetry, notes that "the modern emphasis on the poet's obligation to be true to his own vision and sensibility means that, even when he deals with large concerns and complex ramifications, he must handle them in his own way, from his own angle, with his own unique insight" (*PP, 33*). It is when Alberti is "true to his own vision" that the poetry of *Capital de la gloria* discloses a fresh and original interpretation of public issues and problems that concern us all.

In the midst of war the poet of *Capital de la gloria* discovers not only that the uniting idea of the death and resurrection of the people aids him in imposing order on the chaos of war but also that poetic discourse itself, as "Para luego" reveals, participates in and helps to structure the presentation and the creation of the meaning of the public event.

"Para luego," dated March 1938, is more than likely one of the last poems that Alberti wrote during the Spanish Civil War, or, to use the poet's own words, "por una poesía simultánea de los hechos," the heading under which the poem appeared in *Hora de España*.[56] The poem was published with its companion piece, "Nocturno," and both works concern the role of poetic discourse in the conflict. "Para luego," however, unlike "Nocturno," does not appear in *Capital de la gloria* in Alberti's *Poesías completas*. Published later as one of the two prologues to his first collection of poetry written while in political exile, *Entre el clavel y la espada*, the poem there bears the new title of "De ayer para hoy." "Para luego" is, however, more than a re-membrance of the past brought forward in time to Alberti's new circumstance of exile. The poem could be considered to be Alberti's own epilogue to the war, "este desorden impuesto" (l. 1), sketched throughout *Capital de la gloria*.

Critics of Alberti's political poetry often cite the opening alexandrine quartet of "Para luego" when referring to the various stages of his poetic production, concluding that this poem, considered as the prologue to *Entre el clavel y la espada*, signals a "new" stage in his poetic trajectory. The "desorden impuesto" to which the poet refers in his poem is often interpreted by such critics to mean Alberti's political poetry written during the thirties, primarily that poetry which is highly political in content and intent. They claim, however, that the poetic word and not the political word returns to the poet only while in exile for there the realm of politics and the "urgente gramática" (l. 2) of political discourse are left behind.[57] "Para luego," how-ever, as I have indicated, was written during the final months of the Civil War, not after it, and is, therefore, one further manifestation of Alberti's domina-tion of the poetic word in the midst of the turmoil of the conflict. The harnessing of the poet's own political impulse together with the enormity of the public event within "la palabra precisa . . . el verbo exacto . . . el justo adjetivo" (ll. 3, 4) is what Alberti seeks throughout his "poesía simultánea de los hechos" and what he has effectively accomplished in many of the poems of *Capital de la gloria*. His contemplative elegiac voice and voice celebrating the future express not only the rejuvenative role of the people in the conflict but also the rejuvenative power of poetic discourse as it reshapes the war and molds it into, as the poet records in "Abril, 1938," the paradoxical "vida muerta y nueva vida" (l. 8).

"Nocturno" reveals that words might not always possess and be capable of the miraculous deciphering powers and the ordering potential attributed to them in "Para luego." In his penetrating analysis of the purpose and value of words in the circumstance of war, the speaker of "Nocturno" senses that words, like all elements placed in the midst of the conflict are, in themselves, "heridas de muerte" (l. 17). Words have been robbed of their vital expressiveness and their ability to represent and recreate thought. In war, words no longer shape, pattern, restructure, and reflect the social reality the poet surveys. Rather, words have become useless instruments of communication, inadequate means of expression and, perhaps, as the speaker suggests with the repeated refrain of "Balas. Balas" (ll. 6, 11, 16), impractical tools in the struggle:

> Cuando tanto se sufre sin sueño y por la sangre   1
> se escucha que transita solamente la rabia,
> que en los tuétanos tiembla despabilado el odio
> y en las medulas arde continua la venganza,
> las palabras entonces no sirven: son palabras.   5
>
> Balas. Balas.
>
> Manifiestos, artículos, comentarios, discursos,
> humaredas perdidas, neblinas estampadas,
> ¡qué dolor de papeles que ha de barrer el viento,
> qué tristeza de tinto que ha de borrar el agua!   10
>
> Balas. Balas.
>
> Ahora sufro lo pobre, lo mezquino, lo triste,
> lo desgraciado y muerto que tiene una garganta
> cuando desde el abismo de su idioma quisiera
> gritar lo que no puede por imposible, y calla.   15
>
> Balas. Balas.
>
> Siento esta noche heridas de muerte las palabras.

The first-person speaker of this poem attempts to record and comprehend the meaning of the omnipresent, public, human emotions of "rabia," "odio," "venganza" (ll. 2, 3, 4) in the conflict, but he is unable to do so within and by means of the medium of his craft. Such complex emotional responses are both exaggerated and inescapable in the circumstance of war, especially a fratricidal war, because, in part, these emotions constitute both the cause and effect of the conflict. Despite their ubiquitous presence, human origin, and menacing nature, the speaker of "Nocturno" cannot accurately explain the meaning of such emotions in war. The words recording these emotions are merely words and "las palabras entonces no sirven: son palabras" (l. 5).

Having comprehended that the emotions stemming from the public event no longer can be expressed and clarified by means of words, the speaker then turns not to what is experienced but rather to what is expressed: "Manifiestos, artículos, comentarios, discursos" (l. 7). Asyndeton, assonance, and alliteration lead the reader to the effect of such discourse. Public proclamations are attempts to document, chronicle, and explain the aims of the struggle. These declarations, however, are also rendered useless in war because each reflects a momentary human attempt to simplify the complex public event. Such efforts have, perhaps, immediate results but not the long-lasting results sought by the speaker of "Nocturno."

Words are merely vague representations of what is actually experienced. This knowledge causes the speaker of "Nocturno" great anguish in his present dual situation of witnessing and writing about war. The gravity and paradoxical nature of the conflict together with the speaker's own linguistic skepticism lead the poetic voice of "Nocturno" to a twofold solution to the dilemma he faces as a witness to and a poet of the war: bullets and silence. Perhaps here, as in no other poem of *Capital de la gloria,* the reader receives a glimpse of the frustration, anguish, and confusion of the poet's personalized voice heard in many poems of the collection as he attempts to make sense of the senselessness that is war and record his own inability to do so. For the poet in the war, "balas" are, then, both an expression and a tool that can be immediately understood and used. Their significance is not elusive and their importance can be readily grasped. "Balas" seem to be, for the speaker of "Nocturno," the only logical means of communication when words have lost their expressive power and their ability to effect results and reflect responses within the circumstance of war.

The speaker of Pablo Neruda's "Canto sobre unas ruinas" of *España en el corazón* also experiences a similar moment of frustration and lack of faith in the verbal medium he uses. In his "song" recording the senseless destruction and death found in the war, the speaker of Neruda's poem comprehends: "todo reunido en nada, todo caído / para no nacer nunca" (ll. 36–37). The speaker is momentarily stunned and therefore unable to use words to construct his vision of the new era of life that will follow the war. For this poetic voice, like the voice heard in Alberti's "Nocturno," words in the midst of omnipresent death and ruin seem to have lost their vitality and their usefulness. Neruda's speaker, unlike Alberti's, however, does not invoke the utilitarian value of "balas." Rather, he transfers his own emotional response to the objects he studies—the ruins of the war:

> ved cómo las palabras que tanto construyeron,
> ahora son exterminio: mirad sobre la cal y entre el mármol deshecho
> la huella—ya con musgos—del sollozo.
>
> (Ll. 47–49)

In Miguel Hernández's "Canción de la ametralladora" the soldier-poet reveals that his own "song" is replaced by the sounds produced by the "máquina de mi alma," "mi arma se dedica a cantar" (ll. 63, 29–30). In war, the first-person speaker realizes that the only instrument of utilitarian value is the very real weapon that is fused with his own will—the people themselves as they actively participate in the struggle:

> De mis hombros desciende,
> codorniz de metal,
> y a su nido de arena
> va la muerte a incubar.
>
> Acaricio su lomo,
> de humeante crueldad.
> Su mirada de cráter,
> su pasión de volcán
> atraviesa los cielos
> cuando se echa a mirar,
> con mis ojos de guerra
> desplegados detrás.
>
> Entre todas las armas,
> es la mano y será
> siempre el arma más pura
> y la más inmortal.
> Pero hay tiempos que exigen
> malherir, además
> de los puños de hierro,
> hierro, más eficaz.
>
> Frente a mí varias líneas
> de asesinos están,
> acechando mi vida,
> campeadora y audaz,
> que acobarda al acecho
> y al cañón más fatal.

Con el alba en el pico,
delirante y veraz,
con rocío, mi arma
se dedica a cantar.
. . . .
canta y vuelve a cantar,
máquina de mi alma
y de mi libertad.
. . . .
Sed la máquina pura
que hago arder y girar:
la muralla de máquinas
de la frágil ciudad
del sudor, del trabajo,
defensor de la paz.
Y al que intente invadirla
de vejez, enturbiad
sus paredes con sangre,
¡disparad!
   (Ll. 1–30, 62–64, 75–84)

Hernández, like Alberti, is well aware of the importance and the necessity of bullets in the conflict. The speaker of Alberti's "Nocturno," however, arrives at this same knowledge through linguistic skepticism and after seemingly endless nights of ignorance and despair in the "Nocturno" of the war. Hernández's speaker, on the other hand, gains this knowledge in the direct experience of combat as an armed soldier-poet.

The irony of Alberti's "Nocturno" is that even though the poet is cognizant of the inadequacies of his medium, he nevertheless effectively debates these inadequacies within and from the point of departure of the language of the poem itself. As the poetry of *Capital de la gloria* reveals, Alberti is not silenced by the war, nor does he avoid attempting to comprehend the complexity of the political scene and the paradoxical nature of the conflict in the poem itself. In war, as a poet of his people, Alberti acts: "en medio de un Madrid casi cercado, *escribo*" (*PC,* 15). Alberti's response to the circumstance of war is a response that reflects his personal reaction to and assessment of the war. In the opening moment of "Madrid-Otoño" the poem's speaker, while walking through the remains of the war-torn capital under siege, discloses his heartfelt desire to communicate: "yo quisiera furiosa, pero impasiblemente / arrancarme de cuajo la voz" (ll. 4–6). In "Nocturno" this same desire is expressed, but in a different way:

Ahora sufro lo pobre, lo mezquino, lo triste,
lo desgraciado y muerto que tiene una garganta

cuando desde el abismo de su idioma quisiera
gritar lo que no puede por imposible, y calla.
(Ll. 12–15)

In both poems the respective speakers confess that each is unable to express the horror, the anguish, the bloodshed, and the absurdity that is war. *Capital de la gloria* reveals, however, that these speakers have in fact expressed and explained the significance of the Spanish Civil War and Rafael Alberti's personal response to it. The speakers' observations, together with the poem's verbal expression and the poet's personal response, in the final analysis, enable the reader to comprehend the significance of the poet's interpretation of the paradox and the pity of war.

In this political poetry of the early thirties, most notably in *Consignas* and *Un fantasma recorre Europa,* Alberti attempts to transform the poem into an instrument that would effect social revolution and reform. The poetry written in the agitative political mode, particularly, is poetry that rejects not only the old political process and spirit but also the way in which the poem previously had been used as a means of expression. Alberti's poetry of the public matters of the early thirties is often as explosive and aggressive as the new spirit of revolution it chronicles and advocates. In 1931 Alberti offered a definition of the "new" poet of his era, and it is this prophetic characterization and self-portrait that the poet of *Consignas* and *Un fantasma recorre Europa* was to fulfill a few years later. He would advocate that "the poets of today" be "cruel, violent, demoniac, frightening."[58] The Rafael Alberti of *Capital de la gloria,* however, unlike the poet of *Consignas,* is not a "demoniac" poet, a bellicose voice offering heated and controversial accounts of the efforts and goals of the people's struggle. When the revolution ceased to be an abstract concept for Alberti and became, instead, an integral part of his own daily existence and the daily existence of those who believed in and fought on behalf of the Popular Front during the Civil War, the poet altered his brazen and belligerent voice of revolt. Immersed in the sociopolitical circumstance of a fratricidal conflict, the poet of *Capital de la gloria* writes not a volcanic account of the struggle but rather an intimate and reflective poetic journal recording his daily responses to this grave public event and disclosing the impact that this event had on the poet experiencing war.

In his poetry of the very early thirties, Alberti extensively used free verse and popular forms, adopting them to his newfound revolutionary style and public manner. During the Spanish Civil War, however, Alberti cultivates the "metro culto" that characterized the initial sonnets of *Marinero en tierra* and many of the poems of *Cal y canto.* Upon examining Alberti's war poetry, we see a decided preference (48 percent) for the alexandrine verse form, most often in quartets (eleven poems). We also find the hendecasyllable (19 percent) found most often in tercets, quartets "de tipo gaita gallega,"[59] *silvas,* and stanzas of varying lengths. Alberti does not, however, abandon popular verse forms in his poetry of the Civil War. The *romance* is often found (22 percent), in addition to one *letrilla* published in *El Mono Azul*[60] and one polymetric popular composition, "Galope." Consonance is the predominant rhyme (61 percent). The opening alexandrine quartet of "Para luego" takes on added significance during the Spanish Civil War not only because at that time "vuelva a mí toda virgen la palabra precisa, / virgen el verbo exacto con el justo adjetivo" (ll. 3–4) but also and importantly because during these years in Alberti's poetic production the poet once again cultivates highly structured, rhythmic and metrical verse forms that, in themselves, further impose order on "este desorden impuesto" (l. 1) of war.

Many of the poems of *Capital de la gloria* were first published, as previously noted, in *Hora de España* and *El Mono Azul.* The former magazine as its statement of purpose indicates, had a "literary objective":

> Quede, pues, en *Hora de España,* y sea nuestro objetivo literario reflejar esta hora precisa de revolución y guerra civil.
> Es cierto que esta hora se viene reflejando en los diarios, proclamas, carteles y hojas volanderas que día por día flotan en las ciudades. Pero todas esas publicaciones que son en cierto modo artículos de primera necesidad, platos fuertes, se expresan en tonos agudos y gestos crispados. Y es forzoso que tras ellas vengan otras publicaciones de otro tono y otro gesto, publicaciones que, desbordando el área nacional, puedan ser entendidas por las camaradas o simpatizantes esparcidos por el mundo, gentes que no entienden por gritos como los familiares de casa, hispanófilos, en fin, que recibirán inmensa alegría al ver que España prosigue su vida intelectual o de creación artística en medio del conflicto gigantesco en que se debate.[61]

Much of Alberti's war poetry of the reflective political modality was published in this magazine, which had as its goal the fostering and developing of the artistic, intellectual, and literary endeavors of many of Spain's most renowned writers of the thirties.[62] Those poems of Alberti that first appeared in *Hora de España,* fourteen in all, were directed to a sophisticated, literary public who demanded more from the poem than a fiery, didactic, simplistic call to political action. The readers of *Hora de España,* like the authors who published in the magazine, expected and received personal visions of and insights into the complexities of the public event deeply affecting them all.

Alberti's use of "el metro culto" in this era could, in part, also be guided by the artistic and literary aims of the magazine in which many of his war poems first appeared. Unlike those poems first published in *Hora de España,* the poems Alberti originally published in *El Mono Azul* often reflected the pamphletary and revolutionary style of this "hoja volandera que quiere llevar a los frentes y traer de ellos el sentido claro, vivaz y fuerte de nuestra lucha antifascita."[63] *El Mono Azul* thus became a political instrument, often a political weapon, to be used in the war against fascism, as Alberti's trilogy to the enemy of the Republic reveals. In contrast to *Hora de España, El Mono Azul* "nunca ha tenido el carácter de una 'hoja literaria,' "[64] and Alberti's political poetry published in the latter magazine often reflects, therefore, the aims and the confrontational style of this "hoja volandera" directed to a reading public distinct from and with different expectations from that of *Hora de España.* Alberti's agitative voice of combat is most often heard in the poems appearing in *El Mono Azul,* while his more reflective, elegiac voice predominates in the poems published in *Hora de España.* The aims of the magazines themselves, thus, further call attention to and aid in differentiating the two distinct political modes of writing prevalent in Alberti's poetry of the thirties.

"Vida muerta y nueva vida"

A brief survey of Alberti's poetic production of the late twenties reveals that the antithetical duality of the opposing forces of death and life, so pronounced in *Capital de la gloria,* also pervades *Sobre los ángeles, Sermones y moradas,* and the series of poems entitled *Yo era un tonto y lo que he visto me ha hecho dos tontos.* However, in the last three collections this thematic pairing has personal and not public significance, individual and not civil importance.

Sobre los ángeles, Sermones y moradas, and *Yo era un tonto* trace the inception, development, and results of a complex spiritual and existential crisis experienced by the poet's "alma en pena" (*PC,* 275), as the title of one of the poems of his 1928 collection so accurately reveals.[65] Alberti, grappling with and attempting to make sense of the scattered pieces of his own being and the inescapable spiritual wasteland that engulfs and overwhelms him, assumes the persona of a bewildered, nomadic, bereaved soul destined to wander the earth in search of inner peace. Throughout these three collections of the late twenties, dark and not fully delineated negative forces of death and destruction clash with positive agents metaphorically embodying luminous and lasting vitality. The poet's assumed personae—be they angelic choirs and lost souls, confused prisoners of the symbolic "moradas" of a soul in anguish, or tragicomic figures of the silent cinema who are metaphoric extensions of the poet's own troubled self—attempt to decipher the complex, personal "catastrophe" experienced by the young poet in the late twenties. Alberti recalls in *La arboleda perdida,* his poetic collection of 1927–1928: "¿Qué hacer, cómo hablar, cómo gritar, cómo dar forma a esa maraña en que me debatía, cómo gritar, cómo erguirme de nuevo de aquella sima de catástrofes en que estaba sumido?" (*AP*, 264). This "catastrophe" and its fateful causes and effects are charted and analyzed not only in *Sobre los ángeles* but also in other poems that Alberti wrote during the same period.

The destruction of the poet's own soul and the personal chaos and confusion that resulted all have their origin in the cataclysm of the self and the poet's own *malestar*. The landscape through which Alberti's "alma en pena" roams reflects, accordingly, the ruinous, miserable state of his soul. This spiritual and emotional wasteland, as "Los ángeles muertos" of *Sobre los ángeles* and "Elegías" of *Sermones y moradas* reveal, is in a state of perpetual disintegration. Death permeates all aspects of matter and discarded, insignificant, broken objects are themselves extensions of the poet's own moribund state. The poetic voices heard in these and in other poems of the period are empty echoes, abandoned and lifeless objects lost in the figurative graveyard reflecting the ruin of the soul.

On 1 January 1930, with the writing of the "Elegía cívica," the thematic duality of death/life prevalent in Alberti's poetry of the late twenties discloses a new dimension. In this political allegory, as we have seen in chapter 2, the confrontation of forces incarnating death and those incarnating life has both a private and a public significance. During the ominous "alba de las náuseas" (l. 29) on this initial day of a new year and decade, the conflict of death/life is engendered by the external circumstances of the political turmoil effecting "cualquier calle recien absorta en la locura" (1.1). When a morbid and foreboding dawn ushers in a new day, forces valuing life and liberty clash with those embodying death and repression. The poet's personalized speaker together with the citizens of Spain whom he represents respond to and attempt to change the prevailing, destructive, tumultuous social conditions. The agent of death and destruction is, however, never directly named in Alberti's first political poem. Its presence is implied throughout the cryptic political allegory that structures Alberti's surrealistic and apocalyptic exploration of the devastation of life resulting from a menacing political regime.

Alberti shifts his attention away from an analysis of the effects of death and destruction on himself as a unique, solitary, sensitive individual to an analysis of the effects of death and destruction on the collective in *Capital de la gloria*. Alberti's poetry of the Spanish Civil War reveals that the thematic dialectic of death/life has an ideological synthesis and significance in the people's new era that will emerge when the conflict has been won. A provocative exploration of the impact that the destruction of the collective lifeblood of Spain will have on the future of the nation, *Capital de la gloria* offers insight into the meaning of death in the midst of war. Alberti's elegiac voice discloses the effect of war on the poet as a man among men, as a man who believes in and is firmly committed to the vital potential of the Spanish people. This poet's commitment to the people, his unique position as a poet of and a spokesperson for the people in the war, his own ideological convictions, and his analysis of self in relation to the public circumstance are the underpinnings of *Capital de la gloria,* Alberti's sustained poetic inquiry into the role of death and the possibility of new life in the struggle.

The poet's spirit, stirred by "tan tremenda sacudida" (l. 4) described in "Abril, 1938" and "los tristes agujeros de sangre, escombro y muerte" (l. 4) described in "Aniversario," reveals his authentic impressions of and response to, as "Monte de El Pardo" discloses, "este desentenderse de la muerte" (l. 5) that is war. Throughout *Capital de la gloria,* the poet's inquiry into the "catastrophe" of war helps him to comprehend the meaning of the loss of life and the possibility of new life in the midst of the public circumstance with which he is concerned. As the closing lines of "18 de Julio," quoted earlier in this chapter, reveal:

> Sufre el mapa de España, grita, llora,
> se descentra del mar y su mejilla
> tanto se decolora,
> que se pierde de grana en amarilla.
> Se retuerce su entraña en tal manera,
> que lo que va a parir ya está en la aurora:
> 18 de Julio: Nueva Era.
>
> (Ll. 27–33)

"Para muchos España era el enigma y la revelación de aquella época de la historia"

How art could interpret public events and how the artist could reveal the meaning of public circumstances in his or her works were questions addressed in the thirties. The Spanish Civil War was a public matter that aroused the sociopolitical consciousness of various artists compelling each to analyze the role of art and the artist in relation to the external world and specific political issues in that world. Affecting each artist in a distinct way and provoking numerous and varied responses, the specter of the Spanish Civil War together with "The pity of war / the pity war distilled" left a lasting impression on many gifted and highly acclaimed artists of the twentieth century.[66] In his memoirs Pablo Neruda recalls: "Para muchos España era el enigma y la revelación de aquella época de la historia" (*CV,* 178). This "enigma" and "revelation" are what many artists of the modern era chose to decipher as each attempted to comprehend the significance of the social, political, and historical process, the public event, and the relation of art and the artist to them.

Rafael Alberti's chronicle of and response to the Spanish Civil War in *Capital de la gloria* is, therefore, not an isolated and unique instance of the modern artist's attempt to grasp the meaning of public circumstances and to place the poet and art within the public domain. For Alberti, together with other prominent poets of the era, the Spanish Civil War meant the "test of western civilization in its most mature and humane form" and the struggle of the people to secure the Just Society.[67] A poet of public events and a poet of the people could not remain silent, and thus Rafael Alberti, W. H. Auden, John Cornford, Cecil Day Lewis, César Vallejo, Pablo Neruda, Emilio Prados, and Miguel Hernández, among others, gave voice to the pressing concerns of Western civilization, thereby enabling it to apprehend, to use Neruda's words, "el enigma y la revelación de aquella época de la historia" (*CV*, 178).

Pablo Neruda in *Confieso que he vivido* explains why, in the thirties, so many artists refused to ignore the gravity and the consequences of the Spanish Civil War. "The spirit of resistance" of the Spanish people inspired these artists as each individually charted the collective experience of the people's war. Focusing primarily on the impact of the Civil War on the poets of the thirties, Neruda indicates: "No ha habido en la historia intelectual una esencia tan fértil para los poetas como la guerra española. La sangre española ejerció un magnetismo que hizo temblar la poesía de una gran época. . . . La guerra de España iba de mal en peor, pero el espíritu de resistencia del pueblo español había contaminado el mundo entero" (*CV*, 173, 176). This "magnetism" was to attract many poets to Spain during 1936–39. Auden's *Spain,* Vallejo's *España, aparta de mí este cáliz,* and Neruda's *España en el corazón* are only a few of the many works of artists who came from abroad in order to participate in and reflect in poetry the "spirit of resistance" of the Spanish people in the struggle. Many of Spain's own poets, in addition to Rafael Alberti, also disclosed the enigma of that war in their verse. Prados's *Destino fiel* and Hernández's *Viento del pueblo* and *El hombre acecha,* for example, along with the works of the poets who came to Spain during the war, represent valid investigations into how art and the artist could effectively mold the public event into poetic form while insightfully penetrating and revealing the impact of this event on the individual poet and the collective of whom he or she sings.

W. H. Auden visited Spain during the months of January–March 1937 with "the desire to do something."[68] For this young British poet, the Spanish Civil War was a clear manifestation of the people's collective will to erect the Just

Society. This is the subject of the long poem *Spain* (1937).[69] John Fuller, in examining Auden's poem, explains that "the poem's large rhetorical structure, contrasting past and future, necessity and the political will, fully supports the poet's call to action. History, the poem dramatically explains, means nothing without the clear decisions of individual responsibility. . . . The poem stirringly underlines the need for personal involvement and risk in the fight against fascism: 'but to-day the struggle.' Without this, the Just City, the whole premise of the needs of humanity, is an impossible dream. If the struggle fails (through the implied failure of the political will), then 'History to the defeated / May say Alas but cannot help or pardon.' "[70]

In *Spain,* Auden writes:

What is your proposal? To build the Just City? I will.
I agree. Or is it the suicide pact, the romantic
        Death? Very well, I accept, for
I am your choice, your decision: Yes, I am Spain.
                        (Ll. 53–56, p. 9)

Without a politically engaged attitude and without political action, will, and risk, the "Just City" of the Just Society will, in Auden's estimation, never be established. Auden urges that the success of the struggle depends on the personal, political involvement of the responsible individual. If this struggle fails, however, then:

The stars are dead. The animals will not love.
We are left alone with our day, and the time is short, and
        History to the defeated
May say Alas but cannot help or pardon.
                        (Ll. 101–4, p. 12)

Sadly enough, the closing lines of Auden's *Spain* were a foreboding, prophetic description of the hopelessness that would be experienced by "the defeated" not only in 1939 when the war ended but also years later whenever the aborted struggle for the Just Society would be recalled.

César Vallejo's poetry of the Spanish Civil War, written during 1937 and published posthumously in 1939 under the title *España, aparta de mí este cáliz,* is, like Auden's long poem, also concerned with the success or failure of the envisioned new society.[71] Vallejo's vision of this society, however, is based on his own highly personal brand of communism and his own personalized portrait of man. For Vallejo, the end result of the Spanish Civil War will be, he hopes, the construction of a new world of peace and fraternal love. From the fratricidal war will emerge, paradoxically, the new fraternal order of love, peace, and life for the new man of the new world.

César Vallejo's vision of man, in general, and his own kind of communism, in particular, have been determined by various factors. James Higgins has observed in *Visión del hombre y de la vida en las últimas obras poéticas de César Vallejo:*

> Así el comunismo de Vallejo fue influido y modificado por ciertos factores personales: su ideal de amor fraternal y su sueño de un mundo regido por el amor; su educación cristiana y su conservación de ciertas actitudes cristianas; su ideal de hogar y la familia; su admiración por los valores del indio peruano. Pero aunque estos factores prestan un tono personal a su comunismo, no por eso deja de ser ortodoxo. Es cierto que el amor es la base de la ideología de Vallejo y que concibe una redención del hombre en términos algo útopicos. Pero esto no significa que crea que el amor ha de obrar algún milagro fantástico. La sociedad será cambiada por la acción colectiva de las masas, por una revolución proletaria, y después el mundo será transformado poco a poco por el trabajo de una humanidad unida que utilice todos los recursos de la ciencia y la tecnología al servicio del hombre. (P. 316)

España, aparta de mí este cáliz is just one example in Vallejo's poetic production of the poet's expressed commitment to his fellowman, his profound love for humanity, and his own interpretation of what Higgins terms "el comunismo Vallejiano."[72] Of his collection of poems concerning the Spanish Civil War, Higgins observes in his introduction to *César Vallejo: An Anthology of his Poetry:*

> In several poems in *Poemas humanos* and in *España . . .* Vallejo is speaking on two complementary levels. On the one hand, he is a revolutionary proclaiming the liberation of the oppressed through the proletarian revolution. But at the same time he is a prophet foretelling the total redemption of man: drawing inspiration from the Bible and employing a religious terminology, he sings of the paradise that will be conquered on earth by a united humanity. In the new universal society which Vallejo foresees not only will the social structure be rectified but the conditions of life will be transformed; not only will injustice be eliminated but evil will be abolished, not only will man be freed from oppression but he will overcome the absurd and attain a full and harmonious life. (P. 67)

Vallejo himself, in "Himno a los voluntarios de la República," proclaims the end result of the proletarian revolution and the people's struggle in Spain when his assumed poetic voice declares:

> ¡Voluntarios,
> por la vida, por los buenos, matad
> a la muerte, matad a los malos!
> ¡Hacedlo por la libertad de todos,
> del explotado y del explotador,
> por la paz indolora—la sospecho

cuando duermo al pie de mi frente
y más cuando circulo dando voces—
y hacedlo, voy diciendo,
por el analfabeto a quien escribo
por el genio descalzo y su cordero,
por los camaradas caídos,
sus cenizas abrazadas el cadáver de un camino!

(Ll. 154–66)

The poems of *España, aparta de mí este cáliz,* as Higgins observes, "celebrate the heroes of the Republic. But for Vallejo this is not simply a struggle of the workers against Fascism: it is an episode of man's struggle to create the new, universal society and the Republic is the symbol of that society. Thus in "Himno de los voluntarios de la República" Vallejo prophesies the reign of peace, harmony and justice that will come into being as a result of the sacrifice of the Republican militiamen."[73] For poets such as Auden, Vallejo, Neruda, Prados, Hernández, and Alberti, among others, the victory of the Popular Front in February 1936 initiated the new political era of the people of Spain and, as they hoped, of the rest of the world. The military uprising of 18 July 1936, however, was an ominous and eventually fatal threat to this vision of a new political era. The Civil War that resulted came to represent, for these committed poets, the struggle of a people to determine its own destiny and to gain, to use Vallejo's words, "la unidad, sencilla, justa, colectiva, eterna."[74]

The publication of Pablo Neruda's *España en el corazón: Himno a las glorias del pueblo en la guerra (1936–1937)* in 1938 is significant within the poet's own poetic trajectory because it indicates, as he himself has stated in his memoirs, the "road" upon which he would later journey as a poet of the people. Neruda's experience of the war in Spain was to change profoundly the orientation of his life and work. He reveals in *Confieso que he vivido:* "Desde entonces mi camino se junta con el camino de todos. Y de pronto veo que desde el sur de la soledad he ido hacia la norte que es el pueblo, el pueblo al cual mi humilde poesía quisiera servir de espada y de pañuelo, para secar al sudor de sus grandes dolores y para darle un arma en la lucha del pan" (pp. 203–4). In the early thirties, Alberti, Prados, Vallejo, and Aragon had already decided to align their life and work with "el camino de todos." Neruda's conversion to the "religion" of his fellowmen, however, occurred during and on account of the war in Spain.

In "Explico algunas cosas," Neruda, firmly grounded in the reality of Madrid in the early days of the siege, reveals not only his individual response to the horror of war but also his firm commitment to the cause of the people:

Y una mañana todo estaba ardiendo
y una mañana las hogueras

salían de la tierra
devorando seres,
y desde entonces fuego,
pólvora desde entonces,
y desde entonces sangre.
. . . .
Frente a vosotros he visto la sangre
de España levantarse
para ahogaros en una sola ola
de orgullo y de cuchillos!
Generales
traidores:
mirad mi casa muerta,
mirad España rota:
pero de cada casa muerta sale metal ardiendo
en vez de flores,
pero de cada hueco de España
sale España,
pero de cada niño muerto sale un fusil con ojos,
pero de cada crimen nacen balas
que os hallarán un día el sitio
del corazón.

¿Preguntaréis por qué su poesía
no nos habla del sueño, de las hojas,
de los grandes volcanes de su país natal?

¡Venid a ver la sangre por las calles
venid a ver
la sangre por las calles,
venid a ver la sangre por las calles!
(Ll. 40–46, 56–79)

Like other poetry written in support of the Republic's cause, *España en el corazón* presents a vision of "La victoria de las armas del pueblo," as one poem is entitled, and thus expresses an optimistic view of the triumph of the people's cause. The closing lines of "Oda solar al Ejército del Pueblo," for example, reveal:

tu luz organizada llega a los pobres hombres
olvidados, tu definida estrella
clava sus roncos rayos en la muerte
y establece los nuevos ojos de la esperanza.
(Ll. 62–65)

Other poems of the collection, however, such as "Canto sobre unas ruinas," disclose the poet's own frustration, despair, and pessimism as he, through his assumed poetic voice, witnesses the ubiquitous ruin brought by war:

todo reunido en nada, todo caído
para no nacer nunca.
. . . .
Ved cómo las palabras que tanto construyeron,
ahora son exterminio: mirad sobre la cal y entre el mármol deshecho
la huella—ya con musgos—del sollozo.

(Ll. 36–37, 47–49)

The Neruda of both "Canto sobre unas ruinas" and "Madrid 1937," along with the Vallejo of "España, aparta de mí este cáliz," foresees and responds to the eventual fall of the Spanish Republic and the resulting dissolution of the dream of the new era. Whereas Vallejo, on the one hand, offers a personal, Marxist solution to the possibility of defeat and encourages the people to continue in the struggle in order to realize the dream of the universal society, Neruda, on the other hand, does not offer a political solution to the dilemma facing the people in the war. Rather, as an observer he often recounts aspects of the seemingly endless tragedy of the war, of the "interminable martiro"[75] where:

Nada, ni la victoria
borrará el agujero terrible de la sangre:
nada, ni el mar, ni el paso
de arena y tiempo, ni el geranio ardiendo
sobre la sepultura.

(Ll. 27–31)

James Higgins observes of Vallejo's *España, aparta de mí este cáliz:* "It is significant that the poems of *España* . . . were written in the knowledge that the Republic would be crushed and yet celebrate the triumph of the revolutionary cause: Vallejo sees beyond immediate failures and disappointments to the eventual triumph of the Revolution and the redemption of man."[76] Alberti, like Vallejo, as an active Marxist committed to the cause of the people, also sees beyond the possible defeat of the Republic and envisions the creation of a new political era and the social and political resurrection of the common man in that era. Neruda, however, in 1936–37, when he wrote *España en el corazón,* had not yet undergone his conversion to communism (*CV,* 185–87). The more pessimistic poems of his collection of war poetry reveal a personal despair and ennui experienced during and on account of the conflict rather than a collective frustration and lack of hope. In *España en el corazón,* "la muerte española, más ácida y aguda que otras muertes" was experienced in a very personal manner.[77] For Neruda, this public event did not represent a struggle involving specific ideological aims to which he himself was committed. Rather, in *España en el corazón* Neruda discloses his own experience of war: "Os voy a cantar todo lo que me pasa."[78] *España en el corazón* thus provides personal eyewitness accounts of what, as the first-person speaker of "Llegada a Madrid de la Brigada Internacional" reveals, "he visto con estos ojos que tengo, con este corazón que mira" (l. 10). The collection, therefore, does not provide the sustained ideological vision of the events of the people's war and the poet's role in them that is offered by Vallejo or Alberti in their poetry. Neruda's own commitment to the people's Marxist future would be a direct result of the Spanish Civil War and would later shape his epic of the Latin American people, *Canto general*.[79]

Although *España en el corazón* is, for the most part, unified by the poet's recording of his personal response to war, many poems of the collection also demonstrate the poet's desire to have the poem serve as a political weapon, or, as Jaime Concha has observed, to have the poem serve as a "verdadera arma de lucha para el pueblo en la guerra."[80] There is, thus, an unevenness in tone and vision in Neruda's collection of war poetry. We find poems that are rallying cries to action ("España pobre por culpa de los ricos," "Almería," "Sanjuro en los Infiernos," "Mola en los Infiernos," "El General Franco en los Infiernos," "La victoria de las armas del pueblo," "Los gremios en el frente," "Triunfo," "Antianarquistas," "Oda solar al Ejército del Pueblo"), poems recounting what has occurred in the war and what yet needs to be accomplished ("Madrid 1936," "Canto a las madres de los milicianos muertos," "Cómo era España," "Llegada a Madrid de la Brigada Internacional," "Batalla del río Jarama," "Tierras ofendidas," "Madrid 1937"), and poems disclosing Neruda's personal interpretation of the public event ("Explico algunas cosas," "Canto sobre unas ruinas"). Neruda's poetry of the Civil War, like Alberti's, is at its best, aesthetically speaking, when his unifying idea is not a call to action or a catalog of battlefields and events but an introspective and reflective analysis of the tragedy of war. In poems such as "Explico algunas cosas," "Canto sobre unas ruinas," and "Paisaje después de una batalla" Pablo Neruda offers insights into the relationship of the individual to the larger, more awesomely destructive public event as the poet attempts to decipher the enigma of Spain's war.

In comparing and contrasting the poetry of the Spanish Civil War of Alberti, Vallejo, and Neruda, the works of the former two poets are both unified and inspired by a similar Marxist-socialist vision of the future, the same vision that formed the ideological foundation of the Popular Front. Neruda's poetry of the people's war in Spain is, however, unified by its singular subject, the war. Grounded in the external reality of the conflict and also in the poet's own internal, emotional reality where the war is deeply felt and reflectively analyzed, Neruda's poetry of the Civil War is, as the title of his collection aptly reveals, "España en el corazón."

Emilio Prados is one of Spain's most prolific poets of the Civil War. *Destino fiel: (Ejercicios de poesía en guerra) (1936–1939),* which won the Premio Nacional de Literatura in 1937, contains numerous poems written during and about the conflict. The subject matter of this collection is both the sociopolitical essence of the struggle and also the poet's own reaction to and vision of the war. For Prados, the goals of the Republican cause in the midst of the war are clear, as the ballad "Digan, digan" explains:

Digan, digan ellos: ¡Digan!,
que ya iluminará el cielo
la verdad por que luchamos
y la verdad del suceso.
. . . .
Sepan que paz y trabajo
buscaba tan sólo el pueblo:
pan seguro y sin temores;
hermandad y claro cielo.
. . . .
Digan, digan; ¡yo lo vi!:
gitanos y marineros,
campesinos, pescadores,
soldados, carabineros,
guardia civil y de asalto
levantarse en un momento
y unirse al proletariado,
que con su puño de acero
sabrá vengar la traición
borrando su paso negro.

¿Quién se atreve? Quien se atreva,
¡la razón va con el pueblo!
Si hoy a la justicia temen,
ellos han abierto el fuego.

Digan, digan por el mundo,
desde un extremo a otro extremo,
que la verdad ya ilumina
su aurora roja en el cielo.
       (Ll. 57–60, 69–72, 129–46)

In the ballad "Arenga," Prados adds another dimension to "la verdad por que luchamos" when the speaker of the poem calls for proletarian solidarity in the struggle:

con llanto pide la unión
por tanto tiempo esperada.
Lejos las palabras torpes

que tan sólo nos separan,
dándole fuerza al fascismo
para ganar sus batallas.
Cuando la muerte se acerca
con tan terrible amenaza,
tan sólo a una voz debemos
dejar paso en la garganta:
¡Unión! ¡Unión, proletarios,
hijos valientes de España!
                    (Ll. 17–28)

Prados, however, also views this fratricidal conflict as a "duro sacrificio de
la guerra,"[81] a seemingly endless succession of hours and days filled with
death and destruction:

La ceniza, el carbón, el miedo, el humo,
la sangre, el trepidar y las banderas:
desolación, ruina
y llanto sobre el suelo.[82]

War is, for this poet, both a public and a personal "cotidiana agonía" (*PPC*,
738–39), as the title of one poem so accurately reveals, a public event to
which he responds in his own individual way:

¡Qué lento paso el día!
¡Qué pie tan largo el de la Muerte!
Hora tras hora llega
arrastrando mi cuerpo
por la calle desierta de su vida
y hora tras hora vuelve
en cadena perpetua
a inaugurarlo entero
por clavarle mejor su dura argolla . . .
. . . .
. . . Miro arriba la noche
y marchan lentas sus estrellas . . .
Miro luego hacia abajo:
sobre la tierra enflaquecida
mi cuerpo sigue y vuelve
sin buscar un descanso,
mi cuerpo sigue y vuelve,
perdido en la misión de su tristeza.
                    (Ll. 1–9, 50–57)

Emilio Prados's poetry of the Spanish Civil War offers both an analysis of
and a response to the events, cause, effect, and meaning of the conflict. His

"Romances (1937–1939),"[83] which constitute the first section of *Destino fiel*, chronicle the deeds of the *pueblo*-protagonist of the struggle and present basically an optimistic vision of "toda su sangre prepara / la edad futura que empieza."[84] This vision of the people's new era is similar to that sketched by Alberti in *Capital de la gloria*. Both poets are not only committed to the heroic actions of the people but also foretell the positive effects these deeds will produce. *Destino fiel* and *Capital de la gloria* demonstrate a firm hope in the future of a free Spain and a new era of peace. Prados summarizes his own optimistic view of Spain's nascent era in the closing lines of "Meditación en la noche." His apostrophe to the war reveals:

> ¡Ay guerra, guerra, inúltimente clamo
> la imagen fiel que logre con su enseña
> fuera arrojar de tu infecundo cuerpo
> el fantasma sin luz con que te alumbras;
> porque el hombre, aprendiendo en sus recuerdos,
> hoy va alegre a los campos de sus luchas
> y si el surco cambió por la trinchera
> y más hondo bajó, con esta hondura
> más fuerte en la raíz que sepa alzarlo
> se sostendrá en el árbol de su gloria!
> ¡Ay dura guerra! ¿De qué voz te engañas?
> ¿Qué brújula te ha uncido con la Muerte?
> ¡Mira a los bellos hijos de la aurora!
> Termina, guerra, que no en vano canto
> la paz que anuncia espigas de victoria.
>
> (Ll. 84–98)

In his poetry of the Spanish Civil War, Prados demonstrates his solidarity with the common people: "os habla un hijo del pueblo."[85] This solidarity also is evident in Prados's political poetry written before the war. Manuel Altolaguirre indicates in the 1937 prologue to Prados's *Llanto en la sangre* that this poet's political verse of the early thirties is firmly committed to the people's struggle for a better future: "La voz del poeta difícil luchaba por la verdad sencilla, contra el dolor injusto, dignificando los trabajos. Los poetas que en Madrid o en el extranjero recibíamos estas noticias nos encaminábamos también hacia el mismo destino, con decisíon inquebrantable como Rafael Alberti, con mayores o menores entretenimientos los demás. Fue necesario que llegara el año de la sangrienta represión de Asturias para que todos, todos los poetas, sintiéramos como un imperioso deber adoptar nuestra obra, nuestras vidas, al movimiento liberador de España" (*PPC*, 560). Emilio Prados's early commitment was later intensified by the advent of the Civil War in Spain. As Carlos Blanco Aguinaga and Antonio Carreira point out in their prologue to Prados's *Poesías completas:* "Su misión en la guerra es la de los demás poetas: propaganda activa en los sindicatos o en el frente, y muy en particular por la radio, donde, como los demás, lee romances escritos al calor de la tragedia cotidiana" (p. xliii). Throughout his poetry of the thirties, Emilio Prados, like Juan Gil-Albert and Rafael Alberti, demonstrates his solidarity with the people, a commitment that has led Lechner to the following conclusion: "Gil-Alberti y Prados nos parecen haber dado, a lo largo de las páginas que escribieron durante la guerra (continuación de su actitud de la anteguerra), el más alto ejemplo de poetas comprometidos" (*CPE,* 194).

This commitment to the people is the "destino fiel" of Emilio Prados, and his poetry of the Spanish Civil War is an extensive "canto" recording the actions, goals, fears, and hopes of the people in the conflict. The poem "Presente oficio" explains, perhaps better than any other poem of the collection, the foundation of Emilio Prados's sustained commitment to the cause of the people:

No, guerra, no te canto.
Cantaré la victoria.
Quiero cantar a sus hermosos hijos
que de la paz levantan,
como palmas de sueño,
y contra ti se agrupan, generosos.
Quiero cantar los hijos que en tus campos
pisan por tus batallas,
indomables, feroces,
y en la largueza de su sacrificio
pulsan tus armas y entran por la muerte
con tales pasos y ademán tan firmes
que tú misma te muestras orgullosa
de hallar tales guerros en tu frente.
. . . .
Guerra, teme su alcance;
mi verso te lo augura.
Hijos son de la paz, con ellos canto.
Si mueren por la paz, con ellos vivo.
Hermanos de mi voz: quiero cantarlos.
Pudieron nacer pájaros: son hombres
y hoy labran con su sangre la alegría.
(Ll. 32–45, 72–78)

It is appropriate that this brief overview of various poets' inquiries into the enigma of the Spanish Civil War should conclude with the poetry of Miguel Hernández, the soldier-poet. Cano-Ballesta observes in *Miguel Hernández: El hombre y su poesía:* "El estallido de la Guerra Civil en julio de 1936 le obliga a tomar una desición. Miguel Hernández, sin dar lugar a dudas, la toma con entereza y entusiasmo por la República. No solamente entrega toda su persona, sino que también su creación lírica se trueca en arma de denuncia, testimonio, instrumento de lucha ya entusiasta, ya silenciosa y desesperada. Como voluntario se incorpora al 5° Regimiento."[86] In a ballad entitled "Memoria del 5.° Regimiento," written in 1937, this poet of the Civil War recalls his decision to enlist and to place his life at the service of the people in the war:

El alba del diecinueve
de julio ne so atrevía
a precipitar el día
sobre su costa de nieve.
Nadie a despertar se atreve
hosco de presentimiento.
Y el viento del pueblo, el viento
que muevo y aliento yo
pasó a mi lado y pasó
hacia el 5.° Regimiento.
(Ll. 1–10)

The poetry of Miguel Hernández written during the Spanish Civil War is, as the poem "Sentado sobre los muertos" of *Viento del pueblo* reveals, a personal "clamor" directed to the collective, an audible weapon to be used in the struggle:

Acércate a mi clamor
pueblo de mi misma leche,
árbol con tus raíces
encarcelado me tienes,
que aquí estoy para amarte
y estoy para defenderte
con la sangre y con la boca
como dos fusiles fieles.
(Ll. 11–18)

Hernández's decision to be a poet of the people and a participant in the people's conflict was one that consumed his entire being. In 1937 he declared: "Vivo para exaltar los valores puros del pueblo y, a su lado, estoy tan dispuesto a vivir como a morir" (*OPC*, 18–19). In the "Nota preliminar" of his *Teatro en la guerra*, Hernández reiterates this commitment: "Había escrito versos y drama de exaltación del trabajo y de condenación del burgués, pero el empujón definitivo que me arrastró a esgrimir mi poesía en forma de arma me lo dieron aquel iluminado 18 de julio. Intuí, sentí venir contra mi vida, como un gran aire, la gran tragedia, la tremenda experiencia poética que se avecinaba, y me metí, pueblo adentro, más hondo de lo que estoy metido desde que me parieran, dispuesto a defenderlo firmamente" (*OPC*, 14–15).[87]

The passage introducing *Viento del pueblo* underscores that Hernández's life as a soldier and a poet of the people's struggle is defined and determined by the *pueblo* itself. For Hernández, the collective is the source of his nourishment and strength. The poet explains that it is the *pueblo* "hacia el que tiendo todas mis raíces alimenta y ensancha mis ansias y mis cuerdas con el soplo cálido de sus movimientos nobles" (*OPC*, 304). In "Recoged esta voz" the poet's first-person lyrical voice expresses his commitment to the common people:

Hombres, mundos, naciones,
atended, escuchad mi sangrante sonido,
recoged mis latidos de quebranto
en vuestros espaciosos corazones,
porque yo empuño el alma cuando canta.

Cantando me defiendo
y defiendo mi pueblo cuando en mi pueblo imprimen
su herradura de pólvora y estruendo
los bárbaros del crimen.
(Ll. 13–21)

Cano-Ballesta summarizes Miguel Hernández's poetry of the Civil War in this way: "Miguel Hernández cree en la voluntad transformadora del hombre. El agitado ambiente de la República, con su vida azarosa de controversias y luchas apasionadas, le arrastra a la creación lírica de testimonio y denuncia. Los acontecimientos van despertando en él la conciencia de responsabilidad colectiva; comprende el poder transformador de la palabra, su posible función social y política. . . . De los libros de poesía en la guerra es *Viento del pueblo* el de tono más viril y apasionado. Enardecido por los magnos acontecimientos escribe poemas vigorosos y entusiastas impregnados de las más intensa vibración humana y el espíritu bélico más ardiente."[88]

"Sentado sobre los muertos" provides a portrait in verse of the *pueblo*-protagonist of Hernández's war poetry. Here the speaker exalts the efforts of the collective as it willingly and heroically confronts death in the conflict:

Aunque te falten las armas,
pueblo de cien mil poderes,
no desfallezcan tus huesos,
castiga a quien malhiere
mientras que te queden puños,
uñas, saliva, y te queden
corazón, entrañas, tripas,
cosas de varón y dientes.

Bravo como el viento bravo,
leve como el aire leve,
asesina al que asesina,
aborrece al que aborrece
la paz de tu corazón
y el vientre de tus mujeres.
No te hierran por la espalda,
vive cara a cara y muere
con el pecho ante las balas,
ancho como las paredes.

                              (Ll. 39–56)

"Nuestra juventud no muere" portrays death in war as a source of new life for the people, a theme, as we have seen, that is often found in the poetry of the Republican cause:

Caídos, sí, no muertos
. . . .
Siempre serán famosas
estas sangres cubiertas de abriles y de mayos
que hacen vibrar las dilatadas fosas
con su vigor que se decide en rayos.

                              (Ll. 1, 7–10)

This theme is further developed in "Recoged esta voz," where it is combined with the motif of the valiant, virile soldiers who are "toros de victorioso desenlace" (l. 119):

Ellos harán de cada ruina un prado,
de cada pena un fruto de alegría,
de España un firmamento de hermosura.
Vedos agigantar el mediodía
y hermosearlo todo con su joven bravura.
. . . .
Naciones, hombres, mundos, esto escribo:
la juventud de España saldrá de las trincheras
de pie, invencible como la semilla,
pues tiene un alma llena de banderas
que jamás se somete ni arrodilla.

Allá van por los yermos de Castilla
los cuerpos que parecen potros batalladores,
toros de victorioso desenlace,
diciéndose en su sangre de generosas flores
que morir es la cosa más grande que se hace.

                              (Ll. 103–21)

The underlying tone of hope of *Viento del pueblo* is especially prevalent in "Juramento de alegría." For the poet in the war, the united, luminous collective of "el ejército del sol, de la alegría" (l. 8) will transform the present circumstance of Spain and will usher in the future of new life of the people:

Es un pleno de abriles,
una primavera caballería,
que inunda de galopes los perfiles
de España: es el ejército del sol, de la alegría.
Desaparece la tristeza, el día
devorador, el marchito tallo,
cuando, avasalladora llamarada,
galopa la alegría en un caballo
igual que una bandera desbocada.
. . . .
Avanza la alegría derrumbando montañas.

(Ll. 5–13, 22)

Miguel Hernández's *Viento del pueblo* displays a passionate intensity, a lyrical force, and a sustained emotional impetus whenever the poet in the war presents his vibrant vision of the people actively engaged in and itself metaphorically incarnating the transformative potential of all of humanity. This optimistic view of the collective could not help but fill with hope the combatants of the war who heard the poems of *Viento del pueblo* recited by the poet himself in the trenches.[89] The civilian population who read Hernández's poetry in the various magazines of the era also must have found it to be inspirational. Fifty years after "la fiebre fratricida / de la guerra,"[90] Miguel Hernández's enthusiastic portrait of the regenerative role of the people in the war affects the reader of *Viento del pueblo,* a collection that was originally conceived in the early months of the conflict with the utmost sincerity and with a firm conviction and faith.

Miguel Hernández published one other collection of war poems, *El hombre acecha (1937–1939).*[91] According to Cano-Ballesta's "Trayectoria de una vida trágica" in the collection of essays entitled *En torno a Miguel Hernández,* this work "estará dominado por un tono más sombrío, amargo y desesperanzador. El poeta se ve que ya vislumbra o teme el desenlace fatal de la guerra. Va descubriendo el dolor, el odio, la maldad del hombre convertido en fiera que acecha a su hermano, según sugiere el mismo título: *El hombre acecha.* El libro está en prensa al terminar la guerra."[92] In *Miguel Hernández: El hombre y su poesía,* the same critic observes of this collection:

El poeta va profundizando en la realidad de su mundo, va conociendo mejor al hombre, que rememora sus garras y se convierte en tigre. Las manos, que eran en *Viento del pueblo* instrumentos creadores, fuentes de riqueza y bienestar, son aquí simples garras de odio, armas de destrucción. . . . No es ya sólo el combatiente del bando contrario—aunque lo incluye preferentemente—quien desciende a la bestia. Para él tenía en *Viento del pueblo* metáforas feroces: "monstruos," "fieras," "hienas," "liebres," "podencos." Ahora, con terrible amargura, las aplica al hombre en general. ¿Y es que faltaban pruebas después de tanta sangre derramada? La evolución de este tipo de metáfora deshumanizadora que rebaja al hombre al nivel de fiera es un índice muy revelador del proceso íntimo que ha tenido lugar en el alma de Miguel Hernández, quien en sus últimos libros se entrega a una larga meditación sobre el hombre y su sed de sangre, sus instintos feroces, sus ansias de destrucción. De poeta de una clase social combatiente se va convirtiendo en vate universal amargamente desilusionado del hombre. (Pp. 31, 32–33)

El hombre acecha, using as its point of departure the sociopolitical circumstance of the fratricidal war, is essentially an inquiry into not only the enigma that is war but also the enigma that is human nature. "La canción primera" opens the collection and immediately introduces the universal plight and contradiction that is man: "el hombre acecha al hombre" (l. 22). Even Nature flees from the ferocious creature that destroys human life:

Se ha retirado el campo
al ver abalanzarse
crispadamente al hombre.

¡Qué abismo entre el olivo
y el hombre se descubre!

El animal que canta:
el animal que puede
llorar y echar raíces,
rememoró sus garras.

Garras que revestía
de suavidad y flores,
pero que, al fin, desnuda
en toda crueldad.

Crepitan en mis manos.
Aparta de ellas, hijo.
Estoy dispuesto a hundirlas,
dispuesto a proyectarlas
sobre tu carne leve.

He regresado al tigre.
Aparta o te destrozo.

Hoy el amor es muerte,
y el hombre acecha al hombre.

The poet's own personalized, first-person, lyrical voice cannot escape from what seems to be man's destiny of becoming an awesome, fierce, dehumanized, evil beast of prey in the circumstance of war.

In *El hombre acecha,* Miguel Hernández judges man and man's actions in war. Going beyond the public event, Hernández ultimately sketches in verse a portrait of man's nature and of what man could and eventually would become if anger, hatred, and despair were to go unchecked. With passionate sincerity, frank honesty, and prophetic awareness, Hernández analyzes the serious flaws in man's nature, flaws that in themselves also underlie the inception of the war that man has created and in which man participates. The enigma that is war, for this soldier-poet, is merely a reflection of the contradiction that is man. Like all reflections, the distorted image is what is observed and scrutinized in the poetic mirror of Miguel Hernández's *El hombre acecha.*

Miguel Hernández, unlike the other Hispanic poets of the Civil War, presents a sustained and unified vision of the underside of man in his last collection of war verse. Alberti, Prados, and Neruda, in a few of their poems of the era, depict the enemy as a base and violent creature who has betrayed the cause of the people. Only Miguel Hernández, however, in *El hombre acecha,* goes beyond the overt, public event of the fratricidal war, the antithetical duality of antagonist/protagonist in the tragic drama of the conflict, and the more simplistic characterization of the complex enemy in the struggle. Hernández comprehends that war exaggerates and emphasizes man's own hidden flaws, base instincts, and enigmatic nature. In his dual analysis of war and man, Hernández discovers that the enemy is not a political force; rather, the enemy is man when fraternal love has been supplanted by unbridled hatred and "Hoy el amor es muerte, / y el hombre acecha al hombre."

The works of these poets of the people's struggle form an important part of what Stanley Weintraub has called the "written legacy" of the Spanish Civil War. Weintraub observes: "There remains that written legacy—the fading Legend of Spain, now and then still reshaped into a form which communicates some remnant of the great burst of hope that momentarily fired a generation which had discovered in Madrid and Guernica, in Teruel and Barcelona, an antidote to a world sunk in cowardice, hypocrisy and cynicism."[93] The poets who took pen in hand in order to write the legacy of the "catastrophe" and the "glory" of the Spanish Civil War responded to a political event that, as one historian writes, "caught the conscience of a generation."[94] This public event and its political consequences urged many great poets of the thirties to make public statements within the discourse of poetry. Such public voices not only proclaimed the collective conscience of all who believed in the People's Struggle but also would forever serve as constant reminders and resounding echoes of the "Last Great Cause."

"El pueblo espera a los poetas con la oreja y el alma tendidas al pie de cada siglo"

Rafael Alberti's *Capital de la gloria* transcends the immediate political event of the Spanish Civil War and offers insight into the concerns of the people, the destiny of Spain and the individual poet's own response to the enigma of war. John Krueger has observed: "Whether or not a poet writing on politics speaks to the great issues of man and answers them finally, whether or not he has the power to inform the thoughts of man in later times, the success of his political verse will depend upon the extent to which he brings both his own personal insight to bear on public issues and a purview that extends beyond any particular issue or event."[95] *Capital de la gloria* does not offer final answers to the questions raised by the Spanish Civil War nor could it ever hope to do so. *Capital de la gloria* is essentially a response to the fratricidal conflict, and as such it is one man's way of deciphering the perplexing enigma of war. Almost fifty years have passed since the 1936–39 conflict in Spain. *Capital de la gloria,* to this day, remains a provocative and enlightening collection of poems written not only concurrently with the battles, bombings, victories, and defeats that were a part of the people's struggle but also with a perceptive understanding of the meaning of these public events.

Rafael Alberti's contemplation of the sobering experience of the Spanish Civil War leads him to a prophetic vision of the role the collective should assume if freedom, justice, and basic human dignity are to be preserved. That his prophecy was not fulfilled in 1939 when the war ended left Rafael Alberti a broken man. Forced to become a political refugee and live in exile, Alberti would continue to recall, write about, and appraise the Spanish Civil War and his concept of the people's role in the new era.[96] In *Entre el clavel y la espada (1939–1940),* his first collection of poetry written in exile after the war, Alberti writes: "Salta, gallo del alba: mira que alcobas encendidas van a abrírsete. Caballo, yerba, perro, toro: tenéis llama de hombre. Aceleraos. Hay cambios en el aire. Errores floridos. Pero . . . Silencio. Oíd. Esperad . . . No os mováis" (*PC,* 446). That the prophecy developed in *Capital de la gloria,* and later presented in *Entre el clavel y la espada* (1939–1940), *Signos del día* (1945–1955), *Coplas de Juan Panadero* (1949), *Primavera de los pueblos* (1955–1957), *Sonríe China* (1958), and *Nuevas coplas de Juan Panadero* (1976–1977), did not begin to come about in Spain until almost fifty years after Alberti wrote his last poems of the Civil War, makes his "voz de elegía" even more pronounced and poignant and his "voz de mañana" even more inspiring and optimistic.[97]

Throughout *Capital de la gloria,* Rafael Alberti's public voice is as energetic and influential as the "viento del pueblo" inspiring it and infusing it with life. In this way, as the soldier-poet Miguel Hernández accurately observed during the Spanish Civil War: "Los poetas somos viento del pueblo: nacemos para pasar soplando a través de sus poros y conducir sus ojos y sus sentimientos hacia las cumbres más hermosas. Hoy, este hoy de pasión, de vida, de muerte, nos empuja de un imponente modo a ti, a mí, a varios, hacia el pueblo. El pueblo espera a los poetas con la oreja y el alma tendidas al pie de cada siglo" (*OPC*, 304).

The opening verses of Miguel Hernández's "Vientos de mi pueblo me llevan" could be considered as a fitting epithet for Rafael Alberti:

Vientos de mi pueblo me llevan,
vientos de mi pueblo me arrastran,
me esparcen el corazón
y me avientan la garganta.
(Ll. 1–4)

Perhaps, though, no description is more appropriate for this poet of the people than that which he himself wrote in his "Autorretrato con parecido":

Yo soy Rafael Alberti. . . . El que vuelve a su patria como poeta en la calle, a nivelar su voz con la del pueblo, a ser suyo en la lucha, a cantarlo, ayudarlo, sostenerlo.

Yo soy Rafael Alberti, ya en la guerra. Su verso tiene el silbo de las balas, la arrancada del toro castigado, la alegría de una flor en las trincheras, el filo de la espada que se alza contra el crimen, el duro verde del laurel, los temblores del viento embanderado, el hervor de la sangre del Madrid no vencido, el grito que no calla ni en la muerte y se hace más alto en la derrota. . . .

Yo soy Rafael Alberti, un poeta español, una voz fervorosa en esas muchedumbres. (*PEC*, 11, 12)

Chapter 5

Afterword

P oetry concerning public themes is not peculiar to the thirties, although it was in that overtly political decade, suspended between two world wars, that many gifted poets consciously decided to use their art in order to summon social change. Poetry with a political subject matter spans the centuries. Songs or odes of praise to political leaders have been found among the ancient pyramid texts, and panegyrics on political heroes occur in early Hebrew, Greek, and Roman poetry. In the late twelfth and early thirteenth centuries, Bertrand de Born and Walther von der Vogelweide wrote a substantial body of political lyrics. Jonathan Swift is famous for his satirical political verse, and the British romantic poets openly denounced the old political order while describing the new. Our own century offers an amazing array of political poets, including Mao TseTung, William Butler Yeats, Siegfried Sassoon, Wilfred Owen, Stephen Spender, W. H. Auden, Edith Sitwell, Langston Hughes, Allen Ginsberg, Robert Lowell, Robert Bly, Leroi Jones, Susan Griffin, Adrienne Rich, Denise Levertov, Louis Aragon, Paul Eluard, George Seferis, Bertolt Brecht, Alexander Blok, Andre Bely, Vladimir Mayakovsky, Pablo Neruda, César Vallejo, Carlos Germán Belli, León Felipe, Luis Cernuda, Miguel Hernández, and of course, Rafael Alberti, to name only some of the more prominent. Throughout the decades, poets have aired their public voices to respond to public affairs, survey the concrete world, and predict the fate of political endeavors.

For Rafael Alberti, one of Spain's most outspoken and influential public voices in this century, the poet cannot be divorced from his or her society. In his political poetry since 1930, Alberti portrays humankind's social reality in its various manifestations and militantly advocates radical social changes. It is this aspect that links Alberti to the other committed writers of the twentieth century. As Maxwell Adereth explains:

> The committed outlook rests above all on the recognition that an artist is part of his environment—the society in which he lives, the ideologies of his time, and the public for whom he creates. No modern writer is free from these influences,

and the greater his understanding of them, the greater his commitment will be. . . .

"Littérature engagée" does not claim that it is necessarily more realistic than other kinds of literature, but simply that it is consciously so. This, in turn, leads it to portray *all* aspects of reality and to bring out what it thinks is the objective significance of the world around us. Since the writer is not . . . an inanimate mirror passively reflecting his surroundings, his interest in the world is dominated by a desire to change it. We touch here upon the most original characteristic of "littérature engagée": . . . it is militant and active. (*CMFL*, 225, 226)

That Rafael Alberti's political poetry of the thirties, especially, manifests this "committed outlook" should be clear from the preceding chapters. The themes of his poems of the thirties reflect the political affairs of Spain and other nations and also the evolving political consciousness of the poet. As he gives voice to the experience of the common people Alberti looks not only to civil affairs but also to the self. The collective experience and the poet's perception of it are joined when the "poeta en la calle" transcends the limitations of self and becomes an integral part of, the vocal representative for, and, sometimes, the energized agitator of his society.

I have tried to show that Rafael Alberti's attitude of commitment together with his optimistic view of the people's role in altering the sociopolitical affairs of state inspire his poetry of the thirties, molding it into a pragmatic discourse that is designed to benefit his fellowmen. A careful study of Alberti's poetry of the thirties makes clear the conception, gestation, and evolution of this attitude, highlights political modes of writing and their aim and value, and calls attention to the poet's own evaluation of political activism and its potential as the subject matter of poetry.

The works I have studied place special demands on the reader. Readers of Alberti's political poetry of the thirties, especially the agitative poetry designed to revolutionize the masses, must be willing to consider the poem not simply as an aesthetic end in itself but rather as a means to an end, a social or political end. Regardless of their political persuasion, readers who enter the world of Alberti's poetry of this era enter into the concrete world of the poet's social circumstance and are often required to appraise the poet's specific political interpretation of this circumstance. At times, readers of these poems must ponder the public issue or event presented in order to understand and vicariously experience the poet's vision of the public domain. At other times, readers are encouraged directly to intervene in public affairs. Readers of Alberti's political poetry must attempt to assume one of these roles if they are to comprehend fully the poetry's content, purpose, and manner of expression.

Alberti's poetry of the thirties has not received the critical attention that it deserves. That it is worth our attention should be apparent from the foregoing chapters and my attempts at analyzing often critically neglected poetic texts, placing these texts within their sociohistorical contexts, and determining their value, be it aesthetic or instrumental. In the preceding chapters, I have tried to clarify the prominent role that Alberti and his poetry played within the evolutionary pattern of the poet's political works of that decade and the ones that were to follow. At the same time I have emphasized the importance of Alberti's political poetry of the thirties within the development of Spanish commitment literature of the twentieth century. Lastly, by setting Rafael Alberti's poetry of the era under consideration in its proper international perspective, I hope I have made clear that this poet's resounding public voice echos that of such poets as Vladimir Mayakovsky and Vladimir Kirilov and predates that heard in the poetic works of such writers as Louis Aragon, Pablo Neruda, and César Vallejo. It is an especially noteworthy public voice, since it helps to place Spanish political poetry at the fore of revolutionary verse in the twentieth century.

Following the defeat of the Republic, Alberti lived in political exile, first in Paris (1939–40), then in Argentina (1940–64), and later in Italy (1964–77). In exile, Alberti's poetry became more highly autobiographical when the poet reflected on the many aspects of his new life that would have special meaning for himself and his family: nostalgia for his homeland; the birth of his daughter Aitana; the sea now seen from a new locale; friends, new and old, some dead, others also in exile; his return to his first vocation, painting; and his recollections of the great artists who inspired him. But, above all, his poetry of this era is a search for equilibrium between the past and present.

The poetry written in exile, although frequently more introspective than that of the thirties, is nevertheless also attentive to "el compás del pulso" of its time. We find Alberti's poems exploring the failure of the Spanish revolution, the aftermath of the Spanish Civil War, the dangers of fascism and imperialism and, finally, the advent of "la primavera de los pueblos," as the poet has entitled one of the collections of this period. In exile, Alberti knows no geographical boundaries: his *pueblo*-protagonist takes on global dimensions when the "poeta en la calle" takes his subjects from western and eastern Europe, the Americas, China, the Soviet Union, and Vietnam. Alberti's political poetry is, thus, not isolated to the volatile thirties.

Throughout Rafael Alberti's poetry we witness various poetic personae, each seeking something he passionately desires. In the twenties, Alberti's many personal poetic voices search for the symbolic "lost paradise" and all that it means for the young poet. The displaced "marinero en tierra" longs for the metaphoric sea of his youth and the world of childhood innocence. The symbolic lost angels of *Sobre los ángeles* wander the earth in hope of discovering the meaning of the destruction of the poet's own soul. After 1930, however, the voices heard in Alberti's poetry pursue social and political goals and continually call for a new and better world for the now-adopted *pueblo*-protagonist.

On the occasion of his fiftieth birthday, Alberti summarized his life and work in verse in "Balada de la bicicleta con alas":

> He escrito y publicado inumerables versos.
> Casi todos hablan del mar
> y también de los bosques, los ángeles y las llanuras.
> He cantado las guerras justificadas,
> la paz y las revoluciones.
> Ahora soy nada más que un desterrado.
>
> (Ll. 7–12)

Thirty years later, Alberti still sings of nature, self, and politics. Today, however, Rafael Alberti is no longer "nada más que un desterrado." With the coming of democracy to Spain in 1977, Alberti returned to his homeland and began a new life in the new era he had, for so many years, sketched in his political verse. Alberti continues to draw inspiration from the collective quest he defined in his poetry of the thirties. In 1977, he was a Communist delegate in the Spanish parliament, a position from which he later resigned in order to devote his efforts to being a poet of the people. Always the committed poet, Rafael Alberti continues to frame in verse his vision of the Just Society.

Alberti's Political Poems
of the Thirties
Listed by the Magazines
in Which They Were Published

Octubre (page numbers are those of the 1977 Topos reprint)
   No. 2 (July–August 1933): 34 and 41. "La iglesia marcha sobre la cuerda floja" and "Allí la paz trabaja el horror a la guerra"
   No. 3 (August–September 1933): 68–69. "Himno de las bibliotecas proletarias"
   Nos. 4–5 (October–November 1933): 114–15. "Un fantasma recorre Europa"
El Mono Azul (page numbers are those of the 1975 Kraus reprint)
   No. 1 (27 August 1936): l. "Letrilla de EL MONO AZUL"
   No. 2 (3 September 1936): 12. "El último duque de Alba"
   No. 6 (1 October 1936): 44. "Radio Sevilla"
   No. 10 (29 October 1936): 76. "Defensa de Madrid"
   No. 11 (5 November 1936): 84. "Defensa de Cataluña"
   No. 14 (26 November 1936): 97. "La última voluntad del duque de Alba"
   No. 15 (11 February 1937): 103. "Los campesinos"
   No. 16 (1 May 1937): 112 and 113. "De río a río" and "A las Brigadas Internacionales"
   No. 23 (8 July 1937): 127. "Elegía a un poeta que no tuvo su muerte"
   No. 25 (22 July 1937): 131. "Quinto Cuerpo de ejército"
   No. 38 (28 October 1937): 157. "El mar está lejos"
   No. 40 (11 November 1937): 161. "Allí la paz trabaja el horror a la guerra"
   No. 45 (May 1938): 171. "1° de Mayo en la España Leal de 1938"
Hora de España (page numbers are those of the original magazine)
   No. 2 (February 1937): 29–32
      "Capital de la gloria"
      "Monte de El Pardo"

"Los campesinos"
"A 'Niebla' mi perro"
"Vosotros no caísteis"
No. 5 (May 1937): 35–38
   "A las Brigadas Internacionales"
   "Lejos de la guerra"
   "De río a río
No. 22 (October 1938): 17–22
   "1° de Mayo en la España Leal de 1938"
   "Odio a muerte"
   "Nocturno"
   "Al nuevo Coronel Juan Guilloto Modesto, lejano compañero de colegio en la
     Bahía de Cádiz"
   "El otoño y el Ebro"
   "Para luego"

Alberti's Political Poems of the Thirties Not Included in *Poesías completas*

From *Octubre:*
> "La iglesia marcha sobre la cuerda floja" (later published in *El burro explosivo*)
> "Himno de las bibliotecas proletarias"
> "Allí la paz trabaja el horror a la guerra" (also published *El Mono Azul*)

From *Consignas:*
> "¡Abajo la guerra imperialista!"
> "Sequía"
> "Aquí y allí"
> "Villancico de Navidad"
> "Balada de los doce leñadores"
> "Mitin"
> "Salutación al Ejército Rojo"

From *Un fantasma recorre Europa:*
> "Indice de familia burguesa española (mis otros tíos, tías, tías y tíos segundos)"
> "¡Salud, Revolución cubana!"
> "U.R.S.S."

From *El burro explosivo:*
> "El burro explosivo: Prólogo"
> "Epitafio a un presidente"
> "Al nuncio de S. S. en España"
> "In memoriam"
> "Gil en campaña"
> "A Gil crucificado"
> "Radio Sevilla" (also published in *El Mono Azul)*
> "El último duque de Alba" (also published in *El Mono Azul*)
> "La última voluntad del duque de Alba" (also published in *El Mono Azul*)

From *Nuestra diaria palabra:*
> "En la entrega de la bandera que el C.P. de Sevilla y el C.C. de las juventudes regalaron al Comité Central de Partido Comunista"
> "Colegio (S.J.)"

From *El Mono Azul:*
> "Letrilla de EL MONO AZUL"
> "Quinto Cuerpo de ejército"
> "El mar está lejos"

From *Hora de España:*
> "Odio a muerte"

From Octubre

La iglesia marcha sobre la cuerda floja

Un, dos, tres.
¿Quién va? ¿Quién es?

—A bendecir la cristiandad.
Mis oraciones
darán más fuego a sus cañones.
Mi agua bendita
redoblará su dinamita.
Nuestra Señora
será la dulce cargadora
de los fusiles
de sus guardias civiles
y Dios, el guía
de su secreta policía.

Un, dos, tres.
¿Quién va? ¿Quién es?

—Ven tú, banquero,
devoto y mártir del dinero.
Cristo te ampara.
Su Santidad y su piara.
El cielo eterno
yo le prometo a tu Gobierno,
paz en la tierra,
si al campesino hace guerra,
vida infinita,
si a los obreros se la quita.

Banquero, hermano,
sube hasta mi, dame la mano,
que si la cuerda
que si la cuerda
se rompe iremos a la mierda.

Himno de las bibliotecas proletarias

A luchar sin descansar,
trabajadores.
¡Sí!
Que de la tierra y de la mar
seremos los vencedores.

A estudiar para luchar,
trabajadores.
¡Sí!
Que ni en la tierra ni en la mar
quedarán explotadores.

Y en el viento se sentirá latir
la bandera de la Revolución.
¡Compañeros, uníos y seguid
la luz de los vencedores!

Y en el viento nuestra marcha abrirá
los caminos que van al porvenir.
¡Proletarios, en pie para luchar
contra los explotadores!

A luchar sin descansar,
trabajadores.
¡Sí!
Que de la tierra y de la mar
seremos los vencedores.

¡A estudiar para luchar,
trabajadores!

Acampemos bajo el sol
de las praderas.
¡Sí!
Bajo la sombra y el temblor
de los montes y riberas.

Y a estudiar para saber
qué son los ríos.
¡Sí!
Qué son las nubes y el llover,
la luz, el aire y los fríos.

De los libros recoged y arrancad
letra a letra lo que nos lleve al fin.
¡Camaradas, llegó la pleamar
para la cultura obrera!

¡Todo es nuestro! Los artes, la razon
de la ciencia, la Historia Natural.
¡Proletarios, repetid la canción
de la primavera obrera!

Acampemos bajo el sol
de las praderas.
¡Sí!
Bajo la sombra y el temblor
de los montes y riberas.

¡Acampemos bajo el sol
de las praderas!

Allí la paz trabaja el horror a la guerra

Allí la paz trabaja el horror a la guerra.
Labora allí la paz,
bloqueada de perros que por dientes enseñan bayonetas.
Y contra ese país
se construyen cañones,
se alimentan caballos,
se llena el mar de buques,
el viento de aviones,
y contra su aire puro,
contra sus hombres puros se preparan los gases de la muerte.
¿Conoces, camarada,
conoces tu país?
De él te viene la estrella que en la lucha te guía,
la fuerza que tu sangre reclama en cada hora.
¿Lo conoces tú bien?
Escucha. Se oyen balas contra la Unión Soviética.

From Consignas

¡Abajo la guerra imperialista!

Europa entera se arma para invadir la Unión Soviética. Obreros de todos los partidos, trabajan en las fábricas de municiones y material de guerra, que son las únicas que la crisis no ha cerrado aún. El ataque a la U.R.S.S. retardaría el éxito de la construcción socialista. Defendamos la patria de todos los trabajadores del mundo.

1

La guerra, viene la guerra,
la guerra que se prepara.
¡Trabajadores de Trubia,
no trabajéis en las fábricas!
España entrará en la guerra
como vasalla de Francia.
Si en Trubia se hacen cañones
y si en Trubia se hacen balas
y si en Sevilla y Toledo
se hacen armas,
estáis haciendo la muerte,
la misma muerte que os mata.
Es contra la Unión Soviética
la guerra que se prepara.

Trabajadores de Trubia,
trabajadores de España,
vuestros cañones zumbando,
silbando vuestras granadas,
vuestros sables, bayonetas,
bombas, fusiles y balas,
irán a dar con las vidas
que trabajan.
Vidas de obreros lejanos,
camaradas.

¡Alerta, trabajadores,
no trabajéis en las fábricas!

2

Llamará el Gobierno,
llamará a sus fuerzas,
sonando clarines,
izando banderas.

Pero los soldados
no irán a la guerra.

Mandará que zarpe
la escuadra que espera,
los fijos cañones
las bocas alerta.
Mas los marineros
no irán a la guerra.

Pedirá a las fábricas
las armas que puedan
repetir de muertos
el mar y la tierra.
Pero los obreros
no irán a la guerra.

Que nuestra consigna,
camaradas, sea:
un único frente
con la roja estrella
y en un rojo Octubre
convertir la guerra.

Sequía

Trata del desconcietro que produce la falta de lluvia en una aldea. Los curas, alejándose siempre de toda concepción científica, contribuyendo al adormecimiento del cerebro de los campesinos, y aprovechándose de su ignorancia, pretenden atraer la lluvia con el milagro. Al sentirse engañados, los campesinos, de una manera anárquica, se rebelan contra el cura y la Virgen. Apareciendo, al final, un camarada del Partido que despierta y encauza su conciencia de clase.

1

No llovía.
El mes de mayo avanzaba,
la tierra seca esperaba
y el trigo no florecía.

No llovía.
En nuestras pobres parcelas
se encontraba la sequía.

Vendrá el hambre.
Aún más hambre todavía.
No llovía.

2

El cuervo del cura
graznaba en la iglesia.
—¡Que llueva, que llueva,
Virgen de la Cueva!

Mujeres y hombres
y niños contestan.
—¡Que llueva, que llueva!

El cuervo se viste
traje de oro y seda.
—Los trigos no crecen,
los campos se secan.
¡Oh reina y señora,
riéganos la tierra!

Por prados de polvo
ya en hombros la llevan.
Y entre el humo y manchas
de gotas de cera,
el cuervo, graznando,
repite a la aldea.
—¡Que llueva, que llueva,
Virgen de la Cueva!

Y hombres y mujeres
y niños contestan.
—¡Que llueva, que llueva!

3

No llueve.
Ocho días, quince, veinte.
El trigo se está enfermando,
se está muriendo,
se muere.
Veinte días que no llueve.

4

¡Eh, camaradas!
Hemos rezado,
hemos gritado,
hemos perdido las gargantas.
Secas nuestras lenguas

y resquebrajadas.
¿Dónde está la lluvia,
camaradas?
La tierra,
como nuestras bocas,
se agrieta,
se muere sin agua.
¿Dónde está la Virgen,
camaradas?
Todos hemos sido
sus bestias de carga.
¿Y la flor del trigo
y de la cebada?
¡Alerta!
La Virgen no manda,
ni manda en el viento,
ni manda en el agua.
¡Al pozo con ella!
¿Quiénes nos engañan?
El cura,
los dueños.
¡Navajas!
¡Mueran, camaradas!

5

No,
camaradas.
Cerrad las navajas.
¡Muera la anarquía!
Mueran
la sangre, la muerte aisladas.
¡Masas!
Todos los hombres unidos.
Del brazo, el campo y la fábrica,
los soldados, los marinos.
¡Masas!
Contra la anarquía,
¡masas!
Contra la religión,
¡masas!
Contra las camisas negras
en Italia,
contra las camisas pardas
en Alemania,

contra las camisas azules
en España.
¡Masas!
Y el Partido Comunista,
rígido, al frente, guiándolas.
Así,
camaradas.

Aquí y allí

En la Unión Soviética, lo más maravilloso son los niños: limpios, sanos, alegres,
patinando por el río Moscoba helado, como bolas de pieles. Fuertes: la verdadera
realidad y porvenir de la Unión Soviética. Y no pude olvidarme de los hijos de los
trabajadores de España, especialmente de esos que vi a los campesinos pobres de
Extremadura.

1

Los niños de Extremadura
van descalzos.
¿Quién les robó los zapatos?

Les hiere el calor y el frío.
¿Quién les rompió los vestidos?
La lluvia
les moja el sueño y la cama.
¿Quién les derribó la casa?

No saben
los nombres de las estrellas.
¿Quién les cerró las escuelas?

Los niños de Extremadura
son serios.
¿Quién fué el ladrón de sus juegos?

2

Pero en la Unión Soviética . . .
                    La risa de los niños
se desprende en trineos por las cuestas heladas.
Sus ojos no conocen el espanto del crimen
ni sus oídos ese clamor que alza la sangre.

Allí, cuando se duermen, su mundo es un teatro
donde el trabajo nace y crece como un juego.

El mapa con que sueñan gira lleno de luces,
pero la que más brilla es una estrella roja.

Saben que ella ilumina otros cielos lejanos
y que calienta el pecho de otros niños y hombres,
niños que cuando duermen sólo ven la locura,
los llantos de la madre, la muerte o el presidio.

Son los hijos de Octubre, del campo y de la fábrica,
la realidad latente del sueño socialista.
Es Dios ante sus ojos un cuadro sin sentido
y los popes un viejo dibujo iluminado.

Son la gloria de Lenin, los martillos y hoces
que seguirán cantando su nombre y su memoria,
los que verán fundirse las naciones en una,
haciendo de la Tierra un planeta tranquilo.

Villancico de Navidad

Parodia político-religiosa de las canciones que se cantan en Nochebuena.

El Padre Santo dice misa.
La reina la escucha en camisa,
Alfonso XIII en calzoncillos.
El Papa
quiere cubrirlos con su capa.
La reina
devotamente se despeina.
El rey
moja en el cáliz sus bigotes.
Aparecen la mula y el buey.
Todos a una beben vino:
un cochino,
otro cochino.
Se emborrachan todos a una.
Al rey lo meten en una cuna.
Al rey
lo lamen la mula y el buey.
El Espíritu Santo se asoma.
La reina le da el pico a la Paloma.
Al Papa
le apuntan en la frente dos pitones.
Con ellos
a sus fieles les da las bendiciones.

Balada de los doce leñadores

Después de las represiones sufridas por los campesinos pobres en su ansia por conseguir los medios más elementales de vida—calor, comida, vivienda, etc.—, al abrirse las cárceles, una nueva luz les ilumina su conciencia. El Partido Comunista les conducirá, desde entonces, a la victoria.

Salieron con hachas
los leñadores.
Eran siete,
eran diez,
eran doce.

Cortaron leña, cortaron
la propiedad de los bosques.
(un tiro en la bruma.
En la yerba, un hombre).
Eran siete,
eran diez,
fueron once.

Tres horas más tarde ardieron
las serrerías del monte.
Toda la madera
relumbró la noche.
Se abrieron y se cerraron
las puertas de las prisiones.
Fueron siete,
fueron diez,
fueron once.

De las cárceles un día
salieron los leñadores.
Salieron hundidos,
más fieros y pobres.

Al Partido Comunista
dieron su fuerza y su nombre.
Y fueron las hachas
las mejores hoces.
Eran siete,
eran diez,
eran once.

Mitin

¡Camaradas!
Se acerca el alba de las manos arriba,
oídla,
el alba del espanto en los ojos biliosos de la usura,
el alba de la huída precipitada de los lechos,
el alba de la toma de los bancos,
el alba del asalto a las minas y fábricas,
el alba de la conquista de la tierra,
el alba de la derrota y expulsión de los ángeles,
el alba del aniquilamiento total de la monarquía celeste.
Ayer aún no se sabía el odio que las piedras y ladrillos guardan hacia las monjas,
hacia las cabezas peladas de los curas sifilíticos,
hacia los mercaderes de la fe y explotadores del analfabetismo en que se hunden
    los pueblos.
¡Arriba!
Las guadañas en alto,
segadores,
las hoces a la altura del hervor y la fiebre de la sangre.
¡Arriba!
Los martillos en alto,
trabajadores,
obreros de las fábricas que os derriban y os tumban en provecho del ansia de los
    buitres.
¡Arriba!
Las piquetas en alto,
hombres oscuros que arrojáis los pulmones y los ojos en la mazmorra negra de las
    minas.
¡Arriba!
Los fusiles en alto,
soldados que ignoráis el convenio con Francia para pronto apuntar vuestros cañones
    contra la Unión Soviética.
¡Arriba!
¡FRENTE UNICO!
Los relojes del Kremlin os saludan cantando la Internacional,
las radios de la U.R.S.S. os envían los hurras del Ejército Rojo,
de Madrid a Lisboa una estrella se agranda cubriendo todo el cielo
y silba el primer tren que no conoce las fronteras antiguas.
¡Arriba, camaradas!
¡Viva la Unión de las Repúblicas Soviéticas Iberas!

Salutación al Ejército Rojo

El Ejército Rojo ha cumplido este año el XV aniversario de su creación. Viniendo de
Sevilla, una noche, en Moscú, por la Plaza Roja nevada y anochecida, oímos unos

cantos. Poco después, avanzando lentamente, las largas bayonetas inclinadas en la mano caída, aparecieron dos patrullas de soldados. Una iniciaba la canción. La otra contestaba el estribillo. Preguntamos: ¿Qué cantan? Nos respondieron: Cantan la juventud y el esfuerzo soviéticos.

Sevilla está lejos, lejos,
en la otra punta de Europa.
Yo vengo desde Sevilla,
desde Sevilla la roja.
Con sangre de los obreros
el Guadalquivir se moja
Allí sin defensa muere
la juventud española.
Hoy el Gobierno de España
reina en Sevilla con pólvora.
Yo vengo a la Unión Soviética
desde Sevilla la roja.

Noche.
Nieve en Moscú, nieve aquí.
Sangre,
sangre en las calles, allí.
Por la nieve,
por la nieve y yo los vi.
Desnudas las bayonetas
van cantando,
por la nieve iban cantando.
Nieve aquí,
sangre allí.

Cantad, compañeros,
cantad, camaradas,
que vuestras canciones
levanten a España.
Sí, cantad más alto,
cantad, campañeros,
a los campesinos,
soldados y obreros.
Su sola defensa,
cantad, sois vosotros.
Sevilla la roja os grita:
¡Viva el Ejército Rojo!

Toda España arde.
Sevilla está en llamas.
Grita Extremadura

cruzada de balas.
En Asturias, huelgas
de minas y fábricas.
¡Cantad, compañeros!
De norte a sur pasa
un temblor de olas
revolucionarias.
Su única defensa,
cantad, sois vosotros.
España la roja os grita:
¡Viva el Ejército Rojo!

Desde la Unión a Sevilla
se yerguen muchas fronteras.
Para tender un camino
hay que morir o barrerlas.
La Revolución de Octubre,
soldados rojos, es nuestra.
Se alzarán con las ciudades
los que trabajan la tierra.
Y de este a oeste, cantando,
sólo pasará una estrella.

Vuelvo a Sevilla la roja,
vuelvo de la Unión Soviética.

From Un fantasma recorre Europa

*Indice de familia burguesa española (mis otros tíos, tías, tías y tíos
segundos)*

Venid, queridos, no sé si muy queridos, si nada queridos, si muy huéspedes
o transeúntes de mi sangre, venid, mi sangre os necesita para veros y
comprobar que fuísteis tontos, locos, engañados, hijos de vuestra clase,
y advertiros que otra se ha alzado frente a ella para muy pronto destruirla
y ser dueña del mundo.

Tías, tíos, tías y tíos terceros, cuartos, nebulosos, perdidos en la noche
cruel de los orígenes, secos afluentes de mi sangre que os llama, o sistema
de venas latientes todavía, venid.

Nicolás, borracho y desnudo sobre una mesa de tres patas, llorando a voces
en las iglesias oscuras, estirado y definitivo en una madrugada sin socorro
e incorporado al polvo bajo el disfraz de San Ignacio.

Guillermo, beodo y trasnochado en el escabel último de las puertas cerradas,
confesor y familiar del arzobispo de la diócesis.

Rafael, trapajo sucio en la punta de un palo, derribando murciélagos al
toque de Ánimas, emigrado y perdido en el trayecto ciego de su sangre.

Ignacio, caliche de todos los quicios en el inexplicable culo de sus
pantalones salomónicos, ojos desparejados y fogarata de coñac en el
vientre a cada vertiginoso misterio del rosario, flatos en las letanías,
explosión última de su cuerpo y visible evasión de su espíritu de vino
    hacia la gloria.

Tomás, cuatro dedos boleados de un tiro de fusil ante el asalto a los limones en el
    jardín del Papa.

Julio, ingeniero, corredor de vinos y poeta de la Virgen.

Javier, bello y analfabeto: la P, la A y la N, KAN.

José María, llamando el triste, beocio, filatélico y habitante en una
pajarera.

Vivos, muertos, lejanos y próximos, desvanecidos en la visita y recono-
cimiento de mi memoria de esta tarde, tíos, tías, sangre aún de pie o ya
en estado de vapor, en las nubes.

Josefa, galápaga de luto, enamorada del Santísimo, perseguida por príapos
imaginarios y nocturnos, errante y pobre por las iglesias y conventos.

Salud, monja de clausura, enterrada en un pozo de humedad desde los quince
años, amedrentada siempre por la bocinas de los autos, que ignora.

Milagros, superviviente en la catástrofe de todos sus hijos, lejana y
rígida en el centro de una sala de hielo, rodeada de retratos.

Ángela, huidiza y oscura, llorosa en las habitaciones de luces entornadas,
loca al final, perdida hoy en la casa de yo no sé qué pueblo.

Carmela, monja Reparadora.

Nieves y Concepción, hermanas Carmelitas.

Y esas, esos de vidas y nombres nublados que yo a veces escucho y siento
circular por el descanso o la fatiga de mi cuerpo, esas y esos, todos,
aquí, esta tarde, presentes en mi alcoba.

Moríos, o preparaos a la lucha, pues otra clase se ha alzado ante la vuestra para muy pronto destruirla y ser dueña del mundo.

¡Salud, Revolución cubana!

Nosotros estamos contigo,
nosotros te ofrecemos nuestro hombro,
nuestros puños cerrados,
toda nuestra energía,
la fuerza que hoy estalla bramando en nuestra sangre
al sentirse y saberse hermana de la tuya,
revolución cubana,
revolución obrera y campesina,
revolución de los trabajadores blancos,
de los trabajadores negros de la isla de Cuba.

Y te envíamos un saludo
y acordonamos desde aquí codo con codo lo largo de tus costas,
rodeadas de barcos que quieren destruirte,
arrancarte de cuajo de tu tierra,
hacer crecer con sangre tus plantaciones de azúcar y tabaco,
revolución obrera y campesina,
hermana,
amiga,
compañera,
revolución de todos los trabajadores de la isla de Cuba,
camarada.

Fuera,
atrás los colonos,
los que quieren hacer de tu riqueza patrimonio extranjero.
Cuba tiene su tierra.
¡Que sea suya!
Atrás los aviones,
los aeroplanos de la muerte que navegan por las rutas de sangre.
Cuba tiene su cielo.
¡Que sea suyo!

Atrás los marineros,
sus fusiles,
los buques que defienden los bancos y las fábricas
de dos,
de tres,
de cinco propietarios.

Cuba tiene su mar.
¡Que sea suyo!

La isla de Cuba tiene sus obreros,
tiene sus campesinos
y su Revolución.
¡Que sea suya!

¡Viva!

U.R.S.S.

(Entrada de noche)

Y ahora vamos por ti,
calumniada,
escupida,
bloqueada de perros que por dientes enseñan bayonetas,
mientras tú te defiendes trabajando,
haciéndote día y noche.
Por ti,
que das naranjas hacia el sur y corrientes eléctricas,
petróleo y oro por el este,
caviar al norte y osos blancos.
Por ti,
atravesándote hoy a oscuras,
espiada,
escupida,
provocada
patria de Lenin y de Octubre.

From El burro explosivo

El burro explosivo: Prólogo

No lo toques ya más,
que así es la rosa.
                    J. R. J.

Este es el burro hinchado en dinamita,
con ojos para ver lo que el ojete;

verga mortal en cada saca y mete,
bomba dentro del cuerpo que visita.

Burro que vuela y que de en medio quita
cuanto suena en los hombres a retrete,
que expulsa el rabo en sesgo de cohete
y los revienta en quien lo precipita.

Burro que borra, barre y que burrea
burreando en zig-zág, burro barreno
que todo lo encaraja y lo empalota.

Mas siendo de artificio también mea,
desprende en plastas moscas de veneno . . .
Y no lo toques más, que el burro explota.

Epitafio a un presidente

Ni a mirra y ámbar, sino a hedor de infierno,
pez muerta, pus, pis seco de letrina,
hiede esta tumba donde se amotina,
gusano funeral, el fuego eterno.

No fué un hombre, fué un Jefe de Gobierno,
una lega, una canca, una gallina,
tímida encarnación luciferina
de un congregante Luis de moco tierno.

Yace el tonto, repito, el Presidente,
aquel que en vida sólo fué Niceto,
risa del hambre de la pobre gente.

Con orín en su mármol firma ahora
este epitafio noble y de respeto:
FUÉ TONTO EN PRIEGO, EN ALCALÁ Y ZAMORA.

Al nuncio de S.S. en España

(Después de la represión de Asturias)

Ya, Monseñor, te aguardan las sangrientas
graderías del feudo vaticano.

Católico Apostólico Romano
es que las montes para rendir cuentas.

Remángate esas púrpuras violentas,
y esa mano de sangre, esa alba mano
grábala al Sacro Pío Onceno Ano,
Ano que tú en España representas.

Grábala, Monseñor, que mientras Roma
te exalta como flor de embajadores
y Gil como nodriza a lo divino,

vucla Niceto en forma de paloma,
excrementando pámpanos y flores,
al cieno celestial, de donde vino.

In memoriam

(Durante la República del bienio negro)

—¿Dónde está Gil? — Con Monseñor en cama.
—¿Dónde Alejandro, el ácrata terrible?
—Vela a los pies, de culo, antimarxible,
aguantando una vela ya sin llama.

—¿Y Niceto? —Repúblico en la grama.
—¿Bovino? —No bovino, sí burrible,
rumiando alguna yerba incomestible
que le alce el rabo y cagajone fama.

—¿Y el 14 de Abril? —Huele a difunto.
—¡Negras alfalfas, que a tan triste feto
coronen antes que la luz lo creme!

—¿Dónde está la República?, pregunto.
¿Dónde, dónde? Respóndeme, soneto.
—No en la CEDA, maricas: en la M.

Gil en campaña

(Elecciones de 1936)

Histérico anda Gil por las Españas,
vomitando Escoriales de despecho,

espermatorreando, ya deshecho,
goterones de hiel por las pestañas.

Negra casulla envuelta en telarañas,
culo de obispo aullando en do de pecho,
do de pecho de culo insatisfecho
que siembra soplos para dar cizañas.

A su pedo, a su voz, confesionarios,
caspas, conventos, mugres, sacristías,
herpes, caries, esputos, purgaciones,

formando un frente unido por rosarios,
surgen en sacrosantas cofradías
para encagajonar las elecciones.

A Gil crucificado

(Después del escándalo del Straperlo)

Le van a dar, le van . . . ¡No! Ya le dieron
un lancetazo en la tetilla izquierda,
brotando, en vez de sangre, pura mierda
por la herida mortal que le infligieron.

Bolsas, bolsos, bolsillos sucumbieron
—la desnudada España lo recuerda—
cuando a Gil de la CEDA o de la CERDA,
ya en la cruz, esa R le añadieron.

"Tengo sed" . . . Y bebió la sangre pura
de cinco mil heroicos asturianos
para ganarse el prometido cielo.

Después, vuelta a la diestra su amargura,
dijo a Lerroux, mirándole a las manos:
"Hoy estarás conmigo en la Modelo."

Radio Sevilla

¡Atención! Radio Sevilla.
Queipo de Llano es quien ladra,
quien muge, quien gargajea,
quien rebuzna a cuatro patas.
¡Radio Sevilla! —"Señores:

aquí, un salvador de España.
¡Viva el vino, viva el vómito!
Esta noche tomo Málaga;
el lunes, tomé Jerez;
martes, Montilla y Cazalla;
miércoles, Chinchón, y el jueves,
borracho y por la mañana,
todas las caballerizas
de Madrid, todas las cuadras,
mullendo los cagajones,
me darán su blanda cama.
¡Oh, qué delicia dormir
teniendo por almohada
y al alcance del hocico
dos pesebreras de alfalfa!
¡Qué honor ir al herradero
del ronzal! ¡Qué insigne gracia
recibir en mis pezuñas,
clavadas con alcayatas,
las herraduras que Franco
ganó por arrojo en Africa!
Ya se me atiranta el lomo,
ya se me empinan las ancas,
ya las orejas me crecen,
ya los dientes se me alargan,
la cincha me viene corta,
las riendas se me desmandan,
galopo, galopo . . . al paso.
Estaré en Madrid mañana.
Que los colegios se cierren,
que las tabernas se abran.
Nada de Universidades,
de Institutos, nada, nada.
Que el vino corra al encuentro
de un libertador de España."
—¡Atención! Radio Sevilla.
El general de esta plaza,
tonto berrendo en idiota,
Queipo de Llano, se calla.

El último duque de Alba

Señor duque, señor duque,
último duque de Alba,
mejor, duque del Ocaso,

ya sin albor, sin mañana.
Si tu abuelo tomó Flandes,
tú jamás tomaste nada,
sólo las de Villadiego,
por Portugal o por Francia.
Si tu abuelo, cruel, ilustre,
lustró de gloria tu casa,
tú lustraste los zapatos,
las zapatillas, las bragas
de algún torero fascista,
que siempre te toreara.
Si tu abuelo a Carlos V
le abría con una lanza
la bragueta emperadora
antes de entrar en batalla,
tú, en cambio, las manos trémulas,
impotente, abotonabas
los calzoncillos reales
del último rey de España.
Si a tu abuelo, el primer duque,
Ticiano le retratara,
tú mereciste la pena
de serlo por Zuloaga.
Un pincel se bañó en oro,
el otro se mojó en caca.
Duque, perdiste la aurora,
celador *honoris causa*
de El Prado, donde, desnuda
la duquesa Cayetana,
tú eras bedel de ombligo
que Goya le destapara.
Talento heredado, duque,
fortuna y gloria heredadas
son cosas que el mejor día,
de un golpe, las lleva el agua.
Vuélvete de Londres, deja,
si te atreves a dejarla,
la triste flor ya marchita,
muerta, de tu aristocracia,
y asoma por un momento
los ojos por las ventanas
de tu palacio incautado,
el tuyo, el que tú habitaras;
súbeles las escaleras,
paséalos por las salas,

por los salones bordados
de victoriosas batallas;
bájalos a los jardines,
a las cocheras y cuadras,
páralos en los lugares
más mínimos de tu infancia,
y verás cómo tus ojos
ven lo que jamás pensaran:
palacio más limpio nunca
lo conservó el pueblo en armas.
Las Milicias comunistas
son el orgullo de España.
Verás hasta los canarios,
igual que ayer, en sus jaulas;
los perros mover la cola
a sus nuevos camaradas;
y verás la que contigo
servidumbre se llamaba,
ya abolidas las libreas,
hablar de ti sin nostalgia.
Señor duque, señor duque,
último duque de Alba:
los comunistas sabemos
que la aurora no se para,
que el alba sigue naciendo,
de pie, todas las mañanas.
Si un alba muerta se muere,
otra mejor se levanta.

La última voluntad del duque de Alba

El labio imbécil, caído;
ojos de lagarto muerto;
la comprobada impotencia
reblandecida, hasta el suelo;
espiritado, mezquino,
triste lombriz en los huesos,
saliva el duque de Alba
su último infame deseo:
—"Id al palacio de Liria,
hoy sucia cuadra del pueblo,
id con bombas incendiarias,
con dinamita, con truenos,
con rayos que lo fulminen

y descuajen sus cimientos.
Que los que no ha ser mío,
prefiero dárselo al fuego."
Duque de Alba, duque de Alba,
en todo mi idioma encuentro
insultos con que clavarte,
palabras que echarte al cuello
como nudos corredizos
que estrangularan tu aliento.
No hay lengua para decirte
lo que nunca te dijeron.
Mas lo que yo no te diga,
te lo dirá un día el pueblo.
Brazo ejecutivo tiene,
puño tajante de hierro.
Acuérdate, señor duque,
triste gargajo siniestro,
el último que tu casta
escupiera como ejemplo,
como muestra de gusano
ya retepodrido y seco:
la historia de tu familia
la clausuras tú, corriendo,
no los cerrojos dorados
que colgaran tus abuelos
sobre las primeras puertas
que tan noblemente abrieron,
sino los más miserables
cerrojos de tu despecho.
Duque de Alba, duque de Alba,
señorito madrileño,
jamás soñaste un palacio
mejor que el que tú has deshecho,
mejor guardado, más limpio,
más lustroso, más espejo,
más del amor de unas manos
que nunca nada tuvieron.
Las manos que lo guardaban
no lloran de sentimiento,
lloran de rabia, de cólera,
y empuñan, alto, el remedio
que ha de terminar con gentes
como tú, canijo, perro,
mixto de cabrón y mona,
ni de España, ni extranjero,

hijo de ninguna parte,
rodado excremento muerto,
último duque de Alba,
alba triste, sin recuerdo.

From Nuestra diaria palabra

En la entrega de la bandera que el C.P. de Sevilla y el C.C. de las
juventudes regalaron al Comité Central del Partido Comunista

Por el río andaluz, por ese río que por preliminares
alza cuna de montes,
viendo la luz en sábanas de frío,
arrastrando, entre toros, olivares
hasta los marineros horizontes;
porque la voz de Lenin su agua moja
y su curso conquista,
no rueda verde el agua, sino roja;
que ya el Guadalquivir es comunista
y la Giralda espera
rizar pronto en su frente esa bandera,

¡Salud, las Juventudes!
¡Honor a los obreros de Sevilla!
El Comité Central—el puño erguido,
que no se dobla y que jamás se humilla—,
ante las multitudes
que ven en él la estrella del Partido,
contra toda la España reaccionaria,
la España en agonía,
recibe esa bandera de alegría,
esa bandera revolucionaria.

Mojada de paisaje
de fina oliva y cielo marismeño,
del Sur, en hombros, a Castilla llega;
aunque en andaluz diga su lenguaje,
el mismo rojo y desvelado sueño
de victoria final iza y despliega;
que es de un color, que es una, que a su lado,
por las armas, verán si se le entrega
todo el poder para el proletariado.

Colegio (S.J.)

Nos dijeron que no éramos de aquí,
que éramos viajeros,
gente de paso,
huéspedes de la tierra,
camino de las nubes.

Nos espantaron las mañanas,
llenándonos de horror los primeros días,
las noches lentas de la infancia.
Nos educaron sólo para el alma.

(Hay allá abajo una cisterna,
un hondo aljibe de demonios,
una orza de azufre,
de negra pez hirviendo.
Hay un triste colegio de fuego,
sin salida.)

Nos espantaron las mañanas.

Pero quien obedezca al que firmó la rosa,
a Aquel que nos concede el desayuno
y surte en el verano la casa de la hormiga,
quien dé crédito y ame
al que dejó a los pobres tirados en el barro
y sentó en cambio a nuestros padres sobre los caballos.
ése verá que le abren paso las estrellas,
los celestes canales que paran en los muelles
donde las almas desembarcan,
en las puertas que dan principio a su reinado.

Nos educaron,
así,
fijos.
Nos enseñaron a esperar
con la mirada puesta más allá de los astros,
así,
extáticos.

Pero ya para mí se vino abajo el cielo.

From El Mono Azul

Quinto Cuerpo de ejército

A Modesto, su jefe

Los pobres de alpargata, rotos, descamisados,
ésos que tantas veces tuvieron por abrigo
de sus huesos diez húmedos ladrillos desvelados
y cuatro mudas, sórdidas paredes por amigo;
ésos, entre los cardos, las piedras, los calores,
miradlos vencedores.

Los que continuamente y entre torvas señales
fueron, por su conducta y limpida fe, escupidos;
sus manos, registradas entre las criminales
huellas de los ladrones, homicidas, bandidos;
entre heridas, gangrena, llantos, gritos, dolores,
miradlos vencedores.

Modesto, cuyo nombre en las aserradoras
suena gloriosamente con un son carpintero;
"Campesino", en las eras y entre las trilladoras;
Lister, entre los duros picos de un son cantero;
por la sangre, las tumbas, la sed, los estertores,
miradlos vencedores.

Ellos, analfabetos, decalzos, cargadores
de vida amarga y sacos sólo grandes de penas;
ellos, los más difíciles, nuevos libertadores
de Madrid y alicates de sus largas cadenas;
ellos, entre las balas, los himnos y las flores,
miradlos vencedores.

El mar está lejos

El mar está lejos;
la guerra está cerca.
Déjame que me vaya y no vuelva.

El mar está cerca;
la guerra está lejos.
Dejo la mar y vuelvo.

Letrilla de EL MONO AZUL

EL MONO AZUL tiene manos,
monos que no son de mono,
que hacen amainar el tono
de monos que son marranos.
No dormía,
ni era una tela planchada
que no se comprometía.

EL MONO AZUL sale ahora
de papel, pues sus papeles
son provocarle las hieles
a Dios Padre y su señora.
¡A la pista,
pistola ametralladora,
mono azul antifascista!

¡Mono azul!: salta, colea,
prudente como imprudente,
hasta morir en el frente
y al frente de la pelea.
(Ya se mea
el general más valiente.)

¡Salud!, mono miliciano,
lleno, inflado, no vacío,
sin importarle ni pío
no ser jamás mono-plano.
Tu fusil
también se cargue de tinta
contra la guerra civil.

From Hora de España

Odio a muerte

Para ellos, los tíficos pantanos,
los pálidos, febriles lodazales,
las pestíferas charcas macilentas,
los vengativos, despiadados mares.
        No los socorra nadie.
Toquen un niño y se les vuelva un tigre;
una mujer, y en zarpa se les cambie;

que al caminar, un duro y seco polvo
les calcine el pulmón y pudra el aire.
        No los conozca nadie.
Todo púas, aristas, dientes, filos.
panoramas de rabia, sed y alambres.
España arisca, de feroces uñas,
agria de piel y lomo intransitable.
        No los entierre nadie.
Morid aquí, productos de hombre y hombre,
híbradas bestias, maricones madres,
lejos de vuestro suelo, triste Italia,
del suelo vuestro, fríos alemanes.
        No los recuerde nadie.

Notes

Chapter 1. Introduction

1. Solita Salinas de Marichal, *El mundo poético de Rafael Alberti* (Madrid: Gredos, 1968), 10.
2. *Marinero en tierra, Poesías, 1924* (Madrid: Biblioteca Nueva, 1925); *La amante, canciones, 1925* (Málaga: Imprenta Litoral, 1926); *El alba del alhelí (1925– 1926)* (Santander: Edición para amigos de José María de Cossío, 1927); *Cal y canto (1926–1927)* (Madrid: Revista de Occidente, 1929); *Sobre los ángeles (1927–1928)* (Madrid: Iberoamericana, 1929). The poems of the series entitled *Yo era un tonto y lo que he visto me ha hecho dos tontos* never appeared as a collection. Fourteen of these poems were, however, published individually in *La Gaceta Literaria,* nos. 58, 60–62, 64–66, 71 (May–December 1929). *Sermones y moradas,* written during 1929–30, remained unpublished as a grouping of poems until 1935, when it appeared in *Poesía: 1924–1930* (Madrid: Cruz y Raya, 1935).
3. "Diario de un día," *Poemas de Punta del Este (1945–1956), PC,* 790. All quotations from Rafael Alberti's poetry, unless otherwise indicated, are from *PC.*
4. "Siervos," l. 9. The auto-denomination "poeta en calle" serves as the title of a collection of Alberti's political poems written during 1931–36 and later published in *Poesía: 1924–1937* (Madrid: Signo, 1938). Alberti's statement originally appeared in *Poesía: 1924–1930,* 2; the translation is by Angel Flores, *A Spectre Is Haunting Europe: Poems of Revolutionary Spain* (New York: Critics Group, 1936), 9. The concept of "commitment" is discussed by Adereth, *CMFL,* 15–51. Also see Jean-Paul Sartre, *What Is Literature?* trans. Bernard Frechtman (New York: Philosophical Library, 1949), which contains the greater part of *Situations II* (Paris: Gallimard, 1947–49), vols. 1–3; Theodor Adorno, "Commitment," *New Left Review* (1974); 87–88; Charles Glicksberg, *The Literature of Commitment* (Lewisburg, Pa.: Bucknell University Press, 1976); Eugene F. Kaelin, "Literature of Commitment" and "Committed Literature, Second Phase," in *An Existentialist Aesthetic: The Theories of Sartre and Merleau-Ponty* (Madison: University of Wisconsin Press, 1966), 91–116, 136–55; John Mander, *The Writer and Commitment* (London: Secker and Warburg, 1961); and Renée Winegarten, *Writers and Revolution: The Fatal Lure of Action* (New York: New Viewpoint-Watts, 1974). Johan Lechner addresses Alberti's position within the evolution of commitment literature in Spain in the early thirties (*CPE,* 67, 87–98, 116).

5. "Con los zapatos puestos tengo que morir (Elegía cívica) (1° de enero de 1930)" was first published in *Poesía: 1924–1930; El burro explosivo* (Madrid: Quinto Regimiento, n.d.) was begun in 1934 and published sometime during the Spanish Civil War; *Nuestra diaria palabra* (Madrid: Héroe, 1936); *De un momento a otro (poesía e historia) (1932–1937)* (Madrid: Europa-América, 1937), *El poeta en la calle (1931–1936)*. The last two collections were gathered into Alberti's *Poesía. 1924–1937* (1938). See Robert Marrast, "Essai de bibliographie de Rafael Alberti," *Bulletin Hispanique* 57 (1955): 147–77, and also the second part of this bibliography in *Bulletin Hispanique* 59 (1957): 430–35. Also see the Alberti bibliography in *PC*.

6. The quotation is from Jean-Paul Sartre, cited in Adereth, *CMFL*, p. 27. The term *pueblo* denotes the common people, the common man, the working class. In Spanish it is a term often used in the broader senses of community and nation. For the sake of convenience, I use the English terms *people, common people,* and *common man* as equivalents.

7. "Aniversario," l. 11.

8. Jaime Concha, prologue, *Pablo Neruda: Poemas inmortales* (Santiago, Chile: Impresa Editora Nacional Quimantu, 1971), 9.

9. In a discussion of the literature of the Spanish Civil War and the writers who wrote on behalf of the People's Cause, John Muste notes that many of these writers "thought they had found in Marxism a means to contain and control the element of violence which is so clearly the center of twentieth-century life and of twentieth-century fiction. . . . To writers born between 1900 and 1940, religion, nationalism, and democratic internationalism were unable to provide meaningful explanations of the upheavals of our time, or even means for comprehending them. This explains the desperation with which so many embraced Marxism in the thirties; it was the last chance, and for a while it seemed the best chance" (*Say That We Saw Spain Die: Literary Consequences of the Spanish Civil War* [Seattle: University of Washington Press, 1966], 191).

10. Sergei Eisenstein writes, "Of all living beings on earth . . . we have the privilege of participating collectively in making a new human history," *P*, 16.

11. Louis MacNeice has observed of the poets of *New Signatures:* "The primary characteristic of these poets is that they are interested in a subject outside themselves—or at any rate in a subject which is not merely a subject for their poetry. . . . being poets, and not propagandists or journalists, they approach their subject, though an outside subject, through themselves" (*MP*, 17).

12. René Wellek and Austin Warren, *Theory of Literature,* 3d ed. (New York: Harcourt Brace Jovanovich, 1975), 73.

13. The approaches of the following theorists and critics have influenced my study: Amado Alonso, *Materia y forma en poesía,* 3d ed. (Madrid: Gredos, 1965); Dámaso Alonso, *Poesía española: Ensayo de métodos y límites estilísticos,* 4th ed. (Madrid: Gredos, 1962); Carlos Bousoño, *Teoría de la expresión poética,* 5th ed. (Madrid: Gredos, 1970); Cleanth Brooks, *The Well Wrought Urn: Studies in the Structure of Poetry* (1947; reprinted, New York: Harcourt Brace Jovanovich, 1975); Philip Wheelwright, *The Burning Fountain: A Study in the Language of*

Symbolism (Bloomington: Indiana University Press, 1968); and William K. Wimsatt, *The Verbal Icon*, 2d ed. (New York: Noonday Press, 1958).

14. Eisenstein, *Film Form: Essays in Film Theory* and *The Film Sense*, ed. and trans. Jay Leyda (Cleveland: World, 1967), 37.

15. "Madrid-Otoño," l. 36; "Abril, 1938," l. 8.

16. "De ayer para hoy," ll. 1, 3, 4.

17. Most notably these critics are Johan Lechner (*CPE*) and Juan Cano-Ballesta (*PEPR*).

18. See for example, Anonymous, "An Andalusian Poet," *Times Literary Supplement* (London), March 6, 1948, pp. 129–30; José Francisco Cirre, *Forma y espíritu de una lírica española (1920–1925)* (Mexico City: Gráfica Panamericana, 1950); Vicente Gaos, *Antología del grupo poético del 27* (Salamanca: Biblioteca Anaya, 1965); Eduardo González Lanuza, "Homenaje a Rafael Alberti," *Sur*, no. 281 (March–April, 1963): 52–62, and *Rafael Alberti* (Buenos Aires: Ediciones Culturales Argentinas, 1965); also Alberto Monterde, *La poesía pura en la lírica española* (Mexico City: Universitaria, 1953).

Chapter 2. The Poet, Society, and the Image of Disorder

1. Cited in Guillermo de Torre, *Historia de las literaturas de vanguardia* (Madrid: Guadarrama, 1965), 447; also cited by Juan Cano-Ballesta, *PEPR*, 137.

2. Gerald Brenan, *The Spanish Labyrinth: An Account of the Social and Political Background of the Civil War* (New York: Macmillan, 1943), 30–85, discusses Alfonso XIII's reign, the *pronunciamiento* of General Primo de Rivera and the confusion, instability, corruption, and repression in this era. Also see Melchor Fernández Almagro, *Historia política de la España contemporánea, 1897–1902*, vol. 3 (Madrid: Alianza, 1968); Eduardo de Guzmán, *1930: Historia política de un año decisivo* (Madrid: Tebas, 1973); Hector Vásquez-Azpiri, *De Alfonso XIII al Príncipe de España* (Barcelona: Nauta, 1973).

3. For the poet's recollection and assessment of this period, see *AP*, especially 146–47, 275–78, 290–93, 301–2.

4. See Wellek and Warren, *Theory of Literature*, 73–135, regarding "extrinsic" approaches to the study of literature.

5. Eisenstein, *FF*, 37–38.

6. Eisenstein writes, "Two film pieces of any kind, placed together, inevitably combine into a new concept, a new quality, arising out of that juxtaposition." This "new quality," he goes on to say, is "the thematic matter . . . the image of the theme itself" (*FS*, 4). In the *Art of Assemblage* (New York: Museum of Modern Art, 1961), William Seitz observes that Eisenstein's principle of montage, as the director himself has stated, is not solely a cinematic method and concept (p. 151). That Alberti was aware of this concept and technique is evident from his memoirs; see *AP*, 278–79. As will be shown in chapter 3, the method of montage also underlies Alberti's "Un fantasma recorre Europa" of 1933. Eisenstein, as a Marx-

ist, "believed that the law of the dialectical conflict and synthesis of opposites could provide principles of dynamic editing in film" (David Bordwell and Kristin Thompson, *Film Art* [Reading, Mass.: Addison-Wesley, 1979], 179). At this point in time, Alberti had not yet undergone his own conversion to Marxism. This would occur during the next two years. It is interesting to note, however, that Alberti's use of his own version of the principle of montage symbolically underscores and perhaps even foreshadows the eventual Marxist dialectic and synthesis that would later characterize his world view and the subject matter and themes of his political poetry written after 1930. This is especially evident, as we shall see, in the poem "Un fantasma recorre Europa."

7. For studies on surrealism and Spain see Vittorio Bodini, *Los poetas surrealistas españoles* (Barcelona: Tusquete, 1971), originally *I Poeti Surrealisti Spagnoli* (Rome: Guilo Einaudi Editore, 1963); Paul Ilie, *The Surrealist Mode in Spanish Literature* (Ann Arbor: University of Michigan Press, 1970); Juan Larrea, *Del surrealismo a Machupicchu* (Mexico City: Editorial Joaquín Mortiz, 1967); Morris, *SS;* Gustav Siebenmann, *Los estilos poéticos en España desde 1900,* trans. Angel San Miguel (Madrid: Gredos, 1973); and Torre, *Historia de las literaturas.* Specifically on Alberti and surrealism, see Bodini, *Los poetas,* 60–66; Ilie, *The Surrealist Mode,* 121–30; Morris, *SS,* 43–48; Eric Proll, "The Surrealist Element in Rafael Alberti," *Bulletin of Hispanic Studies* 18 (April 1941): 70–82, and Siebenmann, *Los estilos poéticas,* 316–23.

8. *El poeta en la calle: Poesía civil, 1931–1965, Selección,* Colección Ebro (Paris: Librairie du Glober, 1966), pp. 9–10, reprinted in *PEC.*

9. Alberti's use of versicles is not unique to the "Elegía cívica." Lengthy poetic lines are common in *Sermones y moradas* and, to a limited extent, in a few of the poems of *Sobre los ángeles.*

10. Morris observes: "The surrealists were too embittered by the war to see any glory in combat under the French flag, on which Aragon defecated in *Le Paysan de Paris* and on which Sadoul and Caupenne spat in the letter they sent young Keller urging him not to enter Saint-Cyr" (*SS,* 67). Alberti's narrator's actions are in line with these. The references are to Aragon, *Le Paysan de Paris,* 10th ed., 219, and "A. M. Keller, reçu premier à l'Ecole Militaire de Saint-Cyr (Seine-et-Oise)," *Le Surrealisme au Service de la Révolution,* no. 1 (July 1930): 34 cited in *SS,* 176.

11. Alberti, "Se reciben bahías," *El Sol* (18 August 1931), reprinted in Robert Marrast, *Alberti, Prosas encontradas: 1924–1942,* 2d ed. (Madrid: Ayuso, 1973), 68, and "Rafael Alberti, prosas retrouvés (1931–1932)," *Bulletin Hispanique* 70 (1968): 494.

12. In November 1929, Alberti had already demonstrated his rebellious spirit and his desire to provoke the public when he delivered a lecture before the Lyceum Club Femenino of Madrid. This rather Dada-inspired, farcical demonstration was later termed a "scandalous" performance. See "Un 'suceso' literario," *La Gaceta Literaria* 3, no. 71 (December 1929): 5, reprinted in *AP,* 282–89; Carlos Alberto Pérez, "Rafael Alberti: Sobre los tontos," *Revista Hispánica Moderna* 32 (1966): 207, also comments on this event. García Lorca's own rebellious spirit and "violent protest" are evident not only in *Poeta en Nueva York* but also in the screenplay

Un viaje a la luna. The latter work was written in 1929 in New York after the poet saw *Un Chien Andalou.* See Morris's discussion of the script in *TLD,* 127–34.

13. *Coplas de Juan Panadero* (Montevideo: Pueblos Unidos, 1949).

14. In a letter to Vittorio Bodini, 7 October 1959, Alberti stated: *"Sobre los ángeles es un libro profundamente español, producto de ciertas catástrofes internas que entonces sufrí, unidas al ambiente de violencia y disconformidad que imperaba en España durante el descenso de la Dictadura de Primo de Rivera. Sermones y moradas, Elegía cívica, aunque parezca que no, Yo era un tonto, participan del mismo aire"* (Bodini, *Los poetas,* 115–16).

15. See Brenan, *Spanish Labyrinth,* 85. One such plot, involving Fermín Galán, is recalled in *AP,* 302. This plot inspired Alberti's first political play, *Fermín Galán (romance de ciego en tres actos, diez episodios y un epílogo)* (Madrid: Plutarco, 1931), reprinted in Alberti, *Teatro de agitación política 1933–1939* (Madrid: Edicusa, 1976).

16. W. Lewis Jones, *King Arthur in History and Legend* (Cambridge: Cambridge University Press, 1933), 75; Fernández Almagro, *Historia política de la España,* 299; Vásquez-Azpiri, *De Alfonso XIII,* 25. It is also possible that with this allusion to "Arturo," Alberti wishes both to underscore and criticize Alfonso's role in the Spanish political arena.

17. Edward Gibbon, *The Decline and Fall of the Roman Empire,* vol. 1 in *Great Books of the Western World,* vol. 40 (Chicago: William Benton, 1952), 31. Vásquez-Azpiri, *De Alfonso XIII,* 10, notes that throughout his reign Alfonso XIII never referred to the people as the *pueblo.* Rather, he preferred to call them *la plebe, la canalla,* and *la soez canalla.* The use of such names was insulting to the people themselves. Brenan, *Spanish Labyrinth,* 58, further points out that during World War I Alfonso XIII remarked, " 'Only myself and the *canaille* are on the side of the Allies.' . . . It was not every King who would habitually have spoken of the immense majority of his subjects—both the middle class and the workers—as the *canaille."* Don Miguel Maura observes, "Un rey que se preciaba de 'popular' y deseaba serlo, no veía ni hablaba al 'pueblo' sino en las ceremonias oficiales de inauguración entre muchedumbres aleccionadas en el entusiasmo, o en esas pobres y encogidas escenas de las audiencias palatinas" (*Así cayó Alfonso XIII,* cited in Vásquez-Azpiri, *De Alfonso XIII,* 16).

18. J. E. Cirlot, *A Dictionary of Symbols,* trans. Jack Sage (New York: Philosophical Library, 1962), 160.

19. Cirlot, *Dictionary of Symbols,* 160–61. It is also possible that the ailing political figure of the poem is an allusion to General Primo de Rivera's failing health during the last years of his life. The "estertores" (l. 9) could allude to his consumption, the disease from which he died in 1931; see Vásquez-Azpiri, *De Alfonso XIII,* 72.

20. All works by Federico García Lorca that are mentioned in the text can be found in *OC.*

21. García Lorca, "Panorama ciego de Nueva York," l. 5, and "Paisaje de la multitud que orina," l. 19.

22. Alberti recalls, "Algunos poemas iniciales del libro que más tarde sería *Poeta en Nueva York,* aparecieron en revistas madrileñas o en otras provenientes de la isla

de Cuba" during the year 1929 (*AP*, 293). It is highly possible that many of García Lorca's poems influenced Alberti's own poetry of this same period. It is also possible, however, that Alberti's poetry influenced García Lorca's. Bodini, *Los poetas*, 109, lists the seven poems of *Poeta en Nueva York* published during García Lorca's lifetime.

23. Morris observes that "Alberti stressed the interdependence of words and pictures when he stated in 1961: 'Je suis un poète visuel, comme tous les poètes andalous, depuis Góngora jusqu'à García Lorca. Ma poésie est une poésie plastique. J'aime beaucoup préciser le contour des choses. . . . Je crois que chez moi le poète est un prolongement du peintre, que le peintre aide le poète' " (*TLD*, 87). "Rafael Alberti a l'agrégation d'espagnol. Un entretien avec Pablo Vives" (*Les Lettres Françaises*, no. 901 [16–22 November 1961]: 4). Morris, *SS*, 47, suggests that there is an intimate correspondence between the surrealist paintings of Maruja Mallo and a few of the poems of *Sobre los ángeles* and *Sermones y moradas*. This second section of the "Elegía cívica" also could be considered as an extension of what the critic terms the "common vision of universal decay and decomposition" painted by the artist and described by the poet.

24. Kenneth Burke, "Four Master Tropes," in *A Grammar of Motives* (1945), cited in *Princeton Encyclopedia of Poetry and Poetics* (Princeton: Princeton University Press, 1974), 840. Alberti makes use of many of these same stylistic techniques, especially the juxtaposition of opposites, accumulations of adverbs and preposi- tional phrases of place, and synecdoche in "Los ángeles muertos" of *Sobre los ángeles*.

25. This image brings to mind García Lorca's cosmic vision of destruction and "la circuncisión de un niño muerto" in "La luna pudo detenerse al fin," *Poeta en Nueva York*.

26. Morris, *SS*, 252, cites one such Daliesque litany of decay: ". . . ¿Que he renegat, potser? . . ." (*L'Amic de les Arts*, no. 30 [December 1928]: 233). Alberti's own catalogs of death and decomposition are found in, for example, "Los ángeles muertos" and, from *Sermones y moradas*, "Espantapájaros" and "Elegías."

27. Morris, *SS*, 4. It is curious that the critic does not discuss Alberti's "Elegía cívica."

28. Stylistically, the second section of Alberti's elegy to Fernando Villalón in "Ese caballo ardiendo por las arboledas perdidas" of *Sermones y moradas* can be related to the fifth section of the "Elegía cívica." In both, repeated syntactic patterns and the use of anaphora form an intricate part of the poems' final gradations.

29. Morris, *SS*, 146.

30. Cirlot, *Dictionary of Symbols*, 6.

31. Cirlot, *Dictionary of Symbols*, points out that the number two symbolically repre- sents "conflict and counterpose or contrapositions; . . . the momentary stillness of forces in equilibrium" (p. 221); the number two is also associated with the "focal point of symbolic Inversion" (p. 222). In Alberti's political allegory "Ele- gía cívica," the conflict, collision, and inversion of the opposing forces of death/life, evil/good, "tú"/"muchedumbre de tacones," occurs "a las dos en punto de la tarde" (l. 43).

32. Cirlot, *Dictionary of Symbols,* 154.

33. Lucille F. Becker, *Louis Aragon* (New York: Twayne, 1971), 19, observes, "In 1930, Aragon participated in the Congress of Revolutionary writers in Kharkov and, upon his return, published in an issue of the Surrealist publication, *Le Surréalisme au service de la révolution,* an article entitled 'Le surréalisme et le devenir révolutionnaire.' This was his final attempt to maintain his autonomy as a Surrealist while recognizing the common interest of the Surrealist and Communist movements. He has since described that article as 'a desperate attempt, the last, to reconcile the attitude that had been mine for years and the new reality with which I came into contact' [*Pour un réalisme socialiste* (Paris: Denoel et Stéel, 1935), p. 16]." Aragon, in the essay-speech "Le retour a la réalité" (25 June 1935), proclaims, "Je réclame le retour à la réalité" (pp. 82–87). Torre notes that during 1935, "Aragon . . . publicaba un librito—*Pour un réalisme socialiste*—en que predicaba el 'retorno a la realidad,' sin dejar de utilizar las mismas frases de Lautréamont, invocadas desde años antes por los superrealistas 'La poesía debe tener por fin la verdad práctica' y 'La poesía debe ser hecho por todos, no por uno' " (*Historia de las literaturas,* 392). Cano-Ballesta points out that the Spain of the 1930s "es un momento en que se maneja conceptos como 'regresar a la realidad, después de la prueba del expresionismo,' 'nueva objetividad,' 'pintura social,' tomados generalmente de las artes plásticas, que desde varias generaciones se han puesto a la vanguardia de los movimientos artísticos, como occure en el mismo surrealismo" (*PEPR,* 138). That Alberti's poetry demonstrated this "return" as early as 1 January 1930 is significant and not to be overlooked.

34. Becker, *Louis Aragon,* 38.

35. Each of the following critics discusses in either a few paragraphs or a few sentences Alberti's extensive political allegory: Bodini, *Los poetas,* 66; Lechner, *CPE,* 57; Morris *TLD,* 80–81; Pedro Salinas, *Literatura española del siglo XX* (Madrid: Alianza, 1970), 190; Emilia de Zuleta, *Cinco poetas españoles* (Madrid: Gredos, 1971), 338–39. An earlier version of my analysis of this poem appears as "Ordering the Chaos: Rafael Alberti's 'Elegía cívica' " *Hispannofila* (in press).

36. Alberti's change in focus is first evident in *Sermones y moradas* and even more apparent in *El hombre deshabitado* (Madrid: Plutarco, 1930). Cano-Ballesta, *PEPR,* 112–13, briefly outlines this evolution, although he does not discuss the "Elegía cívica." *Sermones y moradas* is both personal and social in that it is an analysis of the troubled state of the *yo*'s own soul (and in this way an extension of *Sobre los ángeles*) and also a brief and not well developed study of the *yo* in relationship to society. It is, however, not political. Alberti neither directly focuses on the affairs of state nor does he offer a political solution regarding how these affairs could or should be changed. In many ways, this collection does, thematically speaking, foreshadow the "Elegía cívica," especially if the motifs of the "ola" and "la ira inocente de un rey" of "Sermon de las cuatro verdades" and "un alba gritó: ¡la guerra!" of "Morada del alma que espera la paz" are considered. In addition, the poet's portrayal of rotting civilization in "Espantapájaros" and "Elegías," as I have pointed out, foreshadows section 2 of the "Elegía cívica." In the latter poem, however, the cause of the figurative decay of human life is identified and criticized, while in the former poems it is abstract. See Ilie,

The Surrealist Mode, 121–30, and G. W. Connell, "The End of a Quest: Alberti's *Sermones y moradas* and Three Uncollected Poems," *Hispanic Review* 32 (July 1965): 290–309, for discussions of this collection.
37. "El alma en pena," l. 1.

Chapter 3. The Poet, the People, and a New Human History

1. Louis Aragon's first visit to the USSR was in 1930; see *Les critiques de notre temps et Aragon* (Paris: Garnier, 1976), 180. Adereth observes: "One of the most important steps he took with his wife was a visit to the Soviet Union in 1930. What he saw there filled him with enthusiasm. Until then, his attachment to Communism had been chiefly an emotional impulse, now he was able to watch a whole people at work. . . . He needed this concrete experience in order to make his commitment complete. When he returned to home he was 'no longer the same man' " (*CMFL*, 89–90). See also Aragon, *Pour un réalisme socialiste,* 53.
2. For Alberti's impressions of the first Five-Year Plan in the USSR of the early thirties, see Marrast, *Prosas encontradas,* 141–63, reproduced in *PEC,* 455–79. Alberti's observations were originally published in *Luz* (22, 26, 28 July and 8 August 1933). In addition to Aragon, César Vallejo was also greatly impressed by the emergent new society of the USSR in the early thirties. James Higgins says: "Vallejo saw the new society in the process of being born in Russia and in Spain. *Rusia en 1931* reveals that he believed that his ideas were in the process of being realized in the Soviet Union" (introduction to *César Vallejo: An Anthology of His Poetry* [Oxford: Pergamon Press, 1970], 72). For Alberti's own observations regarding his friendships with the writers of the *Unión Internacional de Escritores Revolucionarios,* see Marrast, *Prosas encontradas,* 149–57. Curiously, Alberti makes no reference to his actual conversion to Marxism in the "Indice autobiográfico" of *PC.*
3. The poetry cited in this chapter is from the 1933 collections *Consignas* and *Un fantasma recorre Europa* (*C* and *UFRE*). The punctuation, capitalization, spacing of lines, and diction correspond to the original and not to the poems as they appear in *PC.* After much investigation, the only copies of the 1933 collections that I could locate and use were found in private libraries in Spain, especially the Biblioteca-Museo José María de Cossío, Tudanca, Spain. Seven of the eleven poems of *Consignas* and three of the six poems of *Un fantasma recorre Europa* do not appear in *PC;* they are reproduced in appendix B. Lechner does not quote these poems; Cano-Ballesta gives their titles and occasionally quotes portions of them, although he does not analyze them in detail. For historical background to the period under consideration and the problems encountered by the First Republic in Spain, see Brenan, *Spanish Labyrinth,* 229–97; Raymond Carr, *Spain, 1808–1975,* 2d ed. (Oxford: Clarendon Press, 1982), 603–51; Melchor Fernández Almagro, *Historia de la República española 1931–1936* (Madrid: Alianza, 1940);

Gabriel Jackson, *A Concise History of the Spanish Civil War* (New York: John Day, 1974), 11–42; Hugh Thomas, *The Spanish Civil War* (London: Pelican Books, 1965), 23–161.

4. This influence is certainly seen in the poetry of Emilio Prados, Arturo Serrano Plaja, Pascual Plá y Beltrán, and Luis Cernuda, and it is evident in the novels of Ramón Sender, Joaquín Arderías, and César Arconada; Luis Buñuel often chronicled in film the years prior to the Spanish Civil War.

5. Aragon, "Le retour a la réalité" (25 June 1935), in *Pour un réalisme socialiste*, 82–87. The poet repeatedly proclaims, "Je réclame la retour à la réalité."

6. See Edward E. Malefakis, *Agrarian Reform and Peasant Revolution in Spain: Origins of the Civil War* (New Haven: Yale University Press, 1970); see chapters 5–8 in particular for observations regarding the agrarian problem prior to the Republic and also the Agrarian Reform Law of 1932. Also see Brenan, *Spanish Labyrinth,* 115–20 and 243–45, and Thomas, *The Spanish Civil War,* 75–79, regarding the Spanish agrarian issue. The agrarian problems of the Republic centered on the fact that large amounts of land were held by a few wealthy landlords, many of them absentee, who hired overseers for their vast estates. The overseers, in turn, hired peasants to work on the lands. This state of affairs was especially prevalent in Andalusia. The peasants formed what Brenan refers to as "the agricultural proletariat of the large estates." The peasants owned no land, were employed only as seasonal labor, and when employed earned a very meager wage. The basic agrarian issue facing the Constituent Cortes in 1931 was how to expropriate the land, divide the estates, and redistribute the land so obtained. The Agrarian Reform Law of September 1932 merely scratched the surface of the age-old agrarian problem in Spain, a problem the country had faced for the last 150 years. In the late twenties, however, the gravity of the rural situation was greatly increased by the economic depression. The economic slump caused agricultural prices to fall; the result was huge tracts of land left uncultivated, large-scale unemployment, and general peasant unrest. It is this complex agrarian problem that underlies "Al volver y empezar" and other poems of the period, especially "Sequía," "La lucha por la tierra," and "Romance de los campesinos de Zorita."

7. Jean-Paul Sartre observes, "The real problem is not . . . that 'Littérature engagée' should deal with all issues in the social world; what is required is that the man of whom it speaks, who is both the other and ourselves, should be immersed in that world," *Que peut la littérature?* 126, cited in Adereth, *CMFL,* 175.

8. Rafael Alberti to José María de Cossío, 11 July 1932, Biblioteca-Museo José María de Cossío, Tudanca, Spain. Used with the permission of the Biblioteca-Museo José María de Cossío.

9. In the "Indice autobiográfico," Alberti recalls, "Cuando estalla la revolución de los mineros de Asturias, me encuentro en Moscú, como invitado al Primer Congreso de Escritores Soviéticos. Durante él conozco a Gorki, Eisenstein y Prokoffiev. También, a André Malraux" (*PC,* 14).

10. See Marrast, *Prosas encontradas,* 149, 151–52.

11. *Octubre: Escritores y artistas revolucionarios,* nos. 1–6 (June 1933–April 1934; reprinted, Vaduz: Liechtenstein, Topos, 1977). The page numbers of *O* cited here

correspond to the 1977 reprint. For a listing of Alberti's poems that first appeared in *Octubre,* see appendix A. Enrique Montero's introduction to the reprint of *Octubre,* "Octubre: Revelación de una revista mítica," pp. ix–xxxvi, is very useful for situating Alberti's political poetry of the early thirties within the framework of the magazine. Also see Cano-Ballesta, *PEPR,* 120–22 and Lechner, *CPE,* 87–97. Lechner asks, "¿Cuál ha sido la aportación de *Octubre* a la poesía comprometida española de este siglo? . . . El primer lugar ocupan los fines didácticos, pragmáticos: todo está supeditado al objectivo de hacer consciente de su situatión social al proletariado rural e industrial . . . y de provocar la agitación política. Los temas de los poemas se derivan de la realidad inmediata o de los que se consideraba realidad alcanzable a corto plazo mediante la revolución inminente. . . . *Octubre* contribuyó sin duda a polarizar la conciencia del público lector y a preparar el ambiente de solidaridad que reinará a partir de los primeros momentos de la Guerra Civil entre los artistas e intelectuales disconformes" (*CPE,* 96–97).

12. David Caute, *Communism and the French Intellectual* (New York: Macmillan, 1964), 322.
13. Louis Aragon, *J'abats mon jeu* (1959), 80, 173, cited in Adereth, *CMFL,* 200.
14. Cited in Adereth, *CMFL,* 201. The critic does not give the date of Aragon's speech. Also see Aragon, "D'Alfred de Vigny a Avdéenko: Les écrivains dans les soviets" (4 April 1935 and 21 April 1935) and "Le retour a la réalité" (25 June 1935), *Pour un réalisme socialiste,* especially 8, 11, 14, and 26–33, and 85–87.
15. Sartre, *Situations II,* 185, refers to "une fonction intégrée et militante" of literature, cited in Adereth, *CMFL,* 34.
16. Monterde, *La poesía pura,* 104.
17. Sartre, *Situations II,* 124. Lechner, in a discussion of Alberti's *El poeta en la calle (1931–1936)* and Emilio Prados's *Calendario incompleto del pan y el pescado,* refers to "un estilo panfletario, incitante, con llamamientos a la agitación, y otro más reflexivo y sosegado" (*CPE,* 71). In a discussion of Spanish commitment poetry written in the Republican Zone during the Spanish Civil War, he refers to "poesía directa" and "poesía reflexiva" (*CEP,* 163). However, Lechner offers no analyses of specific poems.
18. Sartre, *Situations II,* 25, cited in Adereth, *CMFL,* 17.
19. This poem is a variation of a "juego de oráculo" defined as "diversión que consiste en dirigir preguntas en verso varias personas a una sola, y en dar ésta respuestas en el mismo metro de las preguntas" (*Diccionario de la lengua española* [Madrid: Espasa Calpe, 1970]). Of the poem "Juego," Lechner writes: "Las referencias a la realidad histórica de aquel período son: la existencia de la actividad de los que formaban el partido comunista, la desunión y la diversón interna de los trabajadores—CNT [Confederación Nacional del Trabajo], UGT [Unión General de Trabajadores], etc.—, pero aquí se acaba el asunto. El que los nobles y los burgueses estén 'bebiéndose el vino, / camarada, comiéndose el pan' se comprende como referencia a una situación determinada, sin que por otra parte puede interpretarse como una realidad histórica objetiva en sentido estricto. Todo lo demás, son aspectos de un sueño utópico—si se excluye por un momento la

matanza que se ha de efectuar blandiendo el martillo y la hoz (¿o es que quería Alberti convertir al noble y al burgués en obrero y campesino, dándoles los atributos de dichas profesiones?)" (*CPE*, 133–34). See Thomas, *The Spanish Civil War*, 45–46 and 64–76, respectively, for the origins of the UGT and the CNT.

20. "¡Abajo la guerra imperialista!" does not appear in *PC*. See appendix B.

21. Vladimir Mayakovsky, "Aloud and Straight," in *Poems*, trans. Dorian Rottenberg (Moscow: Progress Publishers, 1976). See "Vo ves golos'" *Polnoe sobranie sochinenni v trinadtsati tomakh* (Moskva: Goslitizdat, 1958), 10: 281. I wish to thank Professor Elizabeth Pribić for her transliterations of Mayakovsky's poetry and for discussing his verse with me.

22. Mayakovsky, "Aloud and Straight."

23. Mayakovsky, "Fine!" 282.

24. After reading Alberti's agitative verse of the early thirties and Mayakovsky's political verse it seems apparent to me that the latter poet's style of the Revolution clearly influenced the former. In addition, Demyan Bedney's *agitki* (bits of agitative propaganda) also come to mind when reading Alberti's agitative poetry of the early thirties. Bedney's *agitki* could also have had a thematic influence on Alberti's poetry, since both poets write of the peasants' desire for land. For a discussion of Bedney's poetry see Alexander Kaun, *Soviet Poets and Poetry* (Berkeley: University of California Press, 1943), 43–46.

25. "Sequía" does not appear in *PC*. See appendix B.

26. *The Compact Edition of the Oxford English Dictionary*, s.v. "Watchword."

27. Kaun, *Soviet Poets*, 43.

28. "Mitin" does not appear in *PC*. See appendix B.

29. Cano-Ballesta draws a similar conclusion when he states that in Alberti's "poesía de urgencia" we find "la ética por encima de la estética" (*PEPR*, 200). Of Alberti's agitative verse of this period Lechner observes: "Quizás sean los más útiles para el combate, los más incentivos, aunque también de menos trascendencia" (*CPE*, 96). An earlier version of many of the ideas discussed in the present study was published as "Poetry for Politics' Sake: Rafael Alberti's *Consignas*," *Crítica Hispánica* 5, no. 1 (June 1983): 47–58.

30. Of the three poems that Alberti first published in *Octubre* (see appendixes A and B) only "Un fantasma recorre Europa" and "La iglesia marcha sobre la cuerda floja" were gathered into later collections of his poetry. The former poem appeared in the collection of the same title, and the latter appeared in *El burro explosivo*. See appendix B.

31. Sartre, *Situations II*, 30, cited in Adereth, *CMFL*, 30.

32. Roland Barthes, "Political Modes of Writing," in *Writing Degree Zero*, trans. Annette Lavers and Colin Smith (New York: Hill and Wang, 1967), 23, 22, 23; originally published as *Le degré zéro de l'ecriture* (Paris: Seuil, 1953).

33. Barthes, *Writing Degree Zero*, 23.

34. The essays collected in *Writing Degree Zero* are, as Susan Sontag points out in the introduction, "a late contribution to that vigorous debate that has engaged the European literary community since the decade before the war on the relation

between politics and literature" (p. ix). She continues, "It would seem that Barthes, though he never mentions the book [Sartre's *What Is Literature?*], had it in mind when he wrote *Writing Degree Zero,* and that his argument constitutes an attempt at refuting Sartre's" (p. xi). Barthes, in his essay on political modes of writing, is attacking the type of political writing in which Alberti, in both *Consignas* and *Un fantasma recorre Europa,* is engaged. Nevertheless, Barthes's ideas concerning the Marxist mode of writing (pp. 22–24) are valuable in the present discussion of Alberti's earliest political poetry.

35. Vladimir Kirilov, "We," ll. 18–20, in Kaun, *Soviet Poets,* 103.

36. In *PC,* line 24 of "La lucha por la tierra" has been altered slightly, reading "o esos tormentos con que nos amenazas como aliado de los terratenientes"; in the original version of the poem, published in *Consignas,* it reads "o esos tormentos con que nos amenazas como aliado de la burguesía."

37. Prados's "¿Quién, quién ha sido?" appeared in *Octubre,* no. 3, (August-September 1933): 60, and also in *Calendario incompleto,* which was later published in *Llanto en la sangre (1933–1936)* (Valencia: Ediciones Españolas, 1937). Also see the prologue in Emilio Prados, *PPC,* xli–xliii, and Blanco Aguinaga, *Emilio Prados: Vida y obra* (New York: Hispanic Institute, 1960) concerning the early thirties and Prados's poetry.

38. *O,* nos. 4–5 (October–November 1933): 26–27.

39. Eisenstein defines "intellectual montage" in *FF,* 37–38. "Pathos" is defined by Eisenstein in *P,* 13.

40. The poem's title reiterates and reaffirms the opening line of the Communist manifesto (Karl Marx and Friedrich Engels, *The Manifesto of the Communist Party,* in *The Essential Left* [London: George Allen and Unwin, 1961], 14). When "Un fantasma recorre Europa" first appeared in *Octubre* it was accompanied by a footnote quoting the entire Marxian dictum. When published in *Un fantasma recorre Europa,* however, the note was omitted from the poem, since the manifesto's opening line served as the epigraph introducing all of the poems of the collection. The note is also omitted from the poem as it later appeared in Alberti's *PC.*

41. There are differences in punctuation and spacing in the original version published in 1933 from that appearing in *PC.* Lechner, *CPE,* 93, accurately notes other modifications in the poem as it appears in *PC:* the lines "Nos persiguen a tiros / ¡Oh!" have been omitted at the close of part 1; the commands "Cerrad / cerrad las cárceles" replace those of "¡Abrid / abrid las cárceles!" at the close of part 2 of the original; and space has been added to the printed page at the close of part 3 in order to set off the final three lines of the poem. Lechner, however, offers no analysis of the text.

42. Bordwell and Thompson, *Film Art,* 179. Alberti recalls the first time that he saw *The Battleship Potemkin* in the article "El 'Potemkin' en Brujas," written in Paris, 1932, and published in *El Sol* (19 April 1932), later reproduced in Marrast, *Prosas encontradas,* 95–97.

43. Eisenstein writes, "Two film pieces of any kind, placed together, inevitably combine into a new concept, a new quality, arising out of that juxtaposition." This

"new quality," he explains, is the "thematic matter . . . the image of the theme itself" (*FS,* 4).

44. Dwight MacDonald, "Eisenstein, Pudovkin and Others," in *The Emergence of Film Art,* ed. Lewis Jacobs, 2d ed. (New York: Norton, 1979), 139, 140.

45. MacDonald, "Eisenstein," 130.

46. Vladimir Mayakovsky, *How Verses Are Made,* trans. Herbert Marshall, 3d ed. (Bombay: Current Book House, 1955), 192.

47. *O,* nos. 4–5 (October–November 1933), 89.

48. Kaun, *Soviet Poets,* 23.

49. See Cano-Ballesta, *PEPR,* 118–19, for his observations regarding the impact such poetry had on the Spain of the thirties. An earlier version of my analysis appeared as "Dialectical Pathos: Rafael Alberti's "Un fantasma recorre Europa. . .' " *Anales de la literatura española contemporánea* 8 (Fall 1983): 31–46.

50. Johannes Becher's poem "No hay trabajo" (*O,* nos. 4–5, [October–November 1933]: 139), translated by Alberti, could have inspired "S.O.S."

51. Carr relates that in the years 1932 and 1933 Spain "saw a sharp fall in iron and steel production, hard times for orange and olive-oil producers, and mounting unemployment. There was no national system of assistance to the half million unemployed; the municipalities were left to do what they could within limited resources. Thus the great pool of agrarian unemployment in the stagnant south seemed to threaten to engulf the Republic itself" (*Spain,* 613–14). Brenan observes of this same era: "One must remember that during this time the working classes were suffering very real hardships. The slump had brought terrible unemployment. In Barcelona only 30 per cent of the workmen of the builders' union were fully employed. Of the 45,000 at work in 1930, only 11,000 were at work in 1933" (*Spanish Labyrinth,* 253). Of the agrarian unemployment situation in the south, Carr says: "In 1930 there were over 200,000 labourers unemployed in Andalusia during the greater part of the year and after 1930 this figure increased rapidly" (*Spain,* 120).

52. Rafael Alberti to José María de Cossío, Berlin, 11 July 1932, Biblioteca-Museo José María de Cossío, Tudanca, Spain. In this letter Alberti discusses and encloses the original version of the poem that he would later publish as "S.O.S." The first version, however, is merely the nucleus of the poem that appears in *Un fantasma recorre Europa.* Originally, "S.O.S." was entitled "Oíd el alba de las manos arriba," a line from Alberti's "Elegía cívica" (l. 28) and also a line that would later reappear in and introduce the poem "Mitin" of *Consignas* (l. 2). The early version of "S.O.S.," used with the permission of the poet, reads as follows:

6 millones de hombres,   1
12 de manos muertas y ojos descerrajados por el hambre que agranda la
    invasión lenta del insomnio.
El cielo se pregunta por el humo,
el humo por el fuego,
el fuego de las fábricas por el carbón que espera dejar de ser al fin paredón   5
    muerto de las minas.
Leed los gritos del periódico que la Tierra descubre día y noche entre náuseas.

10 millones de hombres,
20 brazos tristes,
como ramas sin lluvia,
caídos secos como ramas.   10
Ese medio planeta sin cultivo,
esas vallas que vedan la posesión común del sol agrario de las granjas,

ríos que piden desviarse,
levantarse hasta el lecho de las yerbas,
el agua: ese factor.   15
La propiedad del mundo consiente almacenarse en el vientre del mar.
El café que se injerta en las raíces de las algas,
las balas de algodón que se hunden mucho más despacio.
Lo dulce del azúcar se disuelve salado.

100 millones,   20
200,
300,
400 millones de pies fijos,
de pies parados en la tierra,
de cuerpos que enrojecen de pasar tanto por el alba.   25

Se yerguen,
se aproximan.
Amigos: nos llaman.

53. Only part 1 of the poem appears in *PC*, with the new title "Los niños de Ex-
    tremadura." A brief version of part 1 of "Aquí y allí" also appeared on the back
    cover of the first issue of *Octubre* (June–July 1933), accompanied by a pho-
    tograph of children reading. The front cover of the same issue has a photograph of
    a peasant woman and a child and is accompanied by the following observation:
    "Así son las mujeres de los campesinos de España que luchan y sufren por la
    posesión de la tierra." In a later issue of *Octubre* (no. 3, August–September
    1933), Alberti published "Himno de las bibliotecas proletarias" (pp. 68–69). In
    this poem he offers a rather simplistic analysis of the educational programs of "la
    cultura obrera," in particular, and the cultural revolution, in general. He urges, for
    example: "De los libros recoged y arrancad / letra a letra lo que nos lleve al
    fin. / ¡Camaradas, llegó la pleamar / para la cultura obrera!" (ll. 36–39). Lenin's
    views concerning the cultural revolution are discussed in "On Co-operation,"
    Selected Works, vol. 2 of *The Marxists*, ed. C. Wright Mills (New York: Dell,
    1965), 246–53.
54. Lechner asks, "¿Cómo no iba a influir en las ideas de los hombres no socialmente
    sensibilizados un nivel de vida de los campesinos que se quedó estancado desde
    1870 hasta 1936?" (*CPE*, 130). In the early thirties many artists were interested in
    and angered by the condition of the Spanish peasantry. This is evident in many of
    the essays published in *Octubre*. See, for example, "Reforma agraria" and
    "Puerto de Sevilla," *O*, no. 3 (August–September 1933): 58, 59.
55. For background on the incidents to which Alberti refers in his introduction to the
    "Romance de los campesinos de Zorita," especially those occurring in Castil-
    blanco, see Brenan, *Spanish Labyrinth*, 256–57; Carr, *Spain*, 234; Malefakis,

Agrarian Reform, 310–13; and Thomas, *The Spanish Civil War*, 74–75. Of the "terrible incident" that occurred at Castilblanco on 31 December 1931, an incident that "caught the attention of the whole country," Thomas reports: "In the wild and empty region of Estremadura there stands a small *pueblo* of 900 inhabitants named Castilblanco. The conditions here were not notably different from elsewhere in the region. There was no special shortage of food. Violence was unknown. The local Branch of the C.N.T., however, asked permission to hold a meeting. This was refused. The Anarchists determined to go ahead. The Civil Guard then came to the defence of the authorities . . . In Castilblanco in 1931 the Civil Guard were as unpopular as elsewhere in Spain. Their fate was terrible. When they tried to prevent the holding of a C.N.T. meeting, the whole population of the village fell upon them. Four were killed. Their heads were beaten in. Their eyes were gouged out. Their bodies were mutilated. . . . And, as in the town of *Fuenteovejuna* in Lope de Vega's play of that name, there was no possibility of bringing the killers to trial. The village, and no single person, was responsible. This tragedy was followed by several comparable but less dramatic events in other *pueblos*" (*The Spanish Civil War*, 74–75).

56. Quoted in Gerardo Diego, *Poesía española* of 1934, cited in Montero, "Octubre," xxxiii.

57. Montero, "Octubre," xxxvi.

58. Domenchina's comments, cited in Cano-Ballesta (*PEPR*, 119–20), originally appeared in "Poesía y crítica," *El Sol* 21 (May 1933): 2.

59. See Marrast, "Essai de bibliographie," 154–55. *El burro explosivo,* which Alberti began in 1934 but did not publish until during the Civil War, includes: "El burro explosivo," "Epitafio a un presidente," "Al nuncio de S.S. en España," "In memoriam," "Gil en campaña," "A Gil crucificado," "El Gil, Gil," "La iglesia marcha sobre la cuerda floja," "Radio Sevilla," "El último duque de Alba," and "La última voluntad del duque de Alba." The last three poems will be discussed in chapter 4. Only "El Gil, Gil" later appeared in *PC*. The rest are reproduced in appendix B. *Nuestra diaria palabra* (1936) includes the following poems: "Dialoguillo de la Revolución y el poeta," "El terror y el confidente," "El perro rabioso," "Geografía política," "En la entrega de la bandera que el C.P. de Sevilla y el C.C. de las juventudes regalaron al Comité Central del Partido Comunista," "Hace falta estar ciego," "Colegio (S.J.)," "Hermana," "Os marcháis viejos padres," and "Siervos." All but "En la entrega de la bandera" were collected in *De un momento a otro* and can be found in *PC*. *13 bandas y 48 estrellas: Poema del Mar Caribe* (Madrid: Impresor Manuel Altolaguirre, 1936), as cited in Cano-Ballesta, *PEPR,* 198, and Marrast, "Essai de bibliographie," 154. These poems were later published in *De un momento a otro* and also appear in *PC*. In *El poeta en la calle (1931–1936)* (1938), Alberti published the following poems from his 1933 collection *Un fantasma recorre Europa:* "Al volver y empezar," "Un fantasma recorre Europa," and "S.O.S." and from *Consignas* he republished the first part of "Aquí y allí," "Juego," "En forma del cuento," "Romance de los campesinos de Zorita," and "La lucha por la tierra."

60. Lechner also highlights the central themes and metrical forms found in the poems

of *El poeta en la calle* (*CPE*, 68–71) and *De un momento a otro* (*CPE*, 71–73). He achieves his aim of situating Alberti's poetry of this period within the overall framework of Spanish commitment poetry of the twentieth century. His observations and conclusions are insightful and serve as a point of departure for any more detailed study of Alberti's poetry of the thirties. Emilia de Zuleta, *Cinco poetas españoles* (Madrid: Gredos, 1971), briefly summarizes a few of the themes and stylistic elements of these two collections of Alberti's poems (pp. 338–44).

61. The Asturian regional CNT, anarchists, socialists, Communists, and semi-Trotskyists of the Workers' and Peasants' Alliance rallied around the cry: "¡Uníos, Hermanos Proletarios!" See Thomas, *The Spanish Civil War*, 118, and his account of the insurrection, 118–24. Also see Brenan, *Spanish Labyrinth*, 284–89 and Carr, *Spain*, 634–36.

62. Thomas, *The Spanish Civil War*, 119, records that the manifesto of the Asturian miners declared, "Comrades . . . we are creating a new society. . . . It is not surprising that the world we are forging costs blood, grief and tears; everything on earth is fecund, soldiers of the Ideal! Put up your rifles! Women eat little, only what is necessary. Long live the Social Revolution" (*La révolution d'Octubre en Espagne*, a pamphlet issued by the government in Madrid in 1935, Peirats, I, pp. 86–87).

63. Thomas, *The Spanish Civil War*, 120–24, discusses the manner in which the rebellion was quelled.

64. On Gil Robles y Quiñones see Thomas, *The Spanish Civil War*, 95–96.

65. "A Gil crucificado," ll. 9–11.

66. Jackson, *A Concise History*, 23.

67. Jackson, *A Concise History*, 25.

68. Salvador Dalí's painting is entitled "Soft Construction with Boiled Beans: Premonition of Civil War."

69. "New-York," ll. 73, 74. I was not able to locate the 1936 edition of *13 bandas y 48 estrellas*, therefore I do not know if any of the poems have been deleted from *PC*. Marrast, "Essai de bibliographie," 154, does indicate that in the 1937 edition of *De un momento a otro*, which recollected those poems first published in *13 bandas*, the second poem of the original 1936 edition was not republished. Cano-Ballesta indicates that he too was unable to locate the first edition of *13 bandas* (*PEPR*, 198).

70. "New-York," l. 2; "Yo también canto a América," ll. 51–52.

71. Alberti's poem is inspired by the Langston Hughes poem of the same title. A translation of the Hughes poem appeared in *O*, no. 3 (August–September 1933): 66.

72. "Un soneto para terminar: Vietnam" (1965) appears in *PEC* along with the poem "Desprecio y maravilla de la guerra del Vietnam" (1968).

73. These questions posed by Sartre serve as the titles of chapters 1–3 of *What Is Literature?*

Chapter 4. The Poet and the Spanish Civil War

1. See Brenan, *Spanish Labyrinth*, 265–332; Carr, *Spain*, 652–94; Jackson, *A Concise History*, 11–86, and Thomas, *The Spanish Civil War*, 23–274.

2. Also see Raymond Carr, ed., *The Republic and the Civil War in Spain* (London: Macmillan, 1971); Robert G. Colodny, *The Struggle for Madrid* (New York: Paine Whitman, 1958); Gabriel Jackson, *The Spanish Republic and the Civil War, 1931–1939* (Princeton: Princeton University Press, 1965); and Gabriel Jackson, *The Spanish Civil War: Domestic Crisis or International Conspiracy* (Boston: Heath, 1967). In addition see Carr's biographical essay in *Spain* for comprehensive lists of the more important books, memoirs, pamphlets, and similar materials on the Civil War.

3. The artists include, among others, W. H. Auden, Julian Bell, Javier Bueño, Bertolt Brecht, John Cornford, Salvador Dalí, John Dos Passos, Ilya Ehrenburg, Lillian Hellman, Ernest Hemingway, Joris Ivens, André Malraux, Archibald Macleish, Pablo Neruda, Pablo Picasso, George Orwell, Ramón Sender, Upton Sinclair, Stephen Spender, and César Vallejo.

4. Spender's article originally appeared in *Left Review* 3, no. 1 (February 1937), cited in *TA*, 63.

5. Thomas Waugh, " 'Men Cannot Act in Front of the Camera in the Presence of Death,' Joris Ivens' *The Spanish Earth*," part 2, *Cineaste* 12, no. 3 (1983): 29.

6. Waugh, "Men Cannot Act," 25.

7. José Bergamín, "Presencia del Mono Azul," *MA*, no. 1 (27 August 1936): 3. All page references to *MA* correspond to the Kraus Reprint edition. For the poems Alberti published in this magazine see appendixes A and B.

8. Pablo Neruda, *España en el corazón: Himno a las glorias del pueblo en la guerra (1936–1937)*, 2d ed. (Santiago, Chile: Ercilla, 1938), 33. All references to this work are to this edition.

9. Miguel Hernández, *Viento del pueblo* (Valencia: Socorro Rojo Internacional, 1937), reprinted in *OPC*. All of Hernández's works mentioned in this book are included in *OPC*.

10. *Capital de la gloria* first appeared as a collection of poems in *De un momento a otro (poesía e historia) (1932–1937)* (1937). Marrast, "Essai de bibliographie," 154–55, states that the war poems written in 1938, in addition to those of the 1937 edition of *De un momento a otro*, were later published in *Poesía: 1924–1937* (1938). Many of Alberti's poems of the Spanish Civil War were first published or appeared simultaneously in *MA* and in *HE*. See appendix A for a listing of Alberti's poems of the era and the corresponding magazine in which they first appeared.

11. "Madrid-Otoño," l. 36. Lechner, *CPE*, 162–63, 174–76, examines the appearance of the theme of what he terms "la muerte fecundante" in the poetry written in the Republican zone during the war. He concludes that Alberti's war poetry, a few of Miguel Hernández's poems, the ballads of Emilio Prados, and numerous poems incorporated into the *Romanceros* of the war reflect this theme.

Since Lechner's aim is to study, as his title indicates, commitment in twentieth-century Spanish poetry, he does not examine in detail the development of this theme in specific poems by Alberti. However, his excellent study serves as a point of departure for my analyses of Alberti's war poems. Emilia de Zuleta, *Cinco poetas españoles,* 342, briefly examines *Capital de la gloria.* She insightfully notes the presence of "el motivo de la muerte como siembra para una vida futura" in Alberti's poetry of the war. Her discussion is somewhat limited, and she does not explicate any of the war poems.

12. "Lejos de la guerra," l. 41.
13. "Para luego," l. 1.
14. "Madrid-Otoño" first appeared in *HE,* no. 2 (February 1937: 29–31, with the title "Capital de la gloria."
15. Thomas, *The Spanish Civil War,* 416–17. On 17 November 1936, the Insurgent forces "combined their ground advances with a supreme effort to break the city's resistance by bombardment" (Jackson, *A Concise History,* 96). Hugh Thomas relates: "Franco, having remarked before Portuguese journalists that he would destroy Madrid rather than leave it to the 'marxists,' greatly intensified the aerial bombardment. The German officers of the new Condor Legion were interested to see the reaction of a civilian population to a carefully planned attempt to set fire to the city quarter by quarter. The bombing concentrated as far as possible on hospitals and other buildings such as the Telefónica, whose destruction would cause special panic. The air raids were accompanied by artillery bombardment from Mount Garabitas. From 16 November until 19 November, the bombing, especially at night, continued and 1,000 people were killed. No great city in history had been so tested—though the attack was a foretaste of what was to happen in a few years to London, Hamburg, Tokyo, and Leningrad—as commentators in Madrid at the time eloquently prophesied. The terrible flames caused the capital to appear like some elemental place of torture. Over the crackle of fire, there could be heard the monotonous refrain, repeated syllabically, like a beat on a distant drum, '¡No pas-ar-án! ¡No pas-ar-án! ¡No pas-ar-án!' " (*The Spanish Civil War,* 416–17). An earlier version of my analysis of "Madrid-Otoño" was published as "Death and Resurrection in Rafael Alberti's *Capital de la gloria,*" *Essays in Literature* 6, no. 2 (Fall 1979): 247–57.
16. The image of "los trajes vacíos" of "Madrid-Otoño" is a variation of the metaphor "el cuerpo deshabitado" of a poem of the same name in *Sobre los ángeles.* This recurrent image is also found in Alberti's play *El cuerpo deshabitado* (Madrid: Plutarco, 1930). In addition, the symbolic metaphor of "el cuerpo vacío" is present in other poems of *Capital de la gloria.* For example, as the poet's assumed voice surveys the war-torn land in his apostrophe "Al General Kleber," he captures the absence of human life in war in the concise images: "lo que era un hombre, ser hueco frío" (l. 13) and "hombres . . . desaparecidos en el viento" (ll. 29–30). A variation of this metaphor appears in *Entre el clavel y la espada* (Buenos Aires: Losada, 1941); in Poem 8 the poet sadly recalls the dead soldiers of the war symbolically represented by "un uniforme / sin nadie / . . . ya

sólo era un traje" (ll. 7–8, 11). Alberti's description of the "silent drama" left by war in "Madrid-Otoño" recalls Herbert Matthews's description of Madrid: "There are six-story houses in the Rosales district, on the western edge of Madrid, where 100-kilo bombs have plowed right through and into the ground exposing parts of rooms on each floor. It is like a strange and horrible stage scene where the fourth wall is nonexistent so that the characters can present a tragedy before an unseen audience. If one were to cut down like that through life in Madrid under siege, what could be seen?" ("Under the Death-spurting Skies of War-torn Madrid," *New York Times Magazine*, 21 February 1937, reprinted in Gabriel Jackson, ed., *The Spanish Civil War* [Chicago: Quadrangle Books, 1972], p. 52).

17. "El último duque de Alba" does not appear in *PC*. First published in *MA*, no. 2 (3 September 1936): 12, it later was included in *El burro explosivo* and is reproduced in appendix B.

18. Alberti recalls in an interview published in the *ABC* (September 1936) that the palace of the Marqués de Heredia Spínola was the headquarters of the Alianza de Intelectuales Antifascistas para la defensa de la cultura: "La residencia de los fastuosos Heredia Spínola se ha convertido—y purificado por ello—en albergue de la Alianza de Intellectuales Antifascistas para la defensa de la cultura. . . . El casón antiguo . . . está poblado hoy de monos azules" (cited in Marrast, *Prosas encontradas*, 188, 194).

19. Francisco Javier Díez de Revenga, *La métrica española de los poetas del 27* (Murcia: Departamento de Literatura Española, Universidad de Murcia, 1973), 93–94.

20. *MA*, no. 41 (18 November 1937): 163.

21. "Madrid por Cataluna," ll. 5–6.

22. *MA*, no. 41 (18 November 1937): 163.

23. Lechner observes of the poetry of the Civil War: "Relacionado con el tema de la solidaridad, basada en el idealismo y abnegación, está el de la muerte fecundante . . . que aparece con tanta frecuencia que no sería difícil dedicarle una antología. . . . Hay muchos ejemplos en que los poetas viniculan la muerte sobrevenida en el campo de batalla, o sencillamente la muerte por la causa del pueblo, dondequiera que acontezca, con gestación de la edad futura; los caídos de hoy—dicen los poetas—son la semilla o constituyen el mantillo de donde brotarán los hombres nuevos, la nueva España. En esta poesía, muerte violenta y resurrección ideal están estrechamente ligadas y encuentran expresión en una imaginería procedente casi siempre del ambiente rural en sus aspectos más elementales . . . segar, sembrar, crecer; espiga, flor, árbol" (*CPE*, 174–76). See also Erika Lorenz, *Der metaphorische Kosmos der modernen spanischen Lyrik (1936–1956)* (Hamburg, 1961), especially 53–81, cited in Lechner, *CPE*, 175.

24. *MA*, no. 1 (27 August 1936): 3.

25. *MA*, no. 45 (May 1938): 171

26. Jackson, *A Concise History*, 145.

27. *HE*, no. 2 (3 February 1937): 34.

28. César Vallejo, "Himno a los voluntarios de la República," *España, aparta de mí*

este cáliz (1939), in *Obra poética completa de César Vallejo* (Havana: Casa de las Américas, 1970), 271–78. All poems by Vallejo are cited from *Obra poética completa.*

29. Higgins, introduction to *Vallejo,* 74.

30. Higgins, *Vallejo,* 76.

31. Higgins, *Visión del hombre y de la vida en las últimas obras poéticas de César Vallejo* (Mexico City: Siglo Veintiuno, 1970), 294, 295.

32. Neruda's "Canto a las madres de los milicianos muertos" appeared in *MA* anonymously, according to Morris Carson, *Pablo Neruda: Regresó el caminante* (Madrid: Playor, 1973), 84. Carson, however, does not cite the issue number in which the poem appeared.

33. Emilio Prados, *Destino fiel (Ejercicios de poesía en guerra) (1936–1939),* in *PPC.* All poems by Prados cited in the text are included in *PPC. Destino fiel* contains many of the ballads that first appeared in *Llanto en la sangre: Romances, 1933–1936* (Valencia: Ediciones Españolas, 1937), the poems of *Cancionero menor para los combatientes (1936–1938)* (Monasterio de Montserrat: Ediciones literarias del Comisariado del Ejército del Este, 1938), and "Poemas varios (1936–1939)," which included uncollected poems, some of which first appeared in various magazines of the era. See the extensive bibliography in *PPC,* lxix–xcv, and also Lechner, *CPE,* 167–70, 192–96.

34. *MA,* no. 15 (11 February 1937): 103; *HE,* no. 2 (February 1937): 32.

35. *MA,* no. 25 (22 July 1937): 131; according to Sánchez Barbudo, "Quinto cuerpo de Ejército" appeared in *Capital de la gloria* (*MA,* no. 41 [18 November 1937]: 163). It was, however, not published in subsequent editions of *De un momento a otro.* The poem is reproduced in appendix B.

36. Lechner, *CPE,* 157, points out that Beimler and Kleber are the heroes of the Madrid defense most often celebrated in the poetry of the Republican zone.

37. On Beimler see Thomas, *The Spanish Civil War,* 433–35, and Lechner, *CPE,* 158.

38. Alberti's "Elegía a un poeta que no tuvo su muerte" appeared in *MA,* no. 23 (8 July 1937): 127. Other elegies to García Lorca include Hernández's "Elegía primera" (*OPC,* 305–8) and Prados's "Estancia en la muerte con Federico García Lorca" (*PPC,* 661–66). The *Romancero general de la guerra de España* (1937) was dedicated to García Lorca (Lechner, *CPE,* 167–68). In addition, as Lechner points out (p. 189), six compositions to García Lorca were published in *HE:* Manuel Altolaguirre, "Elegía a nuestro poeta" (no. 3 [March 1937]: 225–38; vol. 1, Kraus Reprint); Luis Cernuda, "Elegía a un poeta muerto" (no. 6 [June 1937]: 33–36; vol. 2, Kraus Reprint); Vicente Aleixandre's prose work "Federico" and Prados's "Estancia en la muerte de Federico García Lorca" (no. 7 [July 1937]: 139–41, 145–50; vol. 2, Kraus Reprint); Juan Gil-Albert, "Dos sonetos a Federico García Lorca" (no. 12 [December 1937]: 163; vol. 3, Kraus Reprint); and Pedro Garfias, "A Federico García Lorca" (no. 14 [February 1938]: 323; vol. 3, Kraus Reprint). The pagination here corresponds to the reprint edition of *HE.* The magazine also published Pablo Neruda's prose work "Federico García Lorca" (no. 3 [March 1937]: 225–38; vol. 1, Kraus Reprint).

39. *MA*, no. 10 (29 October 1936): 76; Prados's "Ciudad sitiada: Romance de la defensa de Madrid" also celebrates the efforts of the city under siege.

40. Manuel García Blanco, "El romancero," in Guillermo Díaz Plaja, *Historia general de las literaturas hispánicas*, vol. 2 (Barcelona: Barna, 1958), 16; also see Lechner's discussion of the various *Romanceros* published during the war (*CPE*, 165–79).

41. García Blanco, "El romancero," 17.

42. See Jackson, *A Concise History*, 88–95, and Thomas, *The Spanish Civil War*, 407–10.

43. *MA*, no. 11 (5 November 1936): 84.

44. "Aniversario," l. 11.

45. Alberti's "Al nuevo Coronel Juan Modesto Guilloto, lejano compañero de colegio en la bahía de Cádiz" first appeared in *HE*, no. 22 (October 1938): 20–21. The poem was written in 1938, as the parenthetical note accompanying its original publication indicates.

46. For information on General Kleber see Thomas, *The Spanish Civil War*, 412–13, and Lechner, *CPE*, 157.

47. "La última voluntad del duque de Alba" first appeared in *MA*, no. 14 (26 November 1936): 97; "Radio Sevilla" first appeared in *MA*, no. 6 (1 October 1936): 44. Alberti's three war ballads sketching features of the enemy were also published in *El burro explosivo*. They do not appear in *Capital de la gloria*, in subsequent editions of *De un momento a otro*, or in *PC*. See appendix B. Alberti's verbal attacks in this trilogy recall Neruda's three poems of *España en el corazón* that scorn and deride the prominent figures that the poet considers to be traitors to the people's cause: "Sanjuro en los Infiernos," "Mola en los Infiernos," and "El General Franco en los Infiernos." These poems do appear in later editions of *Residencia en la tierra, III*, which incorporate *España en el corazón*. Miguel Hernández's "Ceniciento Mussolini" of *Viento del pueblo* (*OPC*, 333–35) is also in this vein.

48. *MA*, no. 1 (27 August 1936): 1.

49. *MA*, no. 31 (2 September 1937): 143.

50. See Thomas, *The Spanish Civil War*, 834 and 618–19.

51. Thomas, *The Spanish Civil War*, 417.

52. When "Radio Sevilla" first appeared in *MA* the poem was accompanied by a cartoon caricature of General Queipo de Llano. He was depicted as a mustached mule with an elongated snout and was smoking a cigar, drinking a glass of wine, and embracing a microphone labeled *Radio Sevilla* while engaged in a bizarre dance. See Thomas, *The Spanish Civil War*, for information regarding Queipo de Llano's siege of Seville and for descriptions of his nightly radio broadcasts (pp. 186–87, 239, and 615).

53. See Carr, *Spain*, 691–92; Jackson, *A Concise History*, 135–43; and Thomas, *The Spanish Civil War*, 686–711.

54. Thomas, *The Spanish Civil War*, 692.

55. "Monte de El Pardo" first appeared in *HE*, no. 2 (February 1937): 31–32.

56. *HE*, no. 22 (October 1938): 22.

57. See, for example, the works of Cirre, Gaos, and González Lanuza cited in the Selected Bibliography.
58. Marrast, *Prosas encontradas*, 80.
59. Díez de Revenga, *La métrica española*, 117.
60. *MA*, no. 1 (27 August 1936): 1.
61. *HE*, no. 1 (January 1937): 5–6; the stated purpose of *HE* is found on the cover of each issue: "Ensayos, poesía, crítica—al servicio de la causa popular." In the "Propósito" of the first issue we find: "El título de nuestra revista eleva implícito su propósito. Estamos viviendo *una* hora de España de trascendencia incalculable. Acaso *su* hora más importante. . . . Quede, pues, en *Hora de España*, y sea nuestro objetivo literario reflejar esta hora precisa de revolución y guerra civil. . . . Nuestros escritos han de estar, pues, en la línea de los acontecimientos, al filo de las circunstancias, teñidos por el color de la hora, traspasados por el sentimiento general. . . . Nuestro pensamiento es éste: Si es la hora del alba, nuestros actos serán levantarnos, asearnos, agarrar las herramientas y empezar la tarea de esta hora. Y todas estas operaciones irán teñidas forzosamente del color de la luz que hay y del frío del amanecer y transida por los sonidos mañaneros y por la animación matutina. Si fuese la hora del mediodía o la del ocaso, nuestros movimientos serían otros, y también la luz de los sonidos. Creemos, en suma que la hora manda. Y debemos atender lo que nos manda la HORA DE ESPAÑA" (pp. 5–6). See Lechner, *CPE*, 179–201, regarding those responsible for compiling the magazine and those who contributed to it.
62. Lechner relates: "Como se ve, en el primer número de *Hora de España* no hay demagogia en los artículos . . . y el tono es intelectualmente elevado: los redactores y colaboradores no ocultan las esperanzas que tienen puestas en un futuro mejor, pero critican a la vez las faltas que descubren en el propio campo; se basan en convicciones firmes, al mismo tiempo que toman distancia hacia sí mismos y desconfían de los slogans que se utilizan en ambas zonas" (*CPE*, 181). He continues: "Si los poemas de tipo directo publicados en *Hora de España* suelen ser, en general, mucho menos directos que los que aparecieron en otras publicaciones, los de tipo reflexivo superan por lo común la realidad de la guerra y se mueven en un nivel en que no sólo se juega el destino del hombre español concreto de aquellos días, sino el del hombre sin límites nacionales ni anecdóticos. No es una poesía de lemas políticos ni tampoco de programas o 'soluciones,' y a menudo faltan referencias directas a la España que está en guerra y no hay más que alusiones al conflicto; otras veces se amplía un ambiente determinado de tal forma que cobra validez universal y se convierte en este terreno, interior, donde el hombre lucha con su propio destino" (*CPE*, 190).
63. *MA*, no. 1 (27 August 1936): 1.
64. *MA*, no. 31 (2 September 1937): 143.
65. See *La arboleda perdida*, 263–65; also see C. M. Bowra, *The Creative Experiment* (London: Macmillan, 1967), 220–53; G. W. Connell, "The autobiographical element in *Sobre los ángeles*," *Bulletin of Hispanic Studies* 40 (1963): 160–73; C. B. Morris, "*Sobre los ángeles*: A Poet's Apostasy," *Bulletin*

of Hispanic Studies 38 (1960): 222–31; "Los imágenes claves de *Sobre los ángeles*," *Insula* 198 (May 1963): 12, 14; and *Rafael Alberti's "Sobre los ángeles": Four Major Themes* (Hull: University of Hull, 1966); Eric Proll, "The surrealist element in Rafael Alberti," *Bulletin of Hispanic Studies* 18 (April 1941): 70–82; Solita Salinas de Marichal, *El mundo poético de Rafael Alberti*, 179–260; and Luis Felipe Vivanco, "Rafael Alberti en su palabra acelerada y vestida de luces," *Introducción a la poesía española contemporánea* (Madrid: Guadarrama, 1957), 223–58.

66. Wilfred Owen, "Strange Meeting," *The Norton Anthology of Modern Poetry,* ed. Richard Ellmann and Robert O'Clair (New York: Norton, 1973), 515–16. Owen writes: "For by my glee many men have laughed, / And of my weeping something had been left, / Which now must die. I mean the truth untold, / The pity of war, the pity war distilled" (ll. 22–25). At the time of his death, as the note accompanying this poem indicates, "Wilfred Owen . . . was preparing a volume of poems. A sketch of the Preface read: 'This book is not about heroes. English Poetry is not yet fit to speak of them. Nor is it about deeds, or lands, nor anything about glory, honour, might, majesty, dominion, or power, except War. Above all I am not concerned with Poetry. My subject is War, and the pity of War. The Poetry is in the pity. Yet these elegies are to this generation in no sense consolatory. They may be to the next. All a poet can do to-day is warn. That is why the true poets must be truthful' " (p. 515). Although Owen's observations concern the First World War, they reveal his insight into the enigma that is war.

67. Bowra, *PP*, 124. Bowra writes: "The Spanish Civil War, which broke out in 1936, not only cost Spain a million dead but appealed to poets all over the world as a test of western civilization in its most mature and human form."

68. Claude Cockburn, *The Review,* nos. 11/12, p. 51, cited in John Fuller, *A Reader's Guide to W. H. Auden* (New York: Farrar, Straus and Giroux, 1970), 258.

69. W. H. Auden, *Spain* (London: Faber and Faber, 1937).

70. Fuller, *Auden*, 258.

71. Vallejo traveled to Spain in December 1936 and in July 1937. Higgins notes that "in the space of 86 days (3 September–27 November 1937) he wrote twenty-three poems of *Poemas humanos* and the poems of *España, aparta de mí este cáliz*" (*Vallejo*, 6).

72. Higgins, *Visión del hombre*, 304.

73. Higgins, *Vallejo*, 67.

74. Vallejo, "Batallas," ll. 91–92.

75. Neruda, "Tierras ofendidas," l. 2.

76. Higgins, *Vallejo*, 77.

77. Neruda, "Llegada a Madrid de la Brigada Internacional," l. 15.

78. Neruda, "Explico algunas cosas," l. 6.

79. Neruda, *Canto general* (Mexico City: Talleres Gráficas de la Nación, 1950) and (Santiago, Chile: Partido Comunista de Chile, 1950).

80. Jaime Concha, prologue to *Pablo Neruda*, 8.

81. Prados, "Despedida a las Brigadas Internacionales," l. 31.

82. Prados, "Aún hay abril," ll. 20–25.

83. Many of Prados's ballads of the war appeared in the first romancero of the Civil War, which was entitled the *Romancero de la guerra civil* and formed a section of *El Mono Azul,* in the second collection of the same title published by the Ministerio de Instrucción Pública y Bellas Artes, Madrid, November 1936, and later in the third collection, gathered and edited by Prados himself, entitled *Romancero general de la guerra de España* (Madrid-Valencia: Ediciones Españolas, 1937; reprinted Milan: G. G. Feltrinelli Institute, 1966). See Lechner, *CPE,* 166–72 and Blanco Aguinaga, lxxi.

84. Prados, "Primero de mayo de 1937," ll. 9–10.

85. Prados, "Arenga," l. 3.

86. Juan Cano-Ballesta, *Miguel Hernández. El hombre y su poesía* (Madrid: Cátedra, 1977), 19.

87. This observation by Hernández originally appeared in the "Nota Preliminar" of *Teatro en la guerra* (Valencia: Nuestro Pueblo, 1937), cited in *OPC,* 15.

88. Cano-Ballesta, *El hombre y su poesía,* 30.

89. *OPC,* 5; see also Cano-Ballesta, *La poesía de Miguel Hernández* (Madrid: Gredos, 1962), 46.

90. Hernández, "España en ausencia," ll. 48–49.

91. According to the introductory notes accompanying *El hombre acecha* in *OPC:* "*El hombre acecha* estaba preparado a principios de 1939. Lo editaba la Delegación de la Secretaría de Propaganda, y fue compuesto en la Imprenta Moderna, de Valencia, donde se corrigieron pruebas y quizá llegaron a obtenerse capillas. Con la derrota de la República los trabajos se cortaron y la edición despareció. En cierto modo, este libro vino a tener un destino como el de su propio autor" (pp. 355–56).

92. Cano-Ballesta, "Trayectoria de una vida trágica," *En torno a Miguel Hernández* (Madrid: Castalia, 1978), 23.

93. Stanley Weintraub, *The Last Great Cause: The Intellectuals and the Spanish Civil War* (New York: Weybright and Talley, 1968), 312.

94. Dante A. Puzzo, *Spain and the Great Powers 1936–1941* (New York, 1962), p. v; cited in Weintraub, *The Last Great Cause,* 2.

95. John Krueger, "Politics and Poetry," *The Princeton Encyclopedia of Poetry and Poetics,* 971.

96. From 1939 through 1977 Alberti lived in political exile abroad. In 1977, with the advent of democracy in Spain, he returned to his homeland. During his years in exile Alberti composed more than fifteen different collections of poetry. Works from this period in Alberti's poetic production have been studied by the following critics cited in the Selected Bibliography: Díez de Revenga, Gullón, Heisel, Llorens, Manteiga, Marcone, May, Morris, Spang, Vivanco, Warner, Zardoya, and Zuleta. In addition, see Angel Crespo, "Realismo y pitagorismo en el libro de Alberti *A la pintura,*" *Papeles de Son Armadans* 88 (July 1963): 93–126; Eugenio Florit, "La poesía reciente de Rafael Alberti," *La Torre* no. 27 (1959): 11–17; Eduardo González Lanuza, "Rafael Alberti: Entre el clavel y la espada," *Sur* 11,

no. 86 (November 1941): 71–76; and Harry Sieber, "Alberti's *Boticelli*," *Kentucky Romance Quarterly* 16 (1969): 329–32.

97. *Sonríe China* (Buenos Aires: Jacobo Muchnik, 1958) later appeared in *PC*, 1068–108, as part 2 of *Primavera de los pueblos;* Alberti's *Nuevas coplas de Juan Panadero (1976–1977)* appears in *PEC*. "Al General Kleber," l. 2; "Madrid por Cataluña," l. 5.

Selected Bibliography

Adereth, Maxwell. *Commitment in Modern French Literature: Politics and Society in the Works of Péguy, Aragon, and Sartre.* New York: Schocken, 1968.

Adler, Mortimer. *Poetry and Politics.* Pittsburgh: Duquesne University Press, 1965.

Adorno, Theodor. "Commitment." *New Left Review* (1974): 87–88.

Alberti, Rafael. *La arboleda perdida: Libros I y II de memorias.* Barcelona: Seix Barral, 1976.

———. *El burro explosivo.* Madrid: Ediciones del Quinto Regimiento, n.d.

———. *Consignas.* Madrid: Octubre, 1933.

———. *Un fantasma recorre Europa.* Madrid: La Tentativa Poética, 1933.

———. *El hombre deshabitado.* Madrid: Plutarco, 1930.

———. Letter to José María de Cossío. 11 July 1932. Biblioteca-Museo José María de Cossío, Tudanca, Santander, Spain.

———. *Nuestra diaria palabra.* Madrid: Héroe, 1936.

———. *Poemas del destierro y de la espera: Antología.* Madrid: Espasa Calpe, 1976.

———. *Poesía, 1924–1937.* Madrid: Signo, 1938.

———. *Poesías completas.* Buenos Aires: Losada, 1961.

———. *El poeta en la calle: Obra civil.* Madrid: Aguilar, 1978.

———. *El poeta en la calle: Poesía civil, 1931–1965: Selección.* Colección Ebro. Paris: Librairie du Globe, 1966.

———. *Teatro de agitación política, 1933–1939.* Madrid: Edicusa, 1976.

Alonso, Amado. *Materia y forma en poesía.* 3d ed. Madrid: Gredos, 1965.

Alonso, Dámaso. *Poesía española: Ensayo de métodos y límites estilísticos.* 4th ed. Madrid: Gredos, 1962.

———. *Poetas españoles contemporáneos.* Madrid: Gredos, 1952.

Alvarez, Olga. "Rafael Alberti cumple 80 años: Una vida marcada por el fantasma de la guerra y por el ejercicio de la poesía." *Spain: Boletín Cultural,* no. 15 (January 1983): 37–38.

"An Andalusian Poet." *Times Literary Supplement,* 6 March 1948, pp. 129–30.

Aproximación a Rafael Alberti y María Teresa León. Barcelona: La Mano en el Cajón, 1976.

Aragon, Louis. *L'homme communiste.* 1946. Reprint. Paris: Gallimard, 1953.

———. *Le paysan de Paris.* 1926. Reprint. Paris: Gallimard, 1961.

———. *Pour un réalisme socialiste.* Paris: Denoël et Stéele, 1935.

Arniz, Francisco M., ed. *Homenaje a Rafael Alberti*. Barcelona: Península, 1977.

Aub, Max. *La poesía española contemporánea*. México City: Imprenta Universitaria, 1954.

Auden, W H. *Spain*. London: Faber and Faber, 1937.

Barthes, Roland. *Writing "Degree Zero."* Trans. Annette Lavers and Colin Smith. New York: Hill and Wang, 1967.

Bayo, Manuel. *Sobre Alberti*. Madrid: CVS, 1974.

Becker, Lucille F. *Louis Aragon*. New York: Twayne, 1971.

Bellver, Catherine G. "La guerra civil española en la poesía de Rafael Alberti." *Explicación de Textos Literarios* 6, no. 1 (1977): 97–100.

Benson, Frederick R. *Writers in Arms: The Literary Impact of the Spanish Civil War*. New York: New York University Press, 1967.

Bodini, Vittorio. "Rafael Alberti." In *Los poetas surrealistas españoles*. Barcelona: Tusquets, 1971.

Bordwell, David, and Kristin Thompson. *Film Art*. Reading, Mass.: Addison-Wesley, 1979.

Bousoño, Carlos. *Teoría de la expresión poética*. 5th ed. Madrid: Gredos, 1970.

Bowra, Cecil M. *The Creative Experiment*. London: Macmillan, 1967. [On Alberti, see pp. 220–53].

———. *Poetry and Politics, 1900–1960*. Cambridge: Cambridge University Press, 1966.

Brenan, Gerald. *The Spanish Labyrinth: An Account of the Social and Political Background of the Civil War*. Cambridge: Cambridge University Press, 1943.

Brooks, Cleanth. *The Well Wrought Urn: Studies in the Structure of Poetry*. 1947. Reprint. New York: Harcourt Brace Jovanovich, 1975.

Butt, John. *Writers and Politics in Modern Spain*. London: Hodder and Stoughton, 1978.

Byrum, Andrea Jane. "The Postwar Poetry of Rafael Alberti: A Master of Lyric." Ph.D. diss., University of Wisconsin–Madison, 1979.

Calinescu, Matei. "Literature and Politics." In *Interrelations of Literature*, ed. Jean-Pierre Barricelli and Joseph Garibaldi. New York: Modern Language Association, 1982.

Cano, José Luis. *La poesía de la Generación del 27*. Madrid: Guadarrama, 1973.

Cano-Ballesta, Juan, ed. *En torno a Miguel Hernández*. Madrid: Castalia, 1978.

———, ed. *Miguel Hernández: El hombre y su poesía*. Madrid: Cátedra, 1977.

———, *La poesía de Miguel Hernández*. Madrid: Gredos, 1962.

———. "La poesía revolucionaria: Rafael Alberti" and "Rafael Alberti, poeta revolucionario (1934–36)." In *La poesía española entre pureza y revolución (1930–1936)*. Madrid: Gredos, 1972.

Carr, Raymond. *The Republic and the Civil War in Spain*. London, Macmillan, 1971.

———. *Spain, 1808–1975*. 2d ed. Oxford: Clarendon Press, 1982.

Carson, Morris. *Pablo Neruda: Regresó el caminante*. Madrid: Playor, 1973.

Castellet, José María. *Veinte años de poesía española, 1939–1959*. Barcelona: Seix Barral, 1960.

Caute, David. *Communism and the French Intellectuals, 1914–1960.* New York: Macmillan, 1964.

Cernuda, Luis. *Estudios sobre poesía española contemporánea.* Madrid: Guadarrama, 1972.

Chevallier, Marie. *Los temas poéticos de Miguel Hernández.* Trans. Arcadio Pardo. Madrid: Siglo Veintiuno de España, 1978.

Ciplijauskaité, Biruté. *El poeta en la poesía.* Madrid: Insula, 1966.

————. *La soledad y la poesía española contemporánea.* Madrid: Insula, 1962.

Cirlot, J. E. *A Dictionary of Symbols.* Trans. Jack Sage. New York: Philosophical Library, 1962.

Cirre, José Francisco. *Forma y espíritu de una lírica española.* Mexico City: Gráfica Panamericana, 1950. [On Alberti, see pp. 72–84].

Colodny, Robert G. *The Struggle for Madrid.* New York: Paine Whitman, 1958.

Connell, G. W. "The autobiographical element in *Sobre los angeles.*" *Bulletin of Spanish Studies* 40 (1963): 160–73.

————. "The end of a quest: Alberti's *Sermones y moradas* and three uncollected poems." *Hispanic Review* 32 (July 1965): 290–309.

————. "A recurring theme in the poetry of Rafael Alberti." *Renaissance and Modern Studies* 3 (1959): 95–110.

Couffon, Claude. *Rafael Alberti.* Poètes d'aujourd'hui. Paris: Pierre Seghers, 1966.

Crespo, Angel. "Realismo y pitagorismo en el libro de Alberti *A la pintura.*" *Papeles de Son Armadans* 88 (July 1963): 93–126.

Daiches, David. *Literature and Society.* New York: Haskell House, 1970.

Debicki, Andrew P. "El 'correlativo objetivo' en la poesía de Rafael Alberti." In *Estudios sobre poesía española contemporánea.* Madrid: Gredos, 1968.

Dehennin, Elsa. *La resurgence de Góngora et la génération poétique de 1927.* Paris: Didier, 1962.

Delogue, Ignacio. *Rafael Alberti.* Florence: La Nuova Italia, 1972.

Demetz, Peter. *Marx, Engels, and the Poets: Origins of Marxist and Literary Criticism.* Chicago: University of Chicago Press, 1967.

Díaz Plaja, Guillermo. *Historia general de las literaturas hispánicas.* Vol. 2. Barcelona: Espiga, 1951.

Díez de Revenga, Francisco Javier. *La métrica española de los poetas del 27.* Murcia: Departamento de Literatura Española, Universidad de Murcia, 1973.

Duncan, Hugh D. *Language and Literature in Society.* Chicago: University of Chicago Press, 1953.

Durán Gili, Manuel. *El superrealismo en la poesía española contemporánea.* Mexico City: n.p., 1950.

————, ed. *Rafael Alberti.* Madrid: Taurus, 1975.

Eagleton, Terry. *Marxism and Literary Criticism.* Berkeley: University of California Press, 1976.

Edwards, Thomas R. *Imagination and Power: A Study of Poetry on Public Themes.* New York: Oxford University Press, 1971.

Eisenstein, Sergei. *Film Form: Essays in Film Theory* and *The Film Sense*. Ed. and trans. Jay Leyda. Cleveland: World, 1967.

————. "Introduction: *The Battleship Potemkin*." In *Potemkin: A Film by Sergei Eisenstein*. Trans. Gillon R. Aitken. New York: Simon and Schuster, 1968.

Eliot, T. S. *The Waste Land and Other Poems*. 1934. Reprint. New York: Harcourt, Brace and World, 1962.

Fernández Almagro, Melchor. *Historia de la República española (1931–1936)*. Madrid: Alianza, 1940.

————. *Historia política de la España contemporánea, 1897–1902*. Vol. 3. Madrid: Alianza, 1968.

Ferrán, Jaime, and Daniel P. Testa, eds. *Spanish Writers of 1936: Crisis and Commitment in the Poetry of the Thirties and Forties: An Anthology of Literary Studies and Essays*. London: Tamesis, 1973.

Ferreres, Rafael. "Sobre la generación poética de 1927." *Papeles de Son Armadans* 11, nos. 32–33 (November–December 1958): 301–14.

Flores, Angel, and Ira Jan Wallach. *A Spectre Is Haunting Europe: Poems of Revolutionary Spain*. New York: Critics Group, 1936.

Florit, Eugenio. "La poesía reciente de Rafael Alberti." *La Torre,* no. 27 (1959): 11–17.

Flower, J. E., J. A. Morris, and E. E. Williams. *Writing and Politics in Modern Britain*. New York: Holmes and Meier, 1977.

Friedrich, Hugo. *Estructura de la lírica moderna*. Trans. J. Petit. Barcelona: Seix Barral, 1959.

Frye, Northrup. *Anatomy of Criticism: Four Essays*. Princeton: Princeton University Press, 1957.

Fuller, John. *A Reader's Guide to W. H. Auden*. New York: Farrar, Straus and Giroux, 1970.

Gaos, Vicente. *Antología del grupo poético del 27*. Salamanca: Biblioteca Anaya, 1965.

García Lorca, Federico. *Obras completas*. 16th ed. Madrid: Aguilar, 1971.

García Sarriá, Francisco. "*Sobre los ángeles* de Rafael Alberti y el surrealismo." *Papeles de Son Armadans* 271–272–273 (1978): 23–40.

Geist, A. L. *Poética de la generación del 27 y las revistas literarias: De la vanguardia al compromiso*. Barcelona: Labor, 1980.

Gibbon, Edward. *The Decline and Fall of the Roman Empire*. Vol. 1. In *Great Books of the Western World,* vol. 40. Chicago: William Benton, 1952.

Glicksberg, Charles. *The Literature of Commitment*. Lewisburg, Pa.: Bucknell University Press, 1976.

González Lanuza, Eduardo. "Homenaje a Rafael Alberti." *Sur,* no. 281 (March–April 1963): 52–62.

————. *Rafael Alberti*. Buenos Aires: Ediciones Culturales Argentinas, 1965.

————. "Rafael Alberti: Entre el clavel y la espada." *Sur* 11, no. 86 (November 1941): 71–76.

González Muela, Joaquín. "¿Poesía amorosa en *Sobre los ángeles?*" *Insula* 80 (August 1952): 5.

————. *El lenguaje poético de la generación Guillén-Lorca*. Madrid: Insula, 1955.

Gracia Ifach, María de. *Miguel Hernández, rayo que no cesa*. Barcelona: Plaza y Janés, 1975.

Guérard, Albert. *Art for Art's Sake*. New York: Lothrop, Lee, and Shepard, 1936.

Gullón, Ricardo. "Alegrías y sombras de Rafael Alberti (primer momento)." *Insula* 198 (May 1963): 1, 5.

————. "Alegrías y sombras de Rafael Alberti (segundo momento)." *Asomante*, no. 1 (1965): 27–37; no. 2 (1965): 22–35.

Guttman, Allen. *The Wound in the Heart: America and the Spanish Civil War*. New York: Free Press, 1962.

Guzmán, Eduardo de. *1930: Historia política de un año decisivo*. Madrid: Tebas, 1973.

Heisel, Margaret Ellen. "Imagery and Structure in the Poetry of Rafael Alberti." Ph.D. diss., University of Kansas, 1971.

Hernández, Miguel. *Obra poética completa*. Ed. Leopoldo de Luis and Jorge Urrutia. Bilbao: Zero, 1976.

Higgins, James. *César Vallejo: An Anthology of his Poetry*. Oxford: Pergamon Press, 1970.

————. *Visión del hombre y de la vida en las últimas obras poéticas de César Vallejo*. Mexico City: Siglo Veintiuno, 1970.

Holland, Henry M. *Politics through Literature*. Englewood Cliffs, N.J.: Prentice-Hall, 1968.

Hora de España. Nos. 1–22. January 1937–October 1938. Reprint. Liechtenstein: Kraus, 1972–74.

Horst, Robert Ter. "The Angelic Prehistory of *Sobre los ángeles*." *Modern Language Notes* 81, no. 2 (1966): 174–94.

Howe, Irving. *A World More Attractive: A View of Modern Literature and Politics*. 2d ed. Freeport, N.Y.: Books for Libraries Press, 1970.

Ilie, Paul. "Surrealist Rhetoric (Alberti)." In *The Surrealist Mode in Spanish Literature*. Ann Arbor: University of Michigan Press, 1970.

Jackson, Gabriel. *A Concise History of the Spanish Civil War*. New York: John Day, 1974.

————. *The Spanish Civil War: Domestic Crisis or International Conspiracy*. Boston: Heath, 1967.

————. *The Spanish Republic and the Civil War, 1931–1939*. Princeton: Princeton University Press, 1965.

Jameson, Fredric. *Marxism and Form*. Princeton: Princeton University Press, 1972.

Jones, W. Lewis. *King Arthur in History and Legend*. Cambridge: Cambridge University Press, 1933.

Josephson, Hannah, ed. *Aragon, Poet of the French Resistance*. New York: Duell, Sloan and Pearce, 1945.

Jover Zamora, José María. *Introducción a la historia de España*. Barcelona: Teide, 1969.

Kaelin, Eugene F. "Literature of Commitment" and "Committed Literature, Second

Phase." In *An Existentialist Aesthetic: The Theories of Sartre and Merleau-Ponty.* Madison: University of Wisconsin Press, 1966.

Kaun, Alexander. *Soviet Poets and Poetry.* Berkeley: University of California Press, 1943.

Knights, L. C. *Public Voices: Literature and Politics with Special Reference to the Seventeenth Century.* Totowa, N.J.: Rowman and Littlefield, 1971.

Krueger, John Q. "Politics and Poetry." In *The Princeton Encyclopedia of Poetry and Poetics.* Princeton: Princeton University Press, 1974.

Larrea, Juan. *Del Surrealismo a Machupicchu.* Mexico City: Joaquín Mortiz, 1967.

Lecherbonnier, Bernard, ed. *Les critiques de notre temps et Aragon.* Paris: Garnier, 1976.

Lechner, Johan. *El compromiso en la poesía española del siglo XX.* Vol. 1. Leiden: Universitaire Pers, 1968. [On Alberti, see pp. 65–73, 87–97, 131–38, 162–73, 179–200].

──────. *El compromiso en la poesía española del siglo XX, 1939–1974.* Vol. 2. Leiden: Universitaire Pers, 1975.

León, María Teresa. *Memoria de la melancolía.* 2d ed. Barcelona: Laia, 1977.

Ley, Charles David. *Spanish Poetry Since 1939.* Washington, D.C.: Catholic University Press, 1962.

Llorens, Vicente, "Rafael Alberti, poeta social: Historia y mito." *Aspectos sociales de la literatura española.* Madrid: Castalia, 1974.

López Estrada, Francisco. *Métrica espanola del siglo XX.* Madrid: Gredos, 1969.

Lukács, György. *Realism in Our Time: Literature and the Class Struggle.* Trans. John Mander and Necke Mander. New York: Harper and Row, 1964.

MacDonald, Dwight. "Eisenstein, Pudovkin, and Others." In *The Emergence of Film Art,* ed. Lewis Jacobs, 2d ed. New York: Norton, 1979.

MacNeice, Louis. *Modern Poetry: A Personal Essay.* 2d ed. Oxford: Clarendon Press, 1968.

Malefakis, Edward E. *Agrarian Reform and Peasant Revolution in Spain: Origins of the Civil War.* New Haven: Yale University Press, 1970.

Mander, John. *The Writer and Commitment.* London: Secker and Warburg, 1961.

Manteiga, Robert. *The Poetry of Rafael Alberti: A Visual Approach.* London: Tamesis, 1978.

Marcone, Rose Marie. "The Poetic Trajectory of Rafael Alberti." Ph.D. diss., Johns Hopkins University, 1966.

Marrast, Robert. "Essai de bibliographie de Rafael Alberti." *Bulletin Hispanique* 42 (1955): 147–77; 49 (1957): 430–35.

──────. *Rafael Alberti: Prosas encontradas: 1924–1942.* 2d ed. Madrid: Ayuso, 1973.

Marx, Karl, and Friedrich Engels. *The Communist Manifesto: The Essential Left.* London: George Allen, 1961.

Matthews, Herbert. "Under the Death-spurting Skies of War-torn Madrid." In *The Spanish Civil War.* Chicago: Quadrangle, 1972.

May, Barbara Dale. *El dilema de la nostalgia en la poesía de Rafael Alberti.* Utah Studies in Language Education. Las Vegas: Peter Lang, 1978.

———. "The Endurance of Dreams Deferred: Rafael Alberti and Langston Hughes." In *Red Flags, Black Flags: Critical Essays on the Literature of the Spanish Civil War,* ed. John Beals Romeiser. Studia humanitatis. Madrid: José Porrúa Turanzas, 1982.

Mayakovsky, Vladimir. *How Verses Are Made.* Trans. Herbert Marshall. 3d ed. Bombay: Current Book House, 1955.

———. *Poems.* Trans. Dorian Roltenberg. Moscow: Progress Publishers, 1976.

———. *Polnoe sobranie sochinenni v trinadstati tomakh.* Vol. 10. Moscow: Goslitizdat, 1958.

Mills, C. Wright, ed. *The Marxists.* New York: Dell, 1965.

Monguió, Luis. "The Poetry of Rafael Alberti." *Hispania* 43 (May 1960): 158–68.

El Mono Azul. Nos. 1–47. August 1936–February 1939. Reprint. Kraus, 1975.

Monterde, Alberto. *La poesía pura en la lírica española.* Mexico: Imprenta Universitaria, 1953.

Montero, Enrique. "*Octubre*: Revelación de una revista mítica." In *Octubre: Escritores y artistas revolucionarios.* Nos. 1–6. June 1933–April 1934. Reprint. Liechtenstein: Topos, 1977.

Morris, Cyril Brian. *A Generation of Spanish Poets, 1920–1936.* Cambridge: Cambridge University Press, 1969. [On Alberti, see pp. 30–40, 104–11, 201–17, 239–41].

———. "Las imágenes claves de *Sobre los ángeles.*" *Insula,* no. 198 (May 1963): 12, 14.

———. "Parallel Imagery in Quevedo and Alberti." *Bulletin of Spanish Studies* 36 (July 1959): 135–45.

———. *Rafael Alberti's "Sobre los ángeles": Four Major Themes.* Hull: University of Hull, 1966.

———. "*Sobre los ángeles:* A Poet's Apostasy." *Bulletin of Hispanic Studies* 37 (1960): 222–31.

———. *Sobre los ángeles: Yo era un tonto y lo que he visto me ha hecho dos tontos.* Ed. Cyril Brian Morris. Madrid: Cátedra, 1981.

———. *Surrealism and Spain, 1920–1936.* Cambridge: Cambridge University Press, 1972. [On Alberti, see pp. 43–48].

———. *This Loving Darkness: The Cinema and the Spanish Writers, 1920–1936.* Oxford: Oxford University Press, 1980. [On Alberti, see pp. 80–111].

Muste, John M. *Say That We Saw Spain Die: Literary Consequences of the Spanish Civil War.* Seattle: University of Washington Press, 1966.

Nantell, Judith. "Death and Resurrection in Rafael Alberti's *Capital de la gloria.*" *Essays in Literature* 6, no. 2 (Fall 1979): 247–57.

———. "Dialectical Pathos in Rafael Alberti's 'Un fantasma recorre Europa.' " *Anales de la literatura española contemporánea* 8 (Fall 1983): 31–46.

———. "Ordering the Chaos: Rafael Alberti's 'Elegía cívica.' " *Hispanófila,* in press.

———. "Poetry for Politics' Sake: Rafael Alberti's *Consignas.*" *Crítica Hispánica* 5, no. 1 (Spring 1983): 47–58.

————. "Rafael Alberti's Vision of Spain, 1930–1955: The Merging of Politics and Poetics." Ph.D. diss., Indiana University, 1978.

Navarro Tomás, Tomás. *Métrica española: Reseña histórica y descriptiva*. 3d ed. Madrid: Guadarrama, 1972.

Neruda, Pablo. *España en el corazón: Himno a las glorias del pueblo en la guerra (1936–1937)*, 2d ed. Santiago, Chile: Ercilla, 1938.

————. *Confieso que he vivido*. Buenos Aires: Losada, 1974.

O'Brien, Conar C. *Writers and Politics*. New York: Pantheon, 1965.

Octubre: Escritores y artistas revolucionarios. Nos. 1–6. June 1933–April 1934. Reprint. Leichtenstein: Topos, 1977.

Onís, Carlos Marcial de. *El surrealismo y cuatro poetas de la generación del 27*. Madrid: José Porrúa Turanzas, 1974.

Ortega, José. "Pablo Neruda: The Making of a Political Poet." *Perspectives on Contemporary Literature* 2, no. 1 (1976): 3–11.

Owen, Wilfred. "Strange Meeting." In *The Norton Anthology of Modern Poetry*, ed. Richard Ellmann and Robert O'Clair. New York: Norton, 1973.

Pérez, Carlos Alberto. "Rafael Alberti: Sobre los tontos." *Revista Hispánica Moderna* 32 (1966): 206–16.

Prados, Emilio. *Poesías completas*. Ed. Carlos Blanco Aguinaga and Antonio Carreira. Mexico City: Aguilar, 1975.

The Princeton Encyclopedia of Poetry and Poetics. Princeton: Princeton University Press, 1974.

Proll, Eric. " 'Popularismo' and 'Barroquismo' in the Poetry of Rafael Alberti." *Bulletin of Spanish Studies* 14 (1942): 59–86.

————. "The Surrealist Element in Rafael Alberti." *Bulletin of Spanish Studies* 18 (1941): 70–82.

Raymond, Marcel. *From Baudelaire to Surrealism*. London: Methuen, 1970.

Richards, Ivor Armstrong. *The Philosophy of Rhetoric*. London: Oxford University Press, 1936.

————. *Principles of Literary Criticism*. London: Oxford University Press, 1924.

Romeiser, John Beals, ed. *Red Flags, Black Flags: Critical Essays on the Literature of the Spanish Civil War*. Studia humanitatis. Madrid: José Porrúa Turanzas, 1982.

Rosenthal, Marilyn. *The Poetry of the Spanish Civil War*. New York: New York University Press, 1978.

Salinas, Pedro. "La poesía de Rafael Alberti." *Literatura española del Siglo XX*. Madrid: Alianza, 1972.

Salinas de Marichal, Solita. *El mundo poético de Rafael Alberti*. Madrid: Gredos, 1968.

————. "Los paraísos perdidos de Rafael Alberti." Insula 198 (May 1963): 4, 10.

Sánchez-Barbudo, Antonio. " 'De un momento a otro' (de Rafael Alberti)." *El Mono Azul*, no. 41 (18 November 1937): 163.

Sartre, Jean-Paul. *Politics and Literature*. Trans. J. A. Underwood and John Calder. London: Calder and Boyars, 1973.

————. *What Is Literature?* Trans. Bernard Frechtman. New York: Philosophical Library, 1949. [Contains the greater portion of *Situations II*].

Sawrey, Richard B. "Rafael Alberti's Poetry of 1926–1930: Representations of Narcissus, Alienation, and Historical Consciousness: A Critical and Structural Study." Ph.D. diss., University of Washington, 1972.

Seitz, William. *Art of Assemblage.* New York: Museum of Modern Art, 1961.

Senabre, Ricardo. *La poesía de Rafael Alberti.* Cursos Internacionales. Salamanca: Universidad de Salamanca, 1977.

Siebenmann, Gustav. *Los estilos poéticos en España desde 1900.* Trans. Angel San Miguel. Madrid: Gredos, 1973.

Sieber, Harry. "Alberti's *Botticelli.*" *Kentucky Romance Quarterly* 16 (1969): 329–32.

Spang, Kurt. *Inquietud y nostalgia: La poesía de Rafael Alberti.* Pamplona: Universidad de Navarra, 1973.

Spender, Stephen. *The Destructive Element: A Study of Modern Writers and Beliefs.* Boston: Houghton, 1938.

———. *The Thirties and After: Poetry, Politics, and People (1933–1975).* London: Macmillan, 1978.

———. "Writers and Politics." *Partisan Review* 34 (1967): 359–81.

Stern, Madeleine B. "Propaganda or Art?" *Sewanee Review* 45 (October–December 1937): 453–68.

Tejada, José Luis. *Rafael Alberti: Entre la tradición y la vanguardia.* Madrid: Gredos, 1977.

Thomas, Hugh. *The Spanish Civil War.* Great Britain: Pelican Books, 1968.

Thomson, George. *From Marx to Mao Tse-Tung: A Study in Revolutionary Dialectics.* London: China Policy Study Group, 1971.

———. *Marxism and Poetry.* London: Laurence and Wishart, 1945.

Torre, Guillermo de. *La aventura estética de nuestra edad.* Barcelona: Seix Barral, 1962.

———. "Contemporary Spanish Poetry." *Texas Quarterly* 4, no. 1 (Spring 1961): 55–78.

———. *Historia de las literaturas de vanguardia.* Madrid: Guadarrama, 1965.

Torrente-Ballester, Gonzalo. *Literatura española contemporánea (1898–1936).* Madrid: Aguado, 1949.

———. *Panorama de la literatura española contemporánea.* 3d ed. Madrid: Guadarrama, 1965.

Trotsky, Leon. *Literature and Revolution.* Trans. Rose Strunksky. Reprint. Ann Arbor: University of Michigan Press, 1970.

———. *La revolución española.* Madrid: Teivos, 1931.

Valbuena Prat, Angel. *Historia de la literatura española.* 4th ed. Vol. 3. Barcelona: Gustavo Gili, 1953.

Valente, José Angel. "La necesidad y la musa." *Insula,* no. 198 (May 1963): 6.

Vallejo, César. *Obra poética completa.* Havana: Casa de las Américas, 1970.

Vázquez-Azpiri, Hector. *De Alfonso XIII al Príncipe de España.* Barcelona: Nauta, 1973.

Videla, Gloria. *El ultraísmo: Estudios sobre movimientos poéticos de vanguardia en España.* Madrid: Gredos, 1963.

Vivanco, Luis Felipe. "Rafael Alberti en su palabra acelerada y vestida de luces." *Introducción a la poesía española contemporánea.* Madrid: Guadarrama, 1957.

Warner, I. R. "Subjective Time and Space in Alberti's *Baladas y canciones de la Quinta del Mayor Loco.*" *Bulletin of Hispanic Studies* 50 (October 1973): 374–84.

Waugh, Thomas. " 'Men Cannot Act in Front of the Camera in the Presence of Death': Joris Ivens' *The Spanish Earth.*" Pt. 1. *Cineaste* 12, no. 2 (1982): 30–33.

———. " 'Men Cannot Act in Front of the Camera in the Presence of Death': Joris Ivens' *The Spanish Earth.*" Pt 2. *Cineaste* 12, no. 3 (1983): 21–29.

Weintraub, Stanley. *The Last Great Cause: Intellectuals and the Spanish Civil War.* New York: Weybright and Talley, 1968.

Weisstein, Ulrich. *Comparative Literature and Literary Theory.* Bloomington: Indiana University Press, 1973.

Wellek, René, and Austin Warren. *Theory of Literature.* 3d ed. New York: Harcourt, Brace and World, 1956.

Wesseling, Pieter. "Conflict and Juxtaposition in Alberti's Poems of the Spanish Civil War." *Hispanófila* 27, no. 1 (September 1983): 39–51.

———. "The Poetry of Rafael Alberti: Traditionalism and Revolution." Ph.D. diss., University of Wisconson–Madison, 1970.

———. "Violence in Counterpoint: Alberti's Poems of 1935." *Neophilologus* 61, no. 2 (April 1977): 220–25.

Wheelwright, Philip. *The Burning Fountain: A Study in the Language of Symbolism.* Bloomington: Indiana University Press, 1968.

Williams, Raymond. *Culture and Society, 1780–1950.* New York: Columbia University Press, 1958.

Wimsatt, William K. *The Verbal Icon.* 2d ed. New York: Noonday Press, 1958.

Winegarten, Renée. *Writers and Revolution: The Fatal Lure of Action.* New York: New Viewpoint-Watts, 1974.

Woodcock, George. *The Writer and Politics.* London: Porcupine, 1948.

Woodring, Carl. *Politics in English Romantic Poetry.* Cambridge, Mass.: Harvard University Press, 1970.

Wyden, Peter. *The Passionate War: The Narrative History of the Spanish Civil War.* New York: Simon and Schuster, 1983.

Zardoya, Concha. "El mar en la poesía de Rafael Alberti." *Poesía española contemporánea.* Madrid: Guadarrama, 1961.

———. "La técnica metafórica Albertiana." *Poesía española del 98 y del 27.* Madrid: Gredos, 1968.

Zuleta, Emilia de. "La poesía de Rafael Alberti." In *Cinco poetas españoles.* Madrid: Gredos, 1971.

Index